Family and Community Engagement in Charter Schools

A Volume in
Family School Community Partnership Issues

Series Editor

Diana Hiatt-Michael
Pepperdine University

Family School Community Partnership Issues

Diana Hiatt-Michael, Series Editor

Family and Community Engagement in Charter Schools (2025)
edited by Brian Robert Beabout

Family and Community Partnerships:
Promising Practices for Teachers and Teacher Educators (2023)
edited by Margaret Caspe and Reyna Hernandez

Composing Storylines of Possibilities:
Immigrant and Refugee Families Navigating School (2022)
edited by Martha J. Strickland

Critical Perspectives on Education Policy and Schools,
Families, and Communities (2020)
edited by Sue Winton and Gillian Parekh

Promising Practices for Engaging Families in STEM Learning (2018)
edited by Margaret Caspe, Taniesha A. Woods, and Joy Kennedy

Family Involvement in Faith-Based Schools (2017)
edited by Diana Hiatt-Michael

The Power of Community Engagement for Educational Change (2015)
edited by Michael P. Evans and Diana Hiatt-Michael

Promising Practices to Empower Culturally and
Linguistically Diverse Families of Children With Disabilities (2014)
by Lusa Lo

Promising Practices for Engaging Families in Literacy (2013)
edited by Holly Kreider, Margaret Caspe, and Diana Hiatt-Michael

Promising Practices for Fathers' Involvement in Children's Education (2013)
edited by Hsiu-Zu Ho and Diana Hiatt-Michael

Promising Practices for Family Engagement in Out-of-School Time (2011)
edited by Holly Kreider and Helen Westmoreland

Promising Practices to Support Family Involvement in Schools (2010)
edited by Diana Hiatt-Michael

Promising Practices to Support Family Involvement in Schools (2010)
edited by Diana Hiatt-Michael

Series titles continued on next page

*Promising Practices for Family and
Community Involvement During High School (2009)*
edited by Lee Shumow

Promising Practices for Partnering With Families in the Early Years (2008)
edited by Mary M. Cornish

*Promising Practices for Teachers to Engage With
Families of English Language Learners (2007)*
edited by Diana Hiatt-Michael

*Promising Practices for Family Involvement in
Schooling Across the Continents (2005)*
edited by Diana Hiatt-Michael

*Promising Practices Connecting Schools to
Families of Children With Special Needs (2004)*
edited by Diana Hiatt-Michael

Promising Practices to Connect Schools With the Community (2003)
edited by Diana Hiatt-Michael

Promising Practices for Family Involvement in Schools (2001)
edited by Diana Hiatt-Michael

Family and Community Engagement in Charter Schools

Editor

Brian Robert Beabout
The University of New Orleans

INFORMATION AGE PUBLISHING, INC.
Charlotte, NC • www.infoagepub.com

Library of Congress Cataloging-in-Publication Data

CIP record for this book is available from the Library of Congress
http://www.loc.gov

ISBNs: 979-8-88730-676-6 (Paperback)

979-8-88730-677-3 (Hardcover)

979-8-88730-678-0 (ebook)

Copyright © 2025 Information Age Publishing Inc.

All rights reserved. No part of this publication may be reproduced, stored in
a retrieval system, or transmitted, in any form or by any means, electronic,
mechanical, photocopying, microfilming, recording or otherwise, without written
permission from the publisher.

Printed in the United States of America

CONTENTS

Introduction to Family and Community Engagement in
    Charter Schools
    Brian Robert Beabout .... *ix*

1. Family-Community Engagement in California's
    Charter Schools
    Delia Castillo *1*

2. Parent Involvement in Charter School Governance
    Charisse Gulosino and Elif Sisli Ciamarra *29*

3. Charter School Governing Boards and Missed Opportunities
    for Community Engagement
    Elise Castillo and Laura E. Hernández *53*

4. Family Engagement in Diverse by Design Charter Schools
    Priscilla Wohlstetter and Elisabeth H. Kim *73*

5. Constrained Collaboration Between Co-Located Charter and
    District Schools
    Brian Robert Beabout and Shanté Williams *97*

6. Families Actively Mobilizing: School-Based Family Wellness
    Groups in Two Oakland Charter Schools
    Cynthia Martinez and Rebecca Anguiano *121*

7. Family Engagement in Charter School Closure Decisions
    Diana Ward *145*

About the Authors *171*

INTRODUCTION TO FAMILY AND COMMUNITY ENGAGEMENT IN CHARTER SCHOOLS

Brian Robert Beabout

As charter schools have steadily increased their presence in the American educational landscape over the last 30 years (National Charter School Facts, 2018), there have been often divergent views of how they interact with their local communities. Some have described charter schools as neoliberal machinations whereby local democratic decision making and local educational needs are supplanted by strict adherence to free market capitalism and unquestioned acceptance of test-based accountability systems (Buras, 2011; Saltman, 2007). From other sources, charter schools have been described as potentially useful mechanisms to deliver public education and enable community control, especially in places where district bureaucracies have underperformed (Fox & Buchannan, 2014; Rofes & Stulberg, 2004). Still, others have drawn attention to the potential for increased racial segregation that can be caused when families are asked to *choose* a public school for their child, rather than attend a unified public system (Frankenberg et al., 2011; Parker, 2000). Given the highly politicized environment surrounding charter schools, it should come as little surprise that there is also divergent research literature on charter schools' approaches to family and community engagement.

As policy instruments, charter schools have been described as playing a variety of roles, including state takeover of low-performing schools (Beabout, 2010; Wright et al., 2018), the creation of white-flight schools in diverse districts (Eckes, 2015; Wilson, 2019), the gentrification of urban

---

Family and Community Engagement in Charter Schools, pp. ix–xiii
Copyright © 2025 by Information Age Publishing
www.infoagepub.com
All rights of reproduction in any form reserved.

x   B. R. BEABOUT

neighborhoods (Hankins, 2007), the integration of segregated schools and districts (Kahlenberg & Potter, 2014), and the creation of niche options unavailable in public school districts (Brown & Vollman Makris, 2018; Lauen et al., 2015). Each of these uses of charter schools likely means different things for the relationships between schools, families, and communities. Mapping this diversity is a key goal of this volume.

Another key objective is to move beyond the often-fiery rhetoric of charter schools to identify the ways in which communities and charters coexist. Sometimes this coexistence is mandated and hegemonic, sometimes it is entrepreneurial and tentative, and sometimes it is powerful and liberatory. But how and why these relations get created and sustained is crucial to understanding this ascendant form of school organization. Despite important early scholarly contributions from several scholars affiliated with this volume (Beabout & Boselovic, 2015; Beabout & Jakiel, 2015; Smith et al., 2011; Wohlstetter & Smith, 2006), there remains a relatively scant literature base on *how* charter schools, families, and communities engage in the varied community contexts in which they exist. If we have done our job, the chapters included here can serve as an important groundwork for further research into this form of public schooling. While charters serve less than 10% of public-school students in the United States, the chapters here suggest that their unique form of governance, predicated precisely on local control, offers important lessons for consideration from scholars, administrators, and policymakers alike.

In Chapter 1, Delia Castillo describes the myriad ways that families and communities interact in the state of California, the U.S. state with more charter school students than any other. This analysis makes important connections between how the policy environment around charter schools influences opportunities and threats faced by schools themselves.

In Chapter 2, Charisse Gulosino and Elif Sisli Ciamarra provide a quantitative examination of the relationship between parent participation in charter school board governance and student academic achievement in Massachusetts. While noting slightly higher performance in schools with parent board participation, issues of self-selection and an external relationship between student socioeconomic makeup and parent board participation raise further questions for future research.

In Chapter 3, Elise Castillo and Laura Hernández qualitatively examine family and community participation in charter school governing boards in both New York and California. Their profiles of four charter boards highlight the challenges of increasing community voice in such formalized settings. While they observed an often a vocalized desire to steer board member composition towards the community and families served by the school(s), the external pressures of fundraising and improving a school's market position often took precedence and sustained whiter, more middle-class board participation.

In Chapter 4, Priscilla Wohlstetter and Elise Kim share the results of their mixed methods study of diverse-by-design (DBD) charter schools in California, Colorado, and New York. While representing just a small percentage of charter schools in the United States, membership in the Diverse Charter Schools Coalition has increased significantly in the last eight years to over 200 members. Their analysis examines the rationales and activities of DBD charter school family and community engagement programming. Their insightful discussion of how community engagement is integrated into the instructional programs at such schools gives several examples of the fundamental shifts that occur when community becomes an aspirational *goal* of a school rather than a static external stakeholder to be engaged with and managed (Furman, 2002).

In Chapter 5, Brian Beabout and Shanté Williams examine the relationships between principals in co-located charter and state-run schools during the post-Katrina period in New Orleans. While sharing a single campus, the principals they studied kept a largely distant relationship from each other; meeting to discuss lunch schedules and parking lot use, but rarely working together on substantive concerns of teaching and learning. The intensely pro-charter political context surrounding their study is identified as a barrier to more meaningful principal collaboration.

In Chapter 6, Rebecca Anguiano and Cynthia Martinez describe a school-based community organizing and popular education program organized at two charter schools in Oakland. They found that when issues of accessibility were addressed, parents could truly grow their power to advocate for their children and their community. This newfound power, however, can lead to tensions with the charter school sponsoring the convening, leading charters school leaders to reconsider their role in the community.

In Chapter 7, Diana Ward examines an area of family and community engagement research that has only recently begun to expand: parental engagement in charter school closures. This review of existing literature points to a history of missteps common in the closure of both district-run schools and charter schools, often resulting in marginalization of families and at times producing overt resistance to closure. Potentially useful practices for managing closure are identified including extending the time frame of closure and investing in full-time communications staff to manage the process.

REFERENCES

Beabout, B. R. (2010). Leadership for change in the educational wild west of post-Katrina New Orleans. *The Journal of Educational Change, 11*(4), 403–424.

Beabout, B. R., & Boselovic, J. (2015). Community engagement as a central activity in new charter schools. In M. P. Evans & D. Hiatt-Michael (Eds.), *The power of community engagement for educational change* (pp. 41–63). Information Age Publishing.

Beabout, B. R., & Jakiel, L. B. (2011). Family engagement in charter schools. In S. Redding, M. Murphy & P. Sheley (Eds.), *Handbook on family and community engagement* (pp. 147–151). Information Age Publishing.

Brown, E., & Vollman Makris, M. (2018) A different type of charter school: In prestige charters, a rise in cachet equals a decline in access. *Journal of Education Policy, 33*(1), 85–117, https://doi.org/10.1080/02680939.2017.1341552

Buras, K. (2011). Race, charter schools, and conscious capitalism: On the spatial politics of whiteness as property (and the unconscionable assault on Black new orleans). *Harvard Educational Review, 81*(2), 296–331. https://doi.org/210.17763/haer.17781.17762.17766l42343qqw17360j17703

Eckes, S. (2015). Haven charter schools: Separate by design and legally questionable. *Equity & Excellence in Education, 48*(1), 49–70.

Fox, R. A., & Buchanan, N. K. (2014). *Proud to be different: Ethnocentric niche charter schools in America.* R&L Education.

Frankenberg, E., Siegel-Hawley, G., & Wang, J. (2011). Choice without equity: Charter school segregation. *Education Policy Analysis Archives, 19*(1). Retrieved June 1, 2011, from http://epaa.asu.edu/ojs/article/view/2779

Furman, G. (Ed.). (2002). *School as community: From promise to practice.* SUNY Press.

Hankins, K. B. (2007). The final frontier: Charter schools as new community institutions of gentrification, urban geography, *28*(2), 113–128. https://doi.org/10.2747/0272-3638.28.2.11

Kahlenberg, R. D., & Potter, H. (2014). *A smarter charter: Finding what works for charter schools and public education.* Teachers College Press.

Lauen, D. L., Fuller, B., & Dauter, L. (2015). Positioning charter schools in Los Angeles: Diversity of form and homogeneity of effects. *American Journal of Education, 121*(2), 213––239.

National Charter School Facts. (2018). Retrieved November 14, 2018, from https://data.publiccharters.org/

Parker, W. (2000). The color of choice: Race and charter schools. *Tulane Law Review, 75*(3), 563–630.

Rofes, E., & Stulberg, L. M. (Eds.). (2004). *The emancipatory promise of charter schools: Toward a progressive politics of school choice.* SUNY Press.

Saltman, K. J. (2007). *Capitalizing on disaster: Taking and breaking public schools.* Routledge.

Smith, J., Wohlstetter, P., Kuzin, C. A., & De Pedro, K. (2011). Parent involvement in urban charter schools: New strategies for increasing participation. *The School Community Journal, 21*(1), 71–94.

Wilson, E. K. (2019). The new white flight. *Duke Journal of Constitutional Law and Public Policy, 14*, 233–284.

Wohlstetter, P., & Smith, J. (2006). Improving schools through partnerships: Learning from charter schools. *Phi Delta Kappan, 87*(6), 464–467.

Wright, J., Whitaker, R. W., II, Khalifa, M., & Briscoe, F. (2018). The color of neoliberal reform: A critical race policy analysis of school district takeovers in Michigan. *Urban Education, 54,* 764–771

CHAPTER 1

FAMILY-COMMUNITY ENGAGEMENT IN CALIFORNIA CHARTER SCHOOLS

Delia Castillo
Pepperdine University

HISTORICAL PERSPECTIVE

Parent and community support have undergirded California's activity in education prior to the charter school movement. Hiatt-Michael (personal communication, December 6, 2021) noted that parent interest in affluent Los Angeles neighborhoods led to alternative public-school offerings during the early 1970s. This parental concern and energy promoted community coalescence that led to the creation of magnet schools, a precursor to the charter school movement. These magnet schools focused on diverse educational offerings, such as performing arts or science/technology, and expanded secondary offerings to public school youth.

Across the continent, Massachusetts education professor Ray Budde envisioned the notion of chartering during the same period. He perceived charter schools as a way to improve student outcomes, parent choice, and opportunities for groups of teachers to receive autonomy in the implementation of new programs in existing schools (Jason, 2017). Budde's idea focused on teacher control of the curriculum and sought to reduce the control of school boards in school-level decision-making. In his vision, teachers were given autonomy in exchange for accountability through expected measurable student outcomes to parents and the community.

Family and Community Engagement in Charter Schools, pp. 1–27
Copyright © 2025 by Information Age Publishing
www.infoagepub.com
All rights of reproduction in any form reserved.

2   D. CASTILLO

While Ray Budde may be regarded as the father of charter schools in concept, Gary Hart, a longtime California politician, is considered the father of California's charter school law. He served as the driving political force to promote the California legislative enactment of SB 1448 in 1992. Hart, along with Sue Burr, a consultant with the state Senate Education Committee, drafted California's Charter School law of 1992. To secure a broad base of support, SB 1448 was modeled after the American Federation of Teachers (AFT) president Al Shanker's charter school model. Shanker, as well as Senator Hart, was a popular figure in California's politics at that time.

Not surprisingly, with such a grassroots interest in education, California was an early adopter of a state charter school law in 1992, second in the U.S. after Minnesota. The 1992 Charter Schools Act (SB 1448) in California evolved during a series of heated discussions and debates across the state and among legislative groups. The interest in educational alternatives by parents and their communities fueled widespread hearings and revisions. This first law predated Clinton's Goals 2000 (passed in 1994) that included parental involvement as a national goal.

Also, SB 1448 established California's first charter law with the legislative intent of the following:

- improve pupil learning;
- increase learning opportunities for students;
- promote the use of different and innovative teaching methods;
- create new opportunities for teachers;
- provide *parents* and students with expanded options to educational opportunities; and
- provide vigorous competition (Cal. Ed Code, 2020, p. 20).

In alignment with the legislative intent of California's charter law, parents, teachers, and community members could open a charter school and, via a nonprofit board, are entrusted to receive funding if they receive authorization by a school board, county board of education or state board of education. Any proposing group had the opportunity to request support from one of these authorizing bodies. Thus, a proposing group could seek support from a wide base of options across the state.

After the passage of the Charter Schools Act, enthusiastic parents and community groups began creating and applying for charter school status. There was now an opening for input and leadership from parents and the community that simply did not exist in the public-school landscape before 1992. The San Carlos Charter Learning Center in northern California received the first charter from the State Board of Education in February 1993 (CDE Charter School Directory, n.d.). Established by a group of community members with 85 students, this charter school has grown to serve 350 students and remains in operation to this day (San Carlos Charter Learning Center Renewal Petition, 2017).

CURRENT LANDSCAPE OF CHARTER SCHOOLS IN CALIFORNIA

Parents and their communities have supported charter schools over the past 30 years. The California values of freedom, independence, and choice undergird the population's interest and support of school choice. In the 2020–2021 school year, California charter schools experienced a 2.3% increase in student enrollment, whereas student enrollment within school districts decreased 3.2% (Veney & Jacobs, 2021). The state continues to lead the nation in charter school number and student population (National Association of Charter School Authorizers, n.d.). In 2018–19, there were approximately 1,306 charter schools and seven all-charter districts serving 652,933 students in California, which is 10.6% of the state's student enrollment (CDE Dataquest, 2019; CDE News Release, 2019; CDE CalEdFacts, n.d).

Charter schools have generally received favorable reviews from parents and their communities over the last 30 years. A 2019 statewide poll found that 59% of California public school parents favor charter schools, a higher proportion than the overall adult population (Baldassare et al., 2019). California's rating is higher than nationwide survey results of public opinion that reveal 50% of parents polled support charter schools (Henderson et al., 2020). This survey also found that Californians and the state's public-school parents are generally open to school choice options with approximately 75% of Californians and 81% of public-school parents support school choice through access to charter schools in lower-income communities. This data indicate that family and community engagement can serve as a driving force in the continuity of the charter movement in California.

The California Charter Schools Act of 1992 started as an experiment, allowing the establishment of only 100 charters. However, since then, California has witnessed exponential growth in the establishment of charter schools. And these new charter schools produced mixed results in performance and raised concerns about charter schools and the state charter law that established them. These concerns led to the 2019 revisions to the original California Charter Schools Act.

4   D. CASTILLO

2019 REVISION OF CALIFORNIA CHARTER SCHOOLS ACT

The lively debate of 1992 was relived in 2019. The overhaul of the California Charter School Act mirrored the 1992 proceedings, involving lawmakers, advocates, parents, and community members who strongly presented concerns, alternative points of view, and offered multiple amendments to the proposed legislative bills. These issues eventually led to compromises and clarifications to the support of charter schools. The final changes approved and signed into law re-affirmed that charter schools are part of California's educational landscape.

The 2019 legislative session adopted significant changes in the Charter Schools Act of 1992 and became effective in 2020. These changes overhauled state law *regulating* charter schools. The 2019 changes established updates in the review of a charter school petition application. These processes require increased transparency from charter school operators and their nonprofit boards. The changes create a balance of power between school district governing boards and charter petitioners (often parents and community members) and their boards. Also, the revision supported high-performing charter schools in that such qualified schools may receive longer renewal terms (Stokes, 2019b).

The current charter school landscape in California has expanded opportunities for family-community engagement because the new act requires charter petitioners to demonstrate widespread community support. Petitioners must include evidence of the need for this charter school in their specific community and provide explanations for how community support will be maintained during the school's life cycle. The 2019 California Charter Schools Act more fully defines parents/community demand for the establishment of a given charter school and requests for continued support by family-community engagement during implementation. A new provision in the amended law requires a charter school to demonstrate it is likely to serve the interests of the entire community in which the school is proposing to locate (California Education Code, 2020).

ANALYSIS OF THE 2019 CALIFORNIA CHARTER SCHOOLS LAW

The CA charter law remains agile in its ability to demand for the establishment of charter schools, which can be largely supported by family-community engagement. New sections in the 2019 Charter Schools Act expressly empower local school communities and school boards to make decisions regarding fiscal impact and need of new charter schools on existing neighborhood schools, calling on charter petitioners to highlight how these programs can address the needs of the community. This assessment requires significant knowledge of the community, its needs, interests, and must offer viable solutions to change the status quo in existing educational programs. Additional provisions made to the amended charter act include accountability measures for charter renewals that are based on charter school academic performance on the California School Dashboard. Specifically, the changes identify a three-tiered system of high-, middle-, and low-performing schools for deciding on the renewal of the charter and its term based on each school's academic performance schoolwide and by student groups compared to the state average and for student groups. A performance classification is issued by the California Department of Education and must be verified by the local charter authorizing body. An important factor of the new accountability criteria is that it sets criteria for denial of middle-performing schools on a school closure, serving a benefit to students (CA Education Code, 2020). This provision for denying charter renewals is key for family-community engagement activism.

ENROLLMENT DEMOGRAPHICS IN CA CHARTER SCHOOLS

Data over 2006–2013 reflect an enrollment increase in charter schools of non-white charter school students. For example, enrollment of Hispanic students in charters nationwide increased from almost 300,000 to over 600,000 and outnumbered Black students in 2012–13 (Finn et al., 2016). The National Alliance for Public Charter Schools (2023) reported increased enrollment in California charter schools of 413,515 in the 2011–12 school year, growing to 603,489 by the 2016–17 school year (National Alliance for Public Charter Schools, 2023). In the 2018–19 school year, almost 10% of California student enrollment was for charter school students (CDE Dataquest, 2019).

Enrollment demographics for charter schools compared to non-charter schools in California demonstrate that charter schools serve more African American students, but slightly fewer Hispanic or Latino and Asian students than traditional public schools. Charter schools in California serve 9% African American compared to 6% in non-charter schools, 66% Hispanic or Latino compared to 72%, 3% Asian students compared to 6% in non-charter schools (CDE Data Quest 2020–21 Enrollment by Ethnicity, 2021). Targeted recruitment can assist charter schools in attracting more diverse families to their schools, such as by providing direct communication and information about the charter school programs and school choice options within a community. Statewide, charter schools serve lower enrollment populations of student subgroups than non-charter school enrollment. For example, in 2020–21, the English learner population was 13.8% compared to 18.2% in non-charter schools and 11.3% of students with disabilities

6   D. CASTILLO

compared to 12.6% in non-charter schools. Charter schools also served a smaller student population of socioeconomically disadvantaged students. In 2018–19, charter schools in California enrolled 59.4% socioeconomically disadvantaged students, which is slightly lower than the 60.5% enrollment in non-charter schools (CDE enrollment, 2020–21). Yet, charter schools have an affirmative obligation to serve and educate English learners and students with disabilities. Charter schools should develop methods for monitoring enrollment demographics against any established or predetermined benchmark. Aligning outreach and recruitment is also a means to establish a more reflective student population that represents the community it serves.

PROMISES OF THE NEW LEGISLATION TO INCREASE FAMILY/COMMUNITY ENGAGEMENT

Access to Diverse Educational Programs for Families in Underserved Areas

The accountability provision found in the recent changes to the CA charter law provides an opportunity for more transparent high-stakes renewal decision-making for charter schools and access to a diverse portfolio of educational programs in underserved areas. Past charter school moratoriums, such as the 2019 suspension of new non-classroom-based charter schools in California, or the 2016 NAACP-supported moratorium on charter schools have sought to limit the reach of charter schools. This is sometimes in opposition to the wishes of low-income communities. Charter schools have been utilized to provide options where low-income parents want them, and this new law will allow that to continue. California charters have often been created in response to community support, including Stockton Collegiate Charter Schools, Gabriella Charter Schools, and Lennox Math, Science and Technology Academy.

Public Charter Schools in California aid in fulfilling the promise of school choice by offering access to diverse educational programs. These programs are outlined in their performance contracts known as charters. The 2019 statewide Public Policy poll found that 81% of public-school parents felt that it is "important or somewhat important for parents in low-income communities to have the choice to send their children to charter schools" (Baldassare et al., 2019, p. 17). The 2019 revision supports charter schools as a parental choice of public schools.

While family and community engagement with schools is often discussed in terms of volunteerism, philanthropy, or parent participation in school-managed events, charter schools provide a mechanism for parents and community members to participate in the design and creation of schools for their community. This is particularly true in traditionally marginalized communities lacking the political power to challenge school boards and school administrators. For example, Gabriella Charter School, founded in 2005, opened its doors in the low socioeconomic Echo Park neighborhood of Los Angeles. Gabriella offers a comprehensive dance program providing instruction in multiple genres, including ballet, jazz, and modern dance, coupled with a rigorous academic curriculum that serves Grades TK–8 (Gabriella Charter School, n.d.). After receiving numerous accolades for its educational program including, a California Distinguished Schools and a Gold Ribbon School Award from the California Department of Education, Gabriella Charter School continues to thrive in one of Los Angeles' county's underserved communities.

In 2017, Gabriella opened its second charter school in the South-Central area of Los Angeles, offering the same award-winning arts-based educational program to a community in need of high-quality educational programs. The first Gabriella Charter School was one of 156 schools cited in the 2017 Great Schools report, *Searching for Opportunities*. This 2017 report identified schools that are providing high-quality educational programs to students of color, namely African American and Hispanic students. Spotlight schools were identified based on criteria, including scores on the Great Schools Index, test score ratings in English-language arts and math, college-career readiness, suspension, and attendance rates, and advanced placement course ratings for the same student groups by race (Great Schools, 2017).

The Great Schools Report also found that only 6% of Hispanic students and 2% of African American students compared with 59% of White students and 73% of Asian students received a high-quality program based on the criteria mentioned above (Great Schools, 2017). However, Lennox, a small school district with a high Hispanic population near Los Angeles International Airport, searched for a way to improve educational options for these students. The administrative sought parent and community support. After much parent input, a charter school was created. Lennox Mathematics, Science and Technology Academy, a charter high school, was authorized by Lennox School District in 2003. This school, with a 64% Hispanic/Latino student population, was identified as one of the spotlight schools providing a successful educational program.

Similarly, community members in Stockton, a midsized city in northern California, were concerned about high-quality programs for their community. Stockton Collegiate International Secondary Schools, established in 2010, was also identified for offering equitable access to high-quality options, including an International Baccalaureate continuum for its K–12 student population (Great Schools, 2017). Stockton Collegiate

8 D. CASTILLO

International Secondary School is one of two schools operated by the same nonprofit board offering an International Baccalaureate-modeled (IB) charter school program in Grades 6–12. Without the allowance for charter school expansion, it is unlikely that any of these successful schools would be in operation, or that district schools would have evolved these features.

Requirements for Parent and Community Support

California's Charter law requires the submission of signatures of 50% meaningfully interested parents or teachers for the projected enrollment in the first year for charter school start-ups and for 50% teacher signatures for conversion charters. This community support is important for authorizing bodies to ascertain community support or opposition. Such was the case in 2019 with a charter school in Oakland, California.

The completed petition is followed by a required public hearing to determine the community's levels of support or opposition for the establishment of a new charter. In the 1992 law, the hearings are held within 30 days of the charter school petition submission with a final determination within 60 days of the submission. Changes to state law will extend the statutory timelines for a public hearing to 60 days and 90 days for a determination meeting. This extended timeframe will allow for a wider period for the community to provide input in support or opposition of the proposed charter or renewal. Charter school inception may limit parent participation because significant decisions are made by the founding team that is recruited by the founder, thus making parental involvement less meaningful than revising an original plan (Beabout & Jakiel, 2011). This extended time period and required community meetings prior to authorization decisions increases the opportunity for community input. Some charter schools are founded by parents and community members, while others are modeled as replications of an existing charter school. Some of these charter schools may arise from support from politicians, such as The SEED School of Los Angeles County, the first public boarding charter high school in the state that will open its doors in the 2022–23 school year (LA Metro, 2020). This school garnered widespread support from philanthropic donors and community partnerships between the Los Angeles Board of Supervisors, Los Angeles Metropolitan Transportation Agency, the public transportation agency, and the SEED Foundation, the charter school operator. Another example of community involvement in charter schools, in this case involving preexisting community organizations.

In California, amendments to the approved charter are handled as material revisions requiring approval from the charter school's governing board and the chartering authority before the implementation of the changes.

Families and community members are provided an opportunity to speak during public comment at a public hearing ahead of a board decision of the material revision. However, family-community engagement may be limited due to stakeholders having to travel to the public meetings, primary home language barriers, and members of the community may be intimidated by official government or school district proceedings and buildings. Charter schools can foster authentic partnerships with families and community members throughout the school life cycle of a charter school.

For example, in March 2019, hundreds of parents and community members came out to a special board meeting of the Oakland Unified School District Board of Education, which included a proposed charter school moratorium action that resulted from the Teacher Strike in February 2019 (Kroopf, 2019). This case demonstrates a community's activism through exercising their voice against a proposed action. Charter school supporters opposed a moratorium on charter schools because this action would single-handedly eliminate access to school choice and diverse school program offerings. Oakland was the second-largest school district in the state to pass a moratorium on charter schools. Oakland Unified in 2016–17 had the fourth-highest concentration of students attending charter schools in California serving approximately 15,000 students in 44 charter schools authorized by the school district and rose to the highest level in 2017–18 (David et al., 2017; Kroopf, 2019). The impact of proposed charter school moratoriums or closures may produce uncertainty for charter school students who attend these schools because these involve lengthy deliberations. The activism parents displayed towards the school district was instrumental in voicing opposition to the proposed moratorium. This example of charter schools and charter school parents uniting against a district policy is one form of engagement.

Community-Inspired, Mission-Focused Charter Schools

The legislative intent of the California Charter Schools Act provides "opportunities for teachers, parents pupils, and community members to establish and maintain schools that operate independently from the existing school district structure" by providing "parents and pupils with expanded choices in the types of educational opportunities that are available within the public school system," and creating "new professional opportunities for teachers, including the opportunity to be responsible for the learning program at the school site" (CA Education Code, 2020, p. 20). Given this support for creating alternatives, this law supports charter schools that provide for active parent groups and strong engagement. The law serves as a template to provide opportunities to new charters and to support existing charter schools to make school site level decisions and engage their community directly. For example, Odyssey Charter School in Pasadena, California, has created an active parent advisory council that has parent and community member representation on its governing board. Odyssey Charter School opened in 1999 and expanded to operate a second charter school in the same community in 2018. Odyssey's motto is "Building community through education" (Odyssey Charter School, n.d.). Throughout the years, Odyssey Charter School has cultivated an active parent and community base that has helped the school with its expansion efforts and through volunteering opportunities demonstrating a commitment to ensuring students receive a high-quality educational program.

This sort of community-based charter school has already been established in the literature. Warren et al. (2009) cited Camino Nuevo Academy, a community-based charter school network operating six charter schools in underserved communities in Los Angeles for its community development strategy (Warren et al., 2009). Camino Nuevo Charter Academy opened its first charter school in 2000 and has grown in enrollment as well as in its support of the community through robust community partnerships with diverse public agencies. Camino Nuevo operates a total of six charter schools, primarily in the MacArthur/Westlake area of Los Angeles, serving approximately 3,400 students in 2017–18 (Camino Nuevo Academy, n.d.a.). Camino Nuevo Charter Academy has articulated partnerships related to civic engagement, arts and culture, college readiness, health and wellness, and support services. Camino Nuevo's Anchor Values include, "we are rooted in the community's richness and in the cultural and environmental context where our students and their families live" (Camino Nuevo Charter Academy, n.d.b.). This school has implemented a robust family and community engagement plan that values parents as partners in education. Opportunities for parents to provide input through advisory committees and School Site Council meetings with school leadership. The school hires parent coordinators that coordinate the array of parent and community engagement activities. Workshop topics include academic themes, parent curriculum/series, socio-emotional needs, specific training for parents serving on advisory committees, and school-sponsored events (Camino Nuevo Charter Academy, n.d.b.). These examples of community-based charter schools offer images of partnerships that, while certainly possible within traditional district-run public schools, might be more easily created and managed in charter schools given the voluntary nature of charter school attendance and the site-based autonomy they possess.

Full-Service Community Charter Schools

Charter schools designed to foster "unique needs and cultural contexts of their local communities" align themselves with the concept of Community Schools (Hiatt-Michael, 2016, p. 16). A 2014 interview with Martin Blank revealed insights about the growth of Full-Service Community Schools across the nation, citing an increase in the number of this school model in the last 15 years. Dr. Blank also referenced Open Charter Magnet School, the first charter magnet program in California that was initiated by a group of parents in 1993. This charter magnet remains operational in the Westside neighborhood of Los Angeles and is achieving high levels of student performance. Significant research indicates that schools utilizing wrap-around services support an increase in parent's self-efficacy (Schurer et al., 2017). Charter schools that offer full-service supports frequently become an integral part of active student integration and participation in the school.

Para Los Niños, Inc. is a charter operator that runs three charter schools, early education centers, Head Start, and Mental Health Clinics in the metropolitan area of Los Angeles, CA. Para Los Niños, Inc. was established in 1979 to support and create opportunities for childcare, and opened its first charter school, Para Los Niños Charter in 2002. Through its multifaceted nonprofit public agency, Para Los Niños offers families and community members much needed full services. These services encompass the following:

- Family services from birth through age 21, offering mental health services, featuring therapeutic and trauma-informed support;
- Youth Workforce services for students ages 14–24, providing paid and unpaid work experience;
- CAL Senderos partners with its charter schools to offer a wellness program during the CATCH Physical Education Program;
- Best START Region, a community-funded program through First 5LA; and
- Innovations 2, a community collaboration project funded by the Los Angeles County Department of Mental Health to offer trauma-informed services and supports through a multi-agency network and partnership (Para Los Niños, n.d.).

Para Los Niños' motto is, "Excellent Education, Powerful Families, and Strong Communities" (Para Los Niños, n.d.). Such wrap-around services necessarily require a broad set of community partnerships and using the

12 D. CASTILLO

charter school as a site of service. Again, while there are also many examples of this in district-run schools, charter schools may have some advantages in terms of local autonomy and site-based decision-making.

Parent and Community Engagement in Charter School Decision-Making

Some charter schools align themselves with Epstein's Level 5 engagement (participation in school decision-making) by providing opportunities for parents and community members to give input through participating on charter governing boards (Epstein & Associates, 2019). Environmental Charter Schools, Inc. established in 2000, created a parent and community representative position for a parent and community member to serve on its board of directors. The group governs four independent charter schools within Los Angeles County.

Sometimes the parent role in decision-making can be less formal, such as participation in public comment periods and charter school board meetings. In 2017, the American Indian Model Schools (AIMS) in Oakland, despite high student performance and achievement, experienced multiple operational concerns leading to heated debates between stakeholders and school management at the charter governing board meetings (Vogel, 2017). Parents and community members grew frustrated over facilities' maintenance needs and asked for information about the school's operating budget. Then, the school's operating budget showed a severe deficit. There was also a fraud investigation against the school's former executive director and founder. The Fiscal Crisis Management and Assistance Team (FCMAT), a third-party consultant, identified fraud allegations against the former executive director in a 2012 Extraordinary Audit conducted on behalf of the charter school's authorizer (Fiscal Crisis Management and Assistance Team, 2012). In 2019, charges were dropped and in a plea deal federal investigators issued the former executive director a one-year probation and a $100 fine (SF Gate, 2019, May). Yet in closed session, the school's governing board approved an increase of the charter's superintendent' salary of $48,000. This move led to community anger and calls from parents and community members for the charter superintendent to quit. Parent and community member frustration led to AIMS' charter authorizer intervening through monitoring these concerns and was cited as stating, "charter law never entertains the idea of charter families electing charter board members," but it is a flaw in legislation (Vogel, 2017, para. 12). Although the AIMS charter parents were not advocating for parent-elected board members, this notion is a similar method utilized in the Chicago Public Schools when they embarked on their well-studied Local School

Council experiment in 1988 following the Chicago School Reform Act. This effort met with mixed success and aimed to introduce parent members representing a majority on school governing boards and to decentralize control and afford local governing bodies a decision-making function over the hiring of the school principal, budgets, and curriculum (Superville, 2014). California saw its share of the establishment of local governing councils through LEARN, local school councils, and school-based management councils. However, this remains an area that is worth pursuing. There are some independent charter schools that designate governing board membership for parents, but do not represent a majority, such as some of the schools that will be described later.

Currently, the Los Angeles Unified School District authorizes 51 affiliated charter schools, which are semi-autonomous charter schools of the district, and that are afforded flexibilities over areas such as: curriculum and professional development, local school governance, and some staffing practices. Some of these affiliated charter schools form strong parent-community partnerships that include the formation of a charter council with representatives from staff, administration, and parent-community. Charter schools permit parent-elected governing boards, encourage building community capacity, and offer a promising opportunity to amplify community voice.

Community Voice in Charter Authorization

A new requirement found in the amended charter law has been added to the grounds for denying a charter school approval. The authorizer (e.g., local or county appellate) must determine whether a charter school is likely to serve the interests of the entire community in which it proposes to locate. Engaging the community in the value of the proposed educational program in which the charter school seeks to locate will require demonstrating how the charter school can meet the needs of this intended community. During the proposal process, parents and teachers are afforded opportunities to demonstrate meaningful interests in the establishment of a charter school. However, it remains unclear whether public comment during the required public hearing is sufficient for the community to voice support or opposition to the proposed charter petition. Hopefully, future work with charter schools may reveal additional mechanisms that should be developed and implemented to demonstrate sufficiency of community need.

The 2019 Act creates a greater responsibility for charter school developers to satisfactorily demonstrate their educational program can meet the interests of the entire community. The Act also poses a requirement to provide evidence that the proposed program will not duplicate current

14 D. CASTILLO

educational programs offered by the school district. This requires that the charter applicant have a detailed understanding of the local educational landscape and how the new charter will add to the educational value. This demonstration will depend on the support of the community as well as the charter authorizing entity. Demonstrating that charter schools are likely to serve the interests of the community will depend on parent advocacy and community engagement. Since governing board members are set up to be the representatives of communities and they are the final decision-makers, these board members will need *to accurately gauge community advocacy and support* in terms of community support or opposition. Board members need to seek parent and community beyond the traditional public board meeting (Hiatt-Michael, 2016). Such board meetings tend to be board member organized and driven. Opportunities for community groups to participate will need to expand to regular engagement at the school sites or other local gathering places. Decision-makers must access groups in support and opposition. The full community voice should prevail in the determination of community needs within any given charter school.

Charter-District Collaboration

A unique example of school district-charter school collaboration can be found between the Wiseburn Unified School District and Da Vinci Schools, Inc., a charter operator of five charter schools in El Segundo and Hawthorne, California. Da Vinci Schools, Inc. was established in 2008 and opened its first charter school in 2009. Initially, Da Vinci Schools, Inc., was an independent charter school operating with an independent board. Within a few years, the school morphed into five schools, each with a different theme and curricular offerings.

Wiseburn School District was a TK–8 School District and wanted to connect with a high school. After much planning and revisions, the members of Wiseburn's school board supported a unique school district and charter school unification plan. This plan was approved by the community in 2013. Three of the five charter high schools operated by Da Vinci Schools became the local or "home high schools" to Wiseburn Unified School District's families (Da Vinci Schools, n.d.). However, they remain as charter schools open to others in Los Angeles County.

At present, of the five Da Vinci independent charter schools, four of these five schools serve as the resident high schools for students residing within the boundaries of the Wiseburn Unified School District. Wiseburn students as well as others receive a wide range of benefits and support from the aerospace industries that surround this charter school. Students are automatically enrolled at one of the four Da Vinci Schools now housed in a state-of-the-art school building in a co-location with the Wiseburn Unified

Family-Community Engagement in California Charter Schools   15

School District headquarters. In a unique charter-district collaboration, Da Vinci Schools and the Wiseburn Unified School District Board of Education co-locate their district and home office spaces.

Parent Advocacy

As parents participate in charter school advocacy, they strengthen their voices through meaningful engagement and support, leading to decision-making (Warren et al., 2016). In 2016, the city council of Huntington Park, California, a high-population, new immigrant Hispanic community, 6-miles from Downtown Los Angeles passed an ordinance initially introducing a 45-day moratorium on charter schools in the city, that eventually grew to a year-long cap. The directive was based on the numerous requests and inquiries about facility permits for charter schools. In response to the city's action that set a moratorium on charter schools, almost one hundred parents and charter supporters delivered a lawsuit to the city that was drafted in conjunction with the leading charter lobby group in the state, the California Charter Schools Association (Clough, 2016). In *CCSA v. City of Huntington Park*, the court determined that "numerous inquiries and requests are insufficient to pass a moratorium ordinance" (Justia, n.d., para 2). Interest in opening a charter school in this community leads to increases in inquiries and requests for facilities-related permits. City lawmakers felt a moratorium was a viable option that was a necessary measure appropriate at the time. At the same time, some of the community members disagreed and mobilized collectively with assistance from CCSA. The parents and community advocates utilized social capital to gain access to information and resources, such as expanding their network and building a coalition with the lobbying group. This example demonstrates a group of parent-community members joining forces with a larger network to exert influence and effectively organize themselves toward collective action, yielding change and strengthening community voice (Castillo, 2013). Grassroots groups can affect sustainable change as members use a network to influence decision-makers with positional power. In this case, strong parent advocates came together to influence the outcome of the moratorium through organizing. This activity reflects Warren, Mapp, and Ruttner's assertion that individual parents advocating for their student's needs become leaders through engaging in participatory action leading to change (Warren et al., 2016).

A leading criticism of community organizing activities in black and brown communities is that the organizing is politically driven and crafted to appear unsolicited, and rooted in the needs of the community, however directed by powerful elites serving their own interests. This refers to the phenomenon known as *astroturf organizing*. Communities of color must be

16   D. CASTILLO

careful in aligning with organizations or groups that might be leading them towards an agenda that is not their own.

CHALLENGES TO SUCCESSFUL COMMUNITY ENGAGEMENT IN CHARTER SCHOOLS

Achieving Equity and Access to Charter Schools

A promise often made by the charter school movement, cited earlier in this chapter, is high-quality charter school educational options for all students. An often overlooked, but crucially important, element of community engagement in charter schools is simply enrolling students from a variety of backgrounds. This establishes long-term connections with a representative makeup of local community sub-populations.

The 2019 California charter law expands a charter school's responsibility for maintaining and serving a balanced student population of English learners, former English learners (known as Reclassified Fluent English Proficient), students with disabilities, and socioeconomically disadvantaged students. In doing so, charter schools must remove barriers that create challenges for students of diverse backgrounds and who experience academic difficulties.

Parents from under-represented populations, especially those without computer access, may not receive information regarding charter school options. Sufficient information is an essential requirement to ensure charter schools can fulfill their pledge to provide *all students access* to equitable and diverse programs. Such information should be available in the communities' languages. Each charter school should be required to establish and show how they maintain fair practices that promote high-quality school programs. Every charter school should maintain a robust recruitment and outreach program towards diverse ethnic and racial groups reflective of the local population. As mentioned earlier, the 2017 *Searching for Opportunities* report identified "systemic gaps in access" to schools demonstrating strong academic performance and how schools are serving students of color (Great Schools, 2017, p. 9). If charter schools are to sustain healthy, two-way relationships with their surrounding communities, it seems fundamental that they admit a student body that is representative of that community. It is also crucial that they provide excellent education to those students.

Hawthorne Math and Science Academy is cited in the list of Spotlight Schools in this *Searching for Opportunities* report. Hawthorne Math and Science Academy was established in 2003 as a dependent charter school to the district and the only charter school authorized by the Hawthorne School District. A dependent charter school is an autonomous charter school authorized by the school district similar to the affiliated charter schools in the Los Angeles Unified School District, previously discussed. It focuses on science, math, and technology Grades 9–12 and has yielded strong results with their African American and Hispanic student populations. From this base of effective delivery of education, the school will be able to build long-term, sustainable relationships with families and community members.

Information Transparency as a Precursor for Family Involvement

Charter schools in California are serving approximately 10% of the state's student enrollment and receive approximately $3.4 billion in state funding (known as LCFF), including $900 million financing earmarked for serving students with high needs (Public Advocates, 2018). The state enacted the LCFF model in 2013 to provide schools local control of their funding and decision-making over their spending plans (Public Advocates, 2018). The Public Advocates 2019 report *Keeping the LCFF Promise Alive* identified critical issues that pose challenges to charter schools and that inhibit transparency of operations and fiscal outlook. Public Advocates, a nonprofit advocacy group, reviewed 70 charter school Local Control Accountability Plans (LCAPs) and highlighted a list of concerns regarding the distribution of information to parents and community members. LCAPs are spending plans covering yearly spending, actionable goals, and objectives for serving high-need student groups. Report findings uncovered striking information, such as only one-third of the LCAPs reviewed were provided online, only 21% provided a metric for measuring how they engaged parents in the decision-making process, and more than two-thirds of the state funds earmarked for serving high needs students were not reflected in the LCAPs. Ninety-one percent of charter school LCAPs reviewed that served 15% or more English learners were not provided in a language other than English.

Changes to state charter law aim to resolve such report findings in the future, including provisions that require charter schools to post their LCAPs on their websites and to provide a translation of LCAPs to primary home languages if a charter school serves 15% English learners. As seen in the AIMS example earlier in this chapter, access to information regarding the school program, facilities, and operations is essential and now also required in primary home language to expand stakeholder communication and increase the public's trust in a charter school.

Access to Charter School's Educational Program Information

Members throughout a variety of communities share their lack of knowledge of the educational options charter schools offer within their geographic areas (Hiatt-Michael, personal communication, December 6, 2021). Parents and community members experience a challenge in being able to fully exercise school choice options within the broader educational marketplace because they are lacking information about the school choices and their educational programs. A new resident walks into the local public school and seldom receives information on options within the area. Providing school communities with key information about charter school educational programs is essential and invaluable. However, parents and community members often find themselves without access to information about a charter school's educational program or status until an impending action, such as a school closure, charter revocation, or a charter renewal is denied. School communities are often left with limited access to information subject to word of mouth or knowledge obtained on a school website.

Family access to specific school information can assist them in making informed decisions about whether to initially enroll and subsequently remain enrolled in the charter school. In addition to transparency for families, a charter school's success in the areas of academic, operational, fiscal and governance inform its status with its authorizing entity and can also impact a charter school's status during renewal determination or when requesting good standing certification needed for fiscal matters or facilities incentives loans.

Although federal and state programs require schools to implement mechanisms for informing stakeholders about a charter school's academic progress and educational program, through reports, such as California's School Accountability Report Card (SARC) and school LCAPs, information provided in these reports is only as valuable to stakeholders when it is readily available to them and is recent.

The School Dashboard, a newly implemented school accountability system published by the state serves a parent-family friendly data reporting system. It reflects a 5-tier color system denoting achievement progress levels made on multiple state performance indicators. Achievement levels on state and local indicators are assigned a color, with blue and green being the highest and orange and red being the lowest. Schools, including charter schools, that receive red levels on indicators over two years, become eligible for continuous support and improvement funding to assist in identifying high-need and implementation of an action plan. Charter schools must develop an action plan in conjunction with stakeholders that will help the school in improving and moving out of low achievement brackets. Similarly, charter schools that experience low levels of student

Family-Community Engagement in California Charter Schools   19

performance achievement become eligible for technical assistance from the county office of education and can partner with other agencies to receive support. However, despite this pronounced system of support, charter schools are not required to notify stakeholders about their status related to high-stakes decisions, such as charter renewal, closures, or revocation.

Families and Charter School Non-Renewals, Closures, and Revocations

Some charter schools have faced challenges in maintaining their charter status, jeopardizing their viability to remain in operation and serve students and families due to student academic performance and other organizational issues. Under the previous iteration of charter law, initial charter terms were authorized for up to five years and had to be renewed before the end of the charter term. However, recent amendments to charter law created a tiered system for making renewal determinations up to seven years, depending on student academic performance. Contrastingly, low student achievement may also jeopardize a charter school's status with its authorizer. The change in law to extend a charter term up to seven years is beneficial in terms of providing stability to communities about the status of their chosen charter school, but a longer period also requires monitoring. For example, in May 2019, Summit Preparatory Charter School, a start-up charter middle school located in South Central Los Angeles, closed its doors early. The authorizing board dictated this school's fate by denying its renewal application, which subsequently caused the charter school to lose its eligibility status for a grant it was counting on to remain financially viable (Stokes, 2019a). Given such outcomes, the charter school's governing board made the hard decision to close its school in May, which was earlier than their approved annual academic calendar, which extended through June. The school district denied this renewal on April 2, 2019, and 30-days later, the charter school's governing board decided to self-close the charter school without filing an appeal at the county- or state- level. There is no public record of the charter school's governing board communicating with parents and the community before making its decision to voluntarily close early. Self-closure decisions are tough on communities, especially when they are unexpected, abrupt, and early. Although more charter schools are created every year in the state, each year also records many closures (California Department of Education, 2018). For example, in 2017–18, 61 charter schools were opened, but the state also witnessed the close of 14 schools that year. Thus, the creation and demise of charter schools in California suggests that there are promises but also many challenges to the viability of charter schools in this historically progressive state. Another example of an unexpected charter school closure occurred in August 2018, only four days into the school year, PUC iPrep Charter Academy, a dual language-themed charter school in the Eagle Rock neighborhood of Los Angeles (Blume, 2018). It is unknown how parents and guardians were notified about the voluntary school closure before the decision. Although charter schools are required to inform parents, authorizers, county office of education, and the California Department of Education after their governing boards have resolved that it will close their schools, prior stakeholder notification is not required. A description of required closure procedures is included in a school's approved charter petition, as publishing criteria for school closures are beneficial (Hawkins, 2019). Documentation and notification of school closure, retention and transfer of records, financial close-out, and disposition of liabilities and assets are generally topics included in the section on Closure procedures in approved charter petitions (California Department of Education, Charter School Closures, n.d.).

Charter School Facilities and School District-Charter School Co-Locations

Finding adequate facilities for establishing a charter school is a looming challenge that is very important for a charter school to serve its intended community. Yet, this is one of seven national challenges for charter schools cited in the Bellweather 2019 report, *The State of the Charter Sector* (LiBetti et al., 2019). Although federal programs have been designed to assist charter schools in the construction, renovation, or expansion of facilities, securing adequate facilities to accommodate their needs remains a significant challenge. The 2019 changes to law enacted by AB 1507 prohibit a new charter school to operate outside of the jurisdiction or boundaries of the authorizing school district (Cal. Ed. Code, 2020). This became an issue, causing the need for this provision in the law, because of the increasing number of charter schools, specifically non-classroom-based charter schools, that were located *outside* of the boundaries of the authorizing entities. A non-district operated charter school creates a burden on the school district in which it resides although the local district did not authorize these charter schools. Also, although accessible to families and communities, these schools that are located outside of the authorizer's boundaries are hard to monitor since the oversight agency might reside miles away from the charter school's physical locations. Schools operating in southern California might be governed by an agency or board in northern California.

Charter schools in California may purchase or lease private facilities or lease District-owned facilities through a Proposition 39 application process.

State policymakers established the Charter Facilities Grant Program in 2001 (commonly known as the SB 740 Facilities Loan Program) for the reimbursement of rental and leasing of charter school facilities based on meeting eligibility requirements (California Legislative Analyst's Office, 2019). The Charter Schools Facilities Program enacted in 2002 to provide charter schools fixed-rate matching loans dispersed through the school district in which a charter school is located (California Legislative Analyst's Office, 2019). However, facilities options in urban areas are at a premium with few options, such as applying for district-owned facilities through the Proposition 39 program. Though these legislative-backed programs offer charter schools funding options for facilities, securing a site remains challenging for many new charter schools. Given that a school's location largely defines what community it serves, high levels of uncertainty around charter school facilities necessarily creates barriers to family and community engagement.

Another facilities solution not involving adding new school facilities is using existing school facilities to house both a district school and a charter school, a practice known as co-location. A 2015 report, *Best of Both Worlds: Can District-Charter Co-Locations Be a Win-Win?* examined four model district-charter collaborations that shed light on promising practices to address co-location challenges (DeArmond et al., 2015). The 2015 report cited cross-collaboration communication through common meetings to discuss shared concerns, building leaders that prioritize co-location coordination, and working on common school culture elements across the two school models. Charter schools on co-locations have been the target of community backlash, such as Gabriella Charter School. Despite Gabriella Charter School' success in serving its community, it has not gone without criticism. In 2016, Gabriella Charter School received support to open its second charter school. However, finding a location on a school campus was difficult due to community opposition. A group of parents and teachers from local schools a group of parents went on a car caravan during the middle of the pandemic to voice concerns and opposition against Gabriella Charter School's second charter school on the campus of Lizarraga Elementary in the Vernon Park area of Los Angeles (Maple and Lizarraga Against Charter Co-location, 2021, May 21). The school ultimately opened on a different district school less than a mile from Lizarraga Elementary. But not without multiple protests from parents from the various district sites. Based on social media posts, protesters even drove to the charter school's governing board members or founders' homes to protest (Stop Charter Co-Location, 2021, August). This type of organized action from groups became popular during the pandemic as people worked from home or met virtually for governing board meetings instead of physically on the school site.

22   D. CASTILLO

Better collaboration among school districts and charter schools would ensure an amicable and satisfying experience for students and families when charter schools need facilities from a school district that may have space due to declining enrollment (Spurrier, 2017). Development of policies addressing these issues of facilities sharing or purchasing by charter schools can prove to be beneficial to expand the conversation between both parties. School districts can expand communication about facilities with stakeholders as a means of improving district-charter collaboration. Stakeholders can organize around facilities-related requests to demonstrate their interest in obtaining district space in their target communities.

The nexus between establishing community interest, need, and accessing facilities in an intended community calls for charter school teams to intentionally use data to share the uniqueness of their program and how this program can best support the community. The use of data prior to petitioning to establish a charter school in a targeted community is key to ensure facilities are obtained in the intended community and can be addressed through the National Charter Schools Resource Center's 3-Step Model for Design, Planning or Replication and Expansion (National Charter Schools Resource Center, 2020). The 3-step model recommendations are to gather data about the families and community to be served, including researching languages spoken by community members and families, determining enrollment patterns, drafting a survey, and engaging a group of core founding members consisting of family members, parents, guardians, and community members to draft a family engagement plan. Developing a survey to gather school interests and challenges currently encountered in the community is also proposed (National Charter Schools Resource Center, 2020). The second step is to understand how community interests or assets align or do not align with the engagement plan. Part of this strategy entails assessing cultural competencies and developing relationships with the community by regularly scheduling touchpoints and holding focus group interviews to learn about unmet needs. The third strategy is to establish new partnerships with community organizations and for staff to attend events held by these organizations (National Charter Schools Resource Center, 2020). As a response to the COVID-19 pandemic charter schools held COVID-19 testing and vaccination clinics in partnership with community health centers or medical clinics. Value Schools, a Charter Management Organization operates four charter schools near downtown Los Angeles hosted COVID-19 vaccination clinics during the months of August and September 2021 prior to the start of the school year for students who were 12 years and older and their families (Values Schools, n.d.).

Charter Schools and Teachers Unions

Modeled after the teacher strike by the teacher's union in the Los Angeles Unified School District in January 2019, three charter schools in South Central Los Angeles operated by The Accelerated School went on strike. Teachers and classified employees at these charter schools are unionized through the United Teachers of Los Angeles (UTLA) and the Service Employees International Union (SEIU). This historic strike was the first charter school strike in the state and ended with 78 charter teacher union members voting to end this eight-day strike and agreeing to a new labor agreement (Smith, 2019). The new agreement includes but is not limited to a three-month severance pay for teachers not elected to continue, a $10,000 signing bonus for teachers who return at the beginning of the school year and increases to employer's healthcare contributions (Smith, 2019). The State of California is experiencing a teacher and substitute teacher shortage due to teachers not returning to teach or due to coronavirus test positivity rates (Hong, 2021).

SUMMARY

The charter school landscape in California has been shaped by family-community engagement since its inception and continued growth. The efforts of California parents, families, community members, and advocates have helped design and drive demand for diverse educational options for almost half a century. The thousand charter schools throughout California, from affluent to below-poverty level districts, demonstrate family interest in educational alternatives. However, more information and communication about their options must be made available to students, families, and the community at large. Strengthening school choice and high-quality educational programs in underserved communities for all students is vital, such as the case in communities of color, where moratoriums on charter schools and recent changes in law threaten their ability to establish a charter school in their community. Yet, as seen through the level of parent and community advocacy, community organizing has helped communities of color amplify their voice in support of charter schools.

The reviews of charter schools that have failed reveal that these schools had limited families and community engagement. Such engagement could have informed parents and the community about the happenings of the school and drawn upon the resources of their community to improve. Lessons learned from their final reviews identify the challenges of charter schools in California and the requirement for success is in deep family and community commitment to their local charter school.

School choice also provides an opportunity for parents and families to exercise change and vote with their feet. In the earlier part of the chapter, the importance of community voice and advocacy was promoted as well as providing examples of mission-focused charter schools with community efforts at the center of a school's purpose. Parents and community members often support school choice, and their influence is a key driver in efforts to maintain California's support of diverse educational programs for its youth.

However, any promises left unaddressed or underdeveloped create challenges. Continued challenges remain and will need resolution through stronger parent and community engagement. Access to information about charter schools is important for all stakeholders, including those that are not achieving their promised potential or under consideration for potential charter non-renewal, revocation, or closure. The challenges identified in this chapter, offer opportunities for increased stakeholder collaboration, and expanded dialogue that can allow parents and community members to engage in mutual conversations related to charter schools, school choice, and high-quality school programs for all students as well as those in California.

REFERENCES

Baldassare, M., Bonner, D., Dykman, A., & Ward, R. (2019, April). *Californians and education*. Public Policy Institute of California. https://www.ppic.org/wp-content/uploads/ppic-statewide-survey-californians-and-education-april-2019.pdf

Beabout, B., & Jakiel, L. B. (2011). Family and community engagement in charter schools. In S. Redding, M. Murphy, & P. Sheley (Eds.), *Handbook on family and community engagement* (pp. 147–151). Information Age Publishing.

Blume, H. (August 24, 2018). *L.A. charter school closes due to low enrollment; campus was in network co-founded by Ref Rodriguez*. https://www.latimes.com/local/education/la-me-edu-puc-charter-closes-20180824-story.html

California Department of Education. (n.d.). *Charter school directory*. https://www.cde.ca.gov/ds/si/cs/ap/rpt.asp

California Department of Education. (n.d.). *Charter school closures*. https://www.cde.ca.gov/sp/ch/csclosurerules.asp

California Department of Education. (n.d.). *Charter Schools CalEd Facts*. https://www.cde.ca.gov/sp/ch/cefcharterschools.asp

California Department of Education. (2018). *Charter school closures, fiscal year 2017–18*. https://www.cde.ca.gov/sp/ch/chclosures1718.asp

California Department of Education. (2019). *2018–19 enrollment by ethnicity for charters and non charter schools*. https://dq.cde.ca.gov/dataquest/dqcensus/EnrCharterEth.aspx?cds=00&agglevel=state&year=2018-19

Family-Community Engagement in California Charter Schools   25

California Department of Education. (2019, March 28). *News release*. https://www.cde.ca.gov/nr/ne/yr19/yr19rel27.asp

California Department of Education. (2021). *2020–21 Enrollment by Ethnicity for Charters and Non Charter Schools*. https://dq.cde.ca.gov/dataquest/dqcensus/EnrCharterEth.aspx?cds=00&agglevel=state&year=2020-21

California Education Code. (2020). California Education Code (2020 Ed.). *Thomas Reuters, 20*, 42–43.

California Legislative Analyst's Office. (2019, March 12). *Overview of charter Schools in California*. https://lao.ca.gov/handouts/education/2019/Charter-School-Overview-031219.pdf

Camino Nuevo Charter Academy. (n.d.a.), *2018 Impact Report*. https://www.caminonuevo.org/2018_Impact_Report.pdf

Camino Nuevo Charter Academy. (n.d.b.), *Parents as partners*. https://www.caminonuevo.org/apps/pages/parents

Castillo, D. (2013). *Influence of grassroots groups to affect educational change* [Doctoral dissertation]. *PQDT* ProQuest, DAI-75/02(E).

Clough, G. (2016, November 4). Parents deliver lawsuit to Huntington Park over charter ban. *LA School Report*. http://laschoolreport.com/parents-deliver-lawsuit-against-huntington-park-over-charter-ban/

David, R., Hesla, D., & Pendergrass, S. A. (2017). *A growing movement: america's largest charter school communities*. National Public Schools Alliance. https://www.publiccharters.org/sites/default/files/documents/2017-10/Enrollment_Share_Report_Web_0.pdf

DeArmond, M., Nelson, E. C., & Burns, A. (2015, August). *The best of both worlds: Can district-charter co-location be a win-win?* https://www.crpe.org/publications/best-both-worlds-can-district-charter-co-location-be-win-win

Da Vinci Schools. (n.d.). *DV fact sheet*. https://www.davincischools.org/wp-content/uploads/2019/09/DV-fact-sheet-oct-2019.pdf

Epstein, J. L., & Associates. (2019). *School, family, and community partnerships: Your handbook for action* (4th ed.). Corwin Press.

Extraordinary Audit of the American Indian Model Charter Schools. Fiscal Crisis and Management Assistance Team. (2012). https://www.fcmat.org/PublicationsReports/AlamedaCOEfinalreport6121292.pdf

Finn, C. E., Manno, B. V., & Wright, B. L. (2016). *Charter schools at the crossroads: predicaments, paradoxes, possibilities*. Harvard Education Press.

Fensterwald, J. (2018, August 13). *Gary Hart, author of California's charter school law, reflects on its impact*. https://edsource.org/2018/gary-hart-author-of-californias-charter-school-law-reflects-on-its-impact/601212

Great Schools! (2017, May). *Searching for opportunities: Examining racial gaps in access to quality schools in California and list of spotlight schools*. https://www.greatschools.org/catalog/reports/searching_for_opportunity.pdf

Hawkins, B. (2019). *Charter authorizing guru Greg Richmond on past 20 years & what's next*. https://www.the74million.org/article/testifying-before-congress-not-as-fun-as-working-with-people-to-talk-about-a-new-school-charter-authorizing-guru-greg-richmond-on-last-20-years-whats-next/

Henderson, M. B., Houston, D., Peterson, P. E., & West, M. R. (Winter 2020). Public support grows for higher teacher pay and expanded school choice. *Education Next.* https://www.educationnext.org/school-choice-trump-era-results-2019-education-next-poll/

Hiatt-Michael, D. (2016). Two concepts of the community engagement: Interviews with Don Davies and Martin Blank. In M. Evans & D. Hiatt-Michael (Eds.), *The power of community engagement for educational change* (pp. 9–20). Information Age Publishing.

Hong, J. (2021, September). *Not enough subs: California schools face severe teacher shortage.* https://calmatters.org/education/k-12-education/2021/09/california-teacher-schools/

Jason, Z. (2017, Summer). *Battle over charter schools.* https://www.gse.harvard.edu/news/ed/17/05/battle-over-charter-schools

Justia. (n.d.). *California Charter Schools Assn. v. City of Huntington Park.* https://law.justia.com/cases/california/court-of-appeal/2019/b284162.html

Kroopf, W. (2019, March 21). *At Oakland school board meeting, debate over school closures and charter schools intensifies.* Oakland North. https://oaklandnorth.net/2019/03/21/at-oakland-school-board-meeting-debate-over-school-closures-and-charter-schools-intensifies/

LA Metro. (2020, October 21). *Metro, County of L.A. and SEED Foundation hold groundbreaking for SEED School of L.A County in South Los Angeles.* https://thesource.metro.net/2020/10/21/metro-county-of-l-a-and-seed-foundation-hold-groundbreaking-for-seed-school-of-l-a-county-in-south-los-angeles/

Letter from our founder. Letter from Our Founder ("Ms. Liza"). (n.d.). https://www.gabriellacharterschools.org/apps/pages/index.jsp?uREC_ID=285709&type=d

LiBetti, A., Burgoyne-Allen, P., Lewis, B., & Schmitz, K. (2019). *The state of charter sector: What you need to know about charter schools today.* Bellweather Education Partners. https://bellwethereducation.org/sites/default/files/State%20of%20the%20Charter%20Sector_Bellwether.pdf

Maple and Lizarraga Against Charter Co-Locations. Facebook. (2021, May 21). https://www.facebook.com/MapleLizarragaJuntos/

National Alliance of Public Charter Schools. (2016). *Demanding a chance: Parents demand for public charter schools continues to grow.* https://www.publiccharters.org/publications/demanding-chance-parents-demand-charter-schools-continues-grow

National Alliance for Public Charter Schools. (2023, December 19). *Charter enrollment by state by year.* https://data.publiccharters.org/digest/tables-and-figures/charter-enrollment-state-year/

National Association of Charter School Authorizers. (n.d.) *California.* https://www.qualitycharters.org/statemaps/states/california/

National Charter Schools Resource Center. (2020, November 23). *Planning for family engagement in the charter school life cycle: A toolkit for school leaders.* https://charterschoolcenter.ed.gov/publication/planning-family-engagement-charter-school-life-cycle-toolkit-school-leaders

Odyssey Charter School. (n.d.). *Our values.* https://odysseycharterschool.org/our-values/

Para Los Niños. (n.d.). *Who we are*. https://www.paralosninos.org/who-we-are/

Public Advocates. (2019). *Keeping the promise of LCFF in charter schools*. https://www.publicadvocates.org/wp-content/uploads/final-report.pdf

San Carlos Charter Learning Center. (2017). *Charter Renewal Petition*. https://scclc.net/wp-content/uploads/2018/09/SCCLC-Renewal-Petition-2017-FINAL-approved-06_01_17.pdf

Schurer Coldiron, J., Bruns, E. J., & Quick, H. (2017). A comprehensive review of Wraparound Care Coordination Research, 1986–2014. *Journal of Child and Family Studies, 26*, 1245–1265. https://doi.org/10.1007/s10826-016-0639-7

Smith, D. (2019, January 16). *Teachers strike at L.A. charter schools too, a first for California*. Los Angeles Times. https://www.latimes.com/local/lanow/la-me-edu-lausd-strike-accelerated-school-20190114-story.html

Spurrier, A. (2019, May). *Changing enrollment, fiscal strain, and facilities challenges in California's urban schools*. https://files.eric.ed.gov/fulltext/ED596447.pdf

Stokes, K. (2019a, May 3). *This South L.A. charter school closed a month early—and won't reopen*. https://laist.com/2019/05/03/why_this_la_charter_school_closed_a_month_early_--and_wont_reopen.php

Stokes, K. (2019b, September 11). *Your guide to the biggest changes to California charter school laws since 1992*. https://laist.com/2019/09/11/california_charter_school_authorizer_bill_compromise_1505.php

Stop Charter Co-location. (n.d.). *Home [Facebook Page]. Facebook*. Retrieved November 28, 2021, from https://www.facebook.com/StopColocation/?__tn__=-UC

Superville, D. R. (2014 October). Chicago's Local School Councils 'Experiment' Endures 25 Years of Change. *Education Week*. November 25, 2021, https://www.edweek.org/leadership/chicagos-local-school-councils-experiment-endures-25-years-of-change/2014/10

Tucker, J. (2019, May 1). *Controversial charter school director avoids jail after fraud charges dropped*. https://www.sfgate.com/bayarea/article/Controversial-charter-school-director-avoids-jail-13811164.php

UTLA. (2019, January 28). *Accelerated schools approve agreement, end strike*.https://www.utla.net/news/accelerated-schools-approve-agreement-end-strike

Values Schools (n.d.). https://www.valueschools.com/apps/pages/Covid19resources

Veney, D., & Jacobs, D. (2021, September). *V H EET 1 - publiccharters.org*. Retrieved November 21, 2021, from https://www.publiccharters.org/sites/default/files/documents/202109/napcs_voting_feet_rd6.pdf.

Vogel, C. (2017, September 13). *Turmoil returns for charter schools*. East Bay Express. https://www.eastbayexpress.com/oakland/turmoil-returns-for-charter-schools/Content?oid=9074129

Warren, M. R., Hong, S., Rubin, C. L., & Uy, P. S. (2009). *Beyond the Bake Sale: A community-based relational approach to parent engagement in schools*. https://citeseerx.ist.psu.edu/viewdoc/download?doi=10.1.1.615.9522&rep=rep1&type=pdf

Warren, M. R., Mapp, K. L., & Kuttner, P. J. (2016). From private citizens to public actors: The development of parent leaders through community organizing. In M. Evans & D. Hiatt-Michael (Eds.), *The power of community engagement for educational change* (pp. 21–41). Information Age Publishing.

CHAPTER 2

PARENT INVOLVEMENT IN CHARTER SCHOOL GOVERNANCE

Charisse Gulosino
The University of Memphis

Elif Sisli Ciamarra
Stonehill College

INTRODUCTION

Research consistently shows charter school parents are more involved in schools than their counterparts at traditional public schools (Bifulco & Ladd, 2005). While nearly all schools seek to engage parents in some capacity, some schools encourage parents to participate in some forms of school decision-making processes through representation of parents in school boards and parent advisory councils, while others provide a service opportunity for parents like booster clubs (Hanafin & Lynch, 2002). Joyce Epstein (2018) offered a framework of six types of parent involvement and classified families as participants in school decisions as the highest level of involvement. Although parent involvement in school governance is considered the highest form of participation in the schooling process, empirical work in this area remains understudied. In this chapter, we focus on parent involvement in charter school governance.

As privately managed institutions, the main governance function in charter schools is performed by a "Board of Trustees," sometimes also

Family and Community Engagement in Charter Schools, pp. 29–52
Copyright © 2025 by Information Age Publishing
www.infoagepub.com
All rights of reproduction in any form reserved.

30   C. GULOSINO and E. S. CIAMARRA

known as a "Board of Directors." Hence, parents can and do get involved in the governance of charter schools by serving on their boards. In this chapter, we present a systematic study of parent involvement in boards and how it changed over time.

The chapter begins by examining several of the rationales given in the literature for schools to engage in parent involvement programs. Second, it examines the growing body of literature that explores parent involvement in charter schools. Next, it focuses on a subset of directors—charter school parents—serving on the school's governing body. The next section describes part of a larger ongoing study of charter school governance in Massachusetts. The results section provides details of parental representation on charter school boards and its correlation to academic outcomes. The chapter concludes by discussing implications of the study and directions for future research.

BACKGROUND

The importance of parent involvement in their children's schooling is well established by empirical studies. A significant body of literature indicates that when parents participate in their children's education, the result is a higher level of academic achievement and academic behaviors, an improvement in homework habits and students' attitudes toward school, increased school attendance, fewer discipline problems, and higher scholastic aspirations (Epstein & Dauber, 1991; Fan & Williams, 2010; Feuerstein, 2000; Garcia-Reid, 2007; Sheldon & Epstein, 2005; Topor et al., 2010). Research consistently shows that parental school involvement is also important in early childhood education (Epstein & Dauber, 1991; Epstein & Sanders, 2002; Jeynes, 2010; Lee & Bowen 2006; Schaub, 2010; Xu & Gulosino, 2006). As such, strategies to expand the breadth and depth of parental school involvement have been the focus of a long line of research and policymaking efforts (Epstein, 2005; Henderson & Mapp, 2002; Hoover-Dempsey & Sandler, 1997).

Forms of Parent Involvement

Parent involvement is a multifaceted concept entailing activities both inside and outside the schoolhouse with the purpose of promoting children's academic and social success (Epstein, 1995; Fishel & Ramirez, 2005; Nokali et al., 2010). Some parent outreach programs focus on strategies to engage parents in educational practices with children at home (Hamlin & Li, 2019; Posey-Maddox, 2012). For example, schools encourage parents to help with homework and school projects and read to their children. Such activities should prompt academic enrichment at home and allow parents to monitor a child's academic progress.

Other programs focus on activities that bring parents into the school, like attending conferences, parent organization meetings, and volunteering in school (Epstein, 1992). While schools have limited control over whether parents create a nurturing home environment for learning (Becker & Epstein, 1982; Epstein, 1992), they have a greater influence on the extent to which parents participate in activities at school (Feuerstein, 2000).

Joyce Epstein's (1995) classic six-type model captures the most well established and widely utilized typology for conceptualizing parent involvement, as follows: (1) parenting; (2) communicating; (3) volunteering; (4) learning at home; (5) decision making; and (6) collaborating with the community (Epstein, 2001). Similarly, Fan and Chen (2001) empirically identify a seven-dimension model for parental involvement and students' academic achievement: television rules, communication, contact with school, parent–teacher association, volunteering, supervision, and education aspiration. Additionally, Sui-Chu and Willms (1996) introduce two basic types of involvement: (1) involvement occurring at home, including discussing school activities and monitoring out-of-school activities; and (2) involvement taking place at school, including making contacts with school staff, and volunteering and attending parent-teacher conferences or other school events. Marcon (1999) further identifies a continuum for parent involvement—extending from passive, marginally involved (i.e., home-school communications) to active and deeply involved (i.e., participation in the organization of the school and its activities; other aspects of school governance). Such typologies are useful because they may be seen as distinct archetypes of parent involvement that produce differential effects on their children's education (Green et al., 2007). This distinction also illuminates important variation between schools in the extent to which parents are treated as partners in the educational process.

Parent Involvement in Charter Schools

Parent involvement is in many cases a central part of charter school applications (Becker et al., 1997). Most charter school legislations require parent involvement in the decision-making process, ranging from leveraging parental support during the application process to require parents to pledge their involvement through parent-school contracts to playing an active role in school decision-making. In 15 states (including Massachusetts), charter schools are initiated by a founding group that must include parents (Center on Educational Governance, 2008). The idea that charter schools fuel parental school involvement is a major consideration behind the growth and appeal of the charter sector (Schneider & Buckley, 2002).

Presumably, the decentralized structure and autonomous nature of charter schools allow a greater hand in decision-making, as opposed to bureaucratic models in a district school board or the state (Finnigan, 2007; Hamlin, 2017). In addition, because the parents presumably choose to send their children to charter schools they support and feel some connection to, they are more likely to get involved in their operations. Because principals and teachers are key players in cultivating parent involvement, this combination of greater autonomy and more flexibility may prompt charter school leaders to develop more locally customized/tailored programs and policies promoting both more and higher levels of parent involvement (Bulkley & Wohlstetter, 2004; Finn et al., 2000). Bifulco and Ladd (2005) find evidence that organizational and institutional characteristics (i.e., small size, school-level autonomy over school policy, and match between parents and schools) of charter schools account for part of the difference in parent involvement vis-à-vis observationally similar traditional public schools.

They noted that part of the differentially high parent involvement in urban charter schools is attributable to the fact that these schools tend to be created in communities with particularly engaged and motivated parents. Parent participation in school events and school operations, for example, bring parents into a mutual agreement about their central role in their children's education, thereby increasing avenues for participation beyond the traditional classifications (i.e., parents serving as decision-makers). Thus, it may be that charter schools sometimes exist because of high levels of parent engagement, rather than serving as the initiators of it.

One notable outreach strategy that has surfaced among charter school operators is the requirement that parents sign contracts when they enroll their children (Cobb & Glass, 1999; Wells, 1998). Some critics of charter schools have claimed that parental involvement requirements may serve as a form of "creaming"—attracting the most motivated or most capable students in the neighborhood. This would deter disadvantaged households (i.e., single-parent families; low-income families; parents with time and resource constraints; parents with language barriers) from sending their children to such charters, out of concern that they would be unable to meet the requirements of the parent contracts (Becker et al., 1997). More recently, however, many charter schools have rebranded these contracts as "parent-school contracts" or "home-school contracts" to emphasize that the goal of school-based parent involvement is assumed by all stakeholders in the schoolhouse, so that the requirements of the contracts are not the sole responsibility of parents.

On the other hand, critics have raised concerns over the disparities in discipline and possible violation of due process in charter schools because of stricter discipline codes and mandatory parental involvement contracts. Charter schools that suspend students at a much higher rate than non-charter schools are particularly subject to public scrutiny and criticism from education activists and legal experts who have raised concerns about compliance with legal obligations and due process requirements. Less evidence exists on the legal scrutiny applied to charter schools who strictly enforce *failure to comply* clauses in parent involvement contracts.

A long line of research suggests that charter schools have greater levels of parent involvement, as they exhibit many of the attributes of "effective schools" (Goldring & Shapira, 1993). In their study, Marschall and Shah (2016) confirm that predominantly Black and predominantly White charter schools both have more parent participation (i.e., parents attending open houses) when compared to their traditional public-school counterparts. Becker et al. (1995) find that charter school parents are more active than their traditional public-school counterparts in assuming a wide range of roles in the school building.

Using data from the Schools and Staffing Survey (SASS) to examine differences in parental involvement in charter and traditional public schools, Bifulco and Ladd (2005) utilize nine measures of parental participation, namely: open house; schoolwide parent-teacher conferences; subject area events; parent education workshops; written school-parent contract; parents as volunteers in school; parents involved in instructional issues; parents involved in governance; and parents involved in budget decisions. The authors confirm that parental involvement is substantially higher in charter schools than in traditional public schools, even after accounting for school location and the characteristics of the student body. Their follow-up empirical work reveals that charter schools may have higher levels of parental involvement because parents who enter the schoolhouse have self-selected to be there (Bifulco & Ladd, 2005), while parents without resources or time/energy to volunteer might also not have the resources and time to seek out a charter school for their child (Brown & Makris, 2018). Charter schools that are succeeding with parental involvement may thus reflect the characteristics of parents who choose, rather than the quality of a school's engagement efforts.

Practitioners and researchers alike have highlighted the damaging ways that parent involvement opportunities interact with race, class, and culture, which contribute to a marginalized perception of low-income families and their relationships with charter schools (Brown & Makris, 2018). When the rules of engagement via parent social networks privilege a disproportionate number of dominant parents (advantaged professionals; middle-and upper-class families), the cultural values and beliefs that deviate from the norm are discounted and give rise to deficit-based assumptions of disadvantaged parents (Harris & Robinson, 2016). Research suggests that minority

34   C. GULOSINO and E. S. CIAMARRA

and low-income parents have a deep understanding of the complex ways that structural and cultural inequity exists in their charter schools, yet their voices, insights, and contributions are rarely central compared to their White, middle-class counterparts (Smith et al., 2011). Researchers have utilized Epstein's model of family involvement to promote new strategies for increasing parent involvement in charter schools (Smith et al., 2011), while other scholars have used the lens of critical race theory (CRT) to highlight race-based perspectives to involvement among charter school parents (Cooper, 2009; Henry, 2019).

Parent Involvement in Charter School Governance

Beyond the volunteerism and fundraising work common to much parental involvement activity, charter schools offer an opportunity for parents, teachers, school administrators, community leaders and residents, and business executives to be actively involved in the governance of their schools and thereby enhance democratic participation in schooling. Those with diverse skills and backgrounds are ideal members for charter school boards to ensure that members could oversee the multitude of school needs. Parent involvement in charter school governance is defined to include the gamut of decision-making roles not typically afforded to parents in traditional public schools. Parents who serve as members of the charter school's board of directors are indicative of their sense of engagement and desire for agency and voice. Having one or more parents on the board ensures that there is a high level of parental involvement in the governance of the school. This perspective acknowledges that charter school performance is strengthened through the participation and active engagement of school's internal and external stakeholders—including parents—in the process of education. Because of its importance as a model for parent participation that is growing and thriving (Dingerson & Ross, 2016), parent involvement in the governance body of the charter school represents a specialized area of inquiry. This focus is also important because boards have been generally overlooked in charter school research.

There is a marked paucity of empirical research on parent involvement in charter school governance. Evidence from qualitative research confirms that when charter school parents play an active role in school governance, they take on responsibilities that include overseeing the facility, administration, budget, and accountability for student learning (Brown & Makris, 2018; Finn et al., 2000). Researchers from the National Center on School Choice at Vanderbilt University provide some evidence that parental involvement and free and reduced- price lunch enrollment rates may be related to a charter school's level of innovation, especially in the areas of school governance, academic support services, and staffing policies (Preston et al., 2011).

As privately managed institutions, the governance function in charter schools is performed by a "Board of Trustees," also known as "Board of Directors." The main duty of the board is to ensure that the goals of a school, as outlined in its charter contract, are met.[1] Hence, the board is responsible for ensuring a year-to-year improvement in academic performance of the school. The board is also accountable for the school's financial wellbeing by approving capital assets, an operating budget, and closely monitoring its ability to meet its budgetary goals. Parents holding directorships is a highly influential way of engaging in how the schools are run.

Despite the seemingly unassailable logic of including parents as decision makers in the schooling of their children, there are competing arguments in the literature on parental representation in charter school boards. According to Hill and Lake (2011), boards that are overrepresented by parents might be problematic for charters, due to their greater attention to their own children rather than the school as a whole and because of a revolving door of parents caused by their children graduating from school inevitably leads to frequent changes in board composition. On the other hand, the Annenberg Institute for School Reform at Brown University (AISR) recommends a percentage of parents and students of at least 50% to provide adequate representation in board governance and involvement in school-based decision-making (Dingerson & Ross, 2016). Consistent with the AISR's charter governance standard, Dingerson and Ross (2016) believe that "Parent and student representation helps ensure input and oversight from those directly involved with the school on a day-to-day basis and helps guard against unethical or illegal behavior" (p. 5). Considering the competing arguments used to explain the role and impact of parents on charter school boards, there is a need for further investigation in this area. In the sections that follow, we take a step towards this direction by documenting which charter schools are more likely to seek out parents to serve on the board and how parent representation on the board evolved over time.

A STUDY OF PARENT REPRESENTATION ON CHARTER SCHOOL BOARDS IN MASSACHUSETTS

Charter school boards are comprised of a range of individuals, often including teachers, parents, school administrators, community leaders, as well as individuals with expertise in business, finance, legal matters and management. Like their corporate and not-for-profit counterparts, charter school board members are selected for their experience and expertise, as well as for their diverse backgrounds (Fama & Jensen, 1983). The board members are initially recruited by school founders based on their willingness to provide resources, expertise, time, and connections that are beneficial to the school. As stated earlier, the Annenberg Institute for School Reform (AISR), a national policy research and reform-support organization, subscribes to the position that at least 50% of charter school boards should comprise of parents and students in order to provide adequate involvement in school-based decision-making (Dingerson & Ross, 2016). Despite the recognition of the potential benefits of parents' voice on charter school boards, there is limited work documenting the extent of parent representation.

Our description of the involvement of parents in the governance of charter schools is designed to address a gap in the existing research literature. In this section, we describe in detail the representation of parents on charter school boards. To this end, we put together a dataset of director characteristics for the charter schools that were operational in Massachusetts between 2001 and 2014. Massachusetts provides a fertile context for examining charter school boards, because unlike other states, Massachusetts law does not mandate that charter governing boards follow specific requirements on who can and cannot serve on their board of trustees (MADOE, 2010). Thus, schools have ample leeway to determine the composition of the board of trustees. In addition, Massachusetts has been a fertile environment for charter schools- the number of charter schools operational in MA doubled from 41 in 2001 to 81 in 2014.

To determine the professional backgrounds of charter school board members, we hand collected biographical information from annual reports and charter applications submitted to the Massachusetts Department of Education, Office of Charter Schools. The charter school annual reports provide board members' names, professional affiliations, and brief biographies. These annual reports also identify how specific individuals are represented on charter board of directors, such as parents, school founders, and staff members (teachers and administrators) serving on the board. Information about parent representation on governing boards is coded as "1" if the person is a parent board member, and "0" otherwise. Our study period covers thirteen years, from 2001 to 2014. Our final dataset consists of 860 data points at the school-level on boards of directors, school characteristics, and academic achievement.

Descriptive Statistics

During our sample period, charter schools in Massachusetts had on average 11.60 members serving on their board of directors (Table 2.1). The size of the boards showed variability, ranging between 4 and 28 members. Parent involvement in board governance has been significant, with 61.98% of the schools having the representation of at least one parent on their boards. To understand the relative significance of parent involvement in charter school board of directors, we also compiled statistics for directors who are founders and staff of the charter schools (Table 2.2). On average, school founders occupied two seats in the boardroom and school staff occupied one seat. We find that 70.35% of the charter schools had at least one of their founders and 45.81% had at least one of their staff as board members. To summarize, parents have a greater involvement on charter school boards when compared to staff, but their presence is not as high as those of the school founders on the board.

Table 2.1

Parent Representation on Charter School Boards of Directors in Massachusetts

Variable	Obs	Mean	Std Dev.	Min	Max
Board Size	860	11.60	3.67	4	28
Number of Parents Serving on a School Board	860	2.07	2.62	0	14
Number of Founders Serving on a School Board	860	2.01	2.30	0	12
Number of Staff Members Serving on a School Board	860	0.95	1.33	0	7
% of schools with at least one parent serving on its board	860	61.98%	0.49		
% of schools with at least one founder serving on its board	860	70.35%	0.46		
% of schools with at least one staff member serving on its board	860	45.81%	0.50		

A second observation we have is that parent representation on charter school boards declined significantly over time. To show this trend, we provide the statistics on the evolution of charter school boards between 2001 and 2014 in Table 2.2 and Figure 2.1. The average board size has virtually remained unchanged from 2001 (11.73 members) to 2014 (11.24 members). However, parent representation on charter school boards declined considerably. In 2001, 70.73% of the schools have at least one parent to sit on charter school boards. By 2014, this percentage has dropped to 52.50%. The downward trend we document is not surprising. Becker et al. (1997) describe the importance of garnering active parent support for the school

38 C. GULOSINO and E. S. CIAMARRA

during the application process and the early years of a charter school's existence. A best practices report by Cannata et al. (2013) noted from their interviews with experts that charter school founders and operators tended to be split on the role that parents should play on the board once the school is fully operational, as this could lead to conflict of interests (notably, separating their role as a parent and their role as a board member).

Table 2.2

Evolution of Charter School Board of Directors in Massachusetts

	Obs.	Board Size	% of schools with at least one parent serving on its board	% of schools with at least one founder serving on its board	% of schools with at least one staff member serving on its board
2001	41	11.73	70.73%	90.24%	51.22%
2002	46	11.54	65.22%	86.96%	45.65%
2003	49	12.02	63.27%	83.67%	46.94%
2004	55	11.91	65.45%	85.45%	50.91%
2005	56	12.05	67.86%	82.14%	58.93%
2006	58	11.90	65.52%	79.31%	50.00%
2007	60	11.73	65.00%	73.33%	50.00%
2008	61	11.66	67.21%	68.85%	50.82%
2009	62	11.60	69.35%	69.35%	51.61%
2010	63	11.44	68.25%	61.90%	49.21%
2011	72	11.64	58.33%	56.94%	41.67%
2012	77	11.08	49.35%	58.44%	36.36%
2013	80	11.34	53.75%	57.50%	36.25%
2014	80	11.24	52.50%	60.00%	35.00%
2001–2014	860	11.60	61.98%	70.35%	45.81%

Other types of board members, notably the so-called school "insiders," showed a significant downward trend as well. Insiders include school founders, principals, teachers, and other staff members. In 2001, 90.24% of the schools had at least one founder represented on charter school boards. In 2014, only 60% of the schools had a founder on their boards. Similarly, at the beginning of our sample period (2001), 51.22% of the schools utilized the services of school staff on their governing boards. By 2014, only 35% of the schools had a school staff represented on their boards. This downward

Figure 2.1

Evolution of MA Charter School Boards (2001–2014)

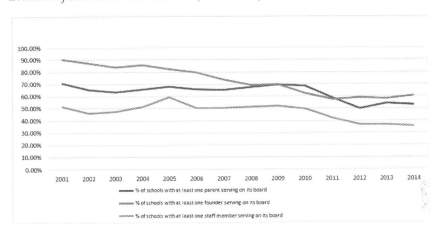

trend is also not surprising. Anecdotal evidence formed through the examination of a few case studies by Cannata et al. (2013) points to the critical role of the governing board to plan an exit strategy for founders and paid staff members sitting on charter boards to avoid a conflict of interest or the appearance of a conflict of interest.

Figure 2.2

Percentage of Charter School Trustees Who Are Parents

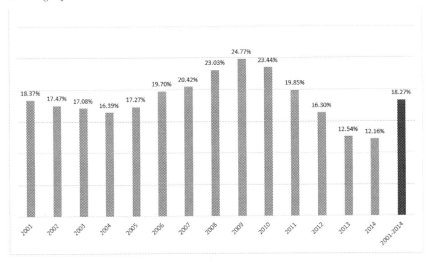

As illustrated in Figure 2.2, the involvement of parents in the governance of charter schools followed a downward trend. At the end of our sample period in 2014, the average percentage representation was 12.16% for parents (i.e., 12.16% of the board members were parents), well below the percentage advocated by the Annenberg Institute. In 2014, only 3.75% of the charter schools had boards exceeding 50% representation of parents, and only 20% of the charter schools had more than 25% of board seats occupied by parents (Figures 2.3 and 2.4). We do not, at this point, advocate for a certain percentage of parent representation, because such a claim should be based on careful empirical research and contextual viability. However, existing research shows that to attain greater voices in governance processes, a more balanced and diverse representation of key social groups/stakeholders should be established, rather than relegating governance decisions to small groups of experts (Allen & Robinson, 2006; Alsbury & Gore, 2015). Developing a common criterion for determining which groups require increased representation in charter school governance is a new avenue of research that should be carefully examined.

Parent Representation and Charter School Characteristics

We next present a descriptive analysis of the differences between schools with and without parental presence on charter school boards. Data on

Figure 2.3

Percentage of MA Charter Schools Whose Boards Have Parent Representation Exceeding 50%

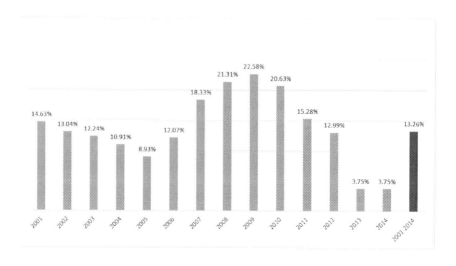

Figure 2.4

Percentage of MA Charter Schools Whose Boards Have Parent Representation Exceeding 25%.

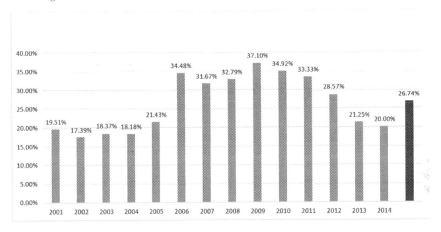

school characteristics include composition of the student body, characteristics of the teachers, and school size (enrollment), and are compiled using the Massachusetts Department of Education Report Cards for 2001–2014. We describe the variables and the data sources in the Data Appendix. Our results in Table 2.3 show significant differences between schools with and without parent-directors. First, parents are more heavily represented on the boards of larger schools. The average enrollment is 472 students in schools that have at least one parent serving on their boards, and 317 students in schools that do not have a parent serving on their boards. The difference in enrollment numbers is statistically significant at the 1% level.

Table 2.3

Comparison of Means Tests—MA Charter School Characteristics

This table presents the comparison of means tests for the school characteristics for charter schools with and without parents serving on their board of directors. All of the variables are described in the Data Appendix.

All Schools		Parent not Present	Parent Present	p – value
Enrollment	413.44	317.41	472.46	0.000***
Percentage of African American Students	26.77	39.08	19.22	0.000***
Percentage of Asian Students	4.89	4.85	4.92	0.927

(Table continued on next page)

42   C. GULOSINO and E. S. CIAMARRA

Table 2.3 (Continued)

Comparison of Means Tests—MA Charter School Characteristics

All Schools	Parent not Present	Parent Present		p – value
Percentage of Hispanic Students	24.25	30.89	20.16	0.000***
Percentage of Native American Students	0.34	0.29	0.38	0.026**
Percentage of Female Students	43.94	44.81	43.41	0.461
Percentage of Non-native English Speakers	17.44	23.47	13.73	0.000***
Percentage with Limited English Proficiency	5.35	8.57	3.37	0.000***
Percentage of Special Education Students	13.94	14.19	13.79	0.432
Percentage of Low-income Students	48.18	64.24	38.27	0.000***
Percentage of Free Lunch	42.59	57.57	33.75	0.000***
Percentage of Reduced Lunch	9.13	11.52	7.77	0.000***
Percentage of High Needs Students	61.35	75.88	47.77	0.000***
Percentage of Licensed Teachers	65.84	59.45	69.78	0.000***
Percentage of Qualified Teachers	86.03	81.88	88.58	0.000***
Student-to-Teacher Ratio	12.02	12.03	12.02	0.938

Parent involvement in school governance is also significantly correlated with charter school demographics. Our results show that on average 19% of the students are African American in schools where parents serve on the board, versus 39% in schools where no parent is represented. Twenty percent of the student body is identified as "Hispanic" in schools with parent-directors, while the percentage of Hispanic students is higher at 31 in schools with no parent-directors. These differences are statistically significant at the 1% level.

Next, we examine the socioeconomic characteristics of the student bodies in charter schools and how it correlated with parent involvement in board governance. In Massachusetts, students are classified as "high needs" if they possess one or more of the following attributes: economically disadvantaged, low-income, and children qualified for receiving subsidies. The percentage of high-needs students is 48 in schools with parents on boards, while it is 76 in schools with no parents. We find that in schools with a parent on the board, 14% of the students are non-native English speakers, while in schools with no parents on the board, this figure climbs to 24%. Three percent of the students have limited English proficiency in schools with parent-directors, and 9% have limited English proficiency in schools with no parent-directors. In contrast, we find no statistically significant relationship between the presence or absence of parents serving on charter schools boards and the percentage of students receiving special education.

Parents show a lower presence on boards of charter schools with more economically disadvantaged students. On average, in schools with parents on the board, 38% of students were low-income, whereas in schools without parent board representation 64% of students were low-income. The percentage of students who qualify for free lunch and who qualify for reduced lunch tells a similar story—parents are more engaged in school governance when a smaller proportion of students are economically disadvantaged.

Finally, we focus on teacher characteristics in charter schools with and without parents serving on the board. In Massachusetts, teachers are deemed "qualified" if they have the following characteristics: a bachelor's degree; a teaching license at any level; and a demonstrated subject matter competency in each of the core subjects they teach. Seventy percent (89) of the teachers are qualified in charter schools with parent-directors. In schools with no parent- directors, the percentage of qualified teachers is lower at 60% (82). There is no statistically significant difference in terms of student-teacher ratios. The student-teacher ratios are virtually identical at 12:1 in charter schools with and without parents serving on the board.

These results collectively tell a consistent story: Parent board involvement is higher in schools with larger numbers of white, English-speaking students, and in schools with more middle-class families. These are schools with lower percentages of minority students, economically disadvantaged students, limited-English proficient (LEP) students and higher percentages of licensed and qualified teachers.

Parent Representation and Academic Achievement

In Table 2.4, we present the comparison of means tests for academic achievement in charter schools with and without parents serving on boards. We use school level average achievement scores as a proxy for academic performance. Following the existing research, we analyze mathematics and ELA test scores (e.g., Carnoy & Loeb 2002). We measure academic performance with two measures calculated using the ELA and Math scores: (1) Composite Performance Index (CPI), a state-generated measure of the extent to which students are progressing toward proficiency, and (2) an academic performance index based on the distribution of student scores in

44 C. GULOSINO and E. S. CIAMARRA

the various performance categories. For example, the index score is equal to 4 times the percent of students in the advanced category plus 3 times the percent of all students in the proficient category plus 2 times the percent of students in the needs improvement category plus 1 times the percent of students in the warning category (Gulosino & Sisli-Ciamarra 2019). Table 2.4 reports the descriptive statistics for the academic performance indicators.

Table 2.4

Comparison of Means Tests—MA Charter School Characteristics

This table presents the comparison of means tests for academic performance in charter schools with and without parents serving on their board of directors. All of the variables are described in the Data Appendix.

All Schools	Parent not Present		Parent Present	p – value
Math Score Index	2.56	2.54	2.56	0.51
Composite Performance Index (Math)	76.96	75.83	77.59	0.12
ELA Score Index	2.73	2.66	2.76	0.00
Composite Performance Index (ELA)	86.10	84.16	87.09	0.00

The results indicate that the presence of parents on the charter school board is not highly correlated with academic performance (Table 2.4). We find that the academic performance in math does not differ in charter schools with and without parents serving on charter school boards. For example, the average math score index in schools with parental representation on school boards is 2.56 out of the maximum score index of 4, as opposed to 2.54 in schools with no parental representation. While the difference in ELA performance is statistically significant, the performance metrics themselves are not materially different. Average ELA score index in schools with parents serving on the board is 2.76, in contrast to 2.66 in schools with no parental representation on school boards. The slightly higher ELA performance when a parent is present on the school board is not surprising given the earlier observation that these schools have a lower percentage of students with limited English language proficiency and more middle and higher- income students.

We recognize that our measures of academic performance are based on the average achievement of students in a school, and do not account for individual variation in achievement between students. Considering the large body of work on the effect of parent involvement on a child's academic performance (Hong & Ho, 2005), one might expect that parent involvement in school governance would be positively correlated with academic achievement. We leave the analysis of student-level academic performance to future studies. Future research should perform a careful analysis of the impact of parents' contribution to academic outcomes using student-level data and by carefully incorporating the possible self-selection of parents into charter school boards.

CONCLUSIONS

While the present study makes an important contribution to understanding the representation of parents on charter school governing boards, considerably more work needs to be done. Future research is necessary to follow up on this study to determine the reasons behind the descriptive findings. Specifically, multivariate analysis of parents on charter school boards would allow for more insight into the mechanisms that link parents serving on the board to school effectiveness. The ultimate question to answer is whether parent involvement on charter school boards contributes to academic achievement. As we have shown in this chapter, charter schools that seek out parents to serve on the board are not a random sample, pointing to the presence of self-selection. Given our results, future empirical research should incorporate the self-selection of parents onto the board by using econometric methods that account for self-selection (Gulosino & Sisli Ciamarra, 2019). One might expect that parent involvement in school governance would be positively correlated with academic performance, yet our initial and descriptive analysis of student achievement does not support this prediction.

Most importantly, however, we observed that parent representation is higher in charter schools that serve more non-minority and wealthier students. This finding points to the possibility that charter school board members have self-selected to be there. Future studies will need to examine the impact of parent self-selection on charter school boards with rigorous instrumental variable research designs. Our result parallels other findings that have raised concerns about the selection process of charter schools in terms of parent commitment requirements (i.e., specific volunteer hours) that ultimately favor the affluent and well-informed (Weiler & Vogel, 2015). Prior work by Smith et al. (2011) noted that in some charters, parents are required to sign a parent contract of 10–72 volunteer hours, on average, a year per family. Similarly, the time commitment for parent board service on charter schools may be too steep for otherwise eligible parents who would be willing to serve but may be unable to comply with board service expectations due to various circumstances, for example, work schedules and job demands. In this sense, much work remains to achieve equitable parent representation on charter school boards.

Future research on parent involvement should also focus on the individual characteristics of parent-directors and analyze whether educational background, job skills, tenure, gender, and outside board memberships have any predictive power for achievement. Future research on parent boards of directors should focus on the directorial characteristics of educational background, job skills, tenure, gender, and outside board memberships in order to determine if certain patterns emerge within and across various subgroups. Future work should also examine the characteristics of parent boards of directors in relation to their attendance and participation at board meetings and membership on charter school board committees. Although charter school boards frequently meet as bodies to discuss key issues and vote on various school-related matters, it is possible for most decision-making to take place in smaller groups or committees. The extent of involvement (voice and agency) of parents in charter school governance provides grounds for future work.

In general, the results of this study highlight an area that requires further consideration. Given that today's charter school boards are held to a more rigorous accountability for the educational performance of schools under their control, this study can only be considered a beginning, and it is important that future studies of parent boards of directors continue to focus on their impact to improvement in school outcomes and equitable representation.

REFERENCES

Allen, A., & Robinson, D. (2006). *Weighing the public-private balance of charter school governance.* The Ohio Collaborative: Research and Policy for Schools, Children, and Families. https://citeseerx.ist.psu.edu/viewdoc/download?doi= 10.1.1.604.9015&rep=rep1&type=pdf

Alsbury, T. L., & Gore, P. (Eds.). (2015). *Improving school board effectiveness: A balanced governance approach.* Harvard Education Press.

Becker, H. J., & Epstein, J. L. (1982). Parent involvement: A survey of teacher practices. *The Elementary School Journal, 83*(2), 85–102.

Becker, H. J., Nakagawa, K., & Corwin, R. G. (1995). *Parent involvement contracts in California's charter schools: Strategy for educational improvement or method of exclusion?* Southwest Regional Laboratory.

Becker, H., Nakagawa, K., & Corwin, R. (1997). Parent involvement contracts in California. *Teachers College Record, 98*(3), 511–536.

Bifulco, R., & Ladd, H. F. (2005). Institutional change and coproduction of public services: The effect of charter schools on parental involvement. *Journal of Public Administration Research and Theory, 16*(4), 553–576.

Brown, E., & Makris, M. V. (2018). A different type of charter school: In prestige charters, a rise in cachet equals a decline in access. *Journal of Education Policy, 33*(1), 85–117.

Bulkley, K. E., & Wohlstetter, P. (Eds.). (2004). *Taking account of charter schools: What's happened and what's next?* Teachers College Press.

Cannata, M., Thomas, G., & Thombre, Z. (2013). *Starting strong. Best practices in starting a charter school.* Vanderbilt Peabody College. https://my.vanderbilt.edu/marisacannata/files/2013/10/Starting_Strong_final.pdf

Carnoy, M., & Loeb, S. (2002). Does external accountability affect student outcomes? A crossstate analysis. *Educational Evaluation and Policy Analysis, 24*(4), 305–331.

Center on Educational Governance. (2008). *Enhancing charter schools through parent involvement.* National Resource Center on Charter School Finance & Governance. https://charterschoolcenter.ed.gov/sites/default/files/files/field_publication_attachment/E nhancing_Charter_Schools-AmyBiehlHS.pdf

Cobb, C. D., & Glass, G. V. (1999). Ethnic segregation in Arizona charter schools. *Education Policy Analysis Archives, 7,* 1.

Cooper, C. W. (2009). Parent involvement, African American mothers, and the politics of educational care. *Equity & Excellence in Education, 42*(4), 379–394.

Dingerson, L., & Ross, C. (2016). *Whose schools? An examination of charter school governance in Massachusetts.* Annenberg Institute for School Reform at Brown University.

Epstein, J. (1992). School and family partnerships. In M. Alkin (Ed.), *Encyclopedia of educational research* (6th ed.) (pp. 1139–1151). Macmillan.

Epstein, J. L. (1995). School/family/community partnerships. *Phi Delta Kappan, 76*(9), 701.

Epstein, J. L. (2001). Introduction to the special section. New directions for school, family, and community partnerships in middle and high schools. *NASSP Bulletin, 85*(627), 3–6.

Epstein, J. L. (2005). Attainable goals? The spirit and letter of the No Child Left Behind Act on parental involvement. *Sociology of Education, 78*(2), 179–3182.

Epstein, J. L. (2018). *School, family, and community partnerships: Preparing educators and improving schools* (2nd ed.). Routledge.

Epstein, J. L., & Dauber, S. L. (1991). School programs and teacher practices of parent involvement in inner-city elementary and middle schools. *The Elementary School Journal, 91*(3), 289–305.

Epstein, J. L., & Sanders, M. G. (2002). Family, school, and community partnerships. In Marc H. Bornstein (Ed.), *Handbook of parenting practical issues in parenting* (Vol. 5, pp. 407–435). Lawrence Erlbaum Associates.

Fama, E. F., & Jensen, M. C. (1983). Separation of ownership and control. *The Journal of Law and Economics, 26*(2), 301–325.

Fan, W., & Williams, C. M. (2010). The effects of parental involvement on students' academic self-efficacy, engagement and intrinsic motivation. *Educational Psychology, 30*(1), 53–74.

Fan, X., & Chen, M. (2001). Parental involvement and students' academic achievement: A meta-analysis. *Educational Psychology Review, 13*(1), 1–22.

Feuerstein, A. (2000). School characteristics and parent involvement: Influences on participation in children's schools. *The Journal of Educational Research, 94*(1), 29–40.

48 C. GULOSINO and E. S. CIAMARRA

Finn, C. E., Manno, B. V., & Vanourek, G. (2000). *Renewing public education: Charter schools in action.* Princeton University Press.

Finnigan, K. S. (2007). Charter school autonomy: The mismatch between theory and practice. *Educational Policy, 21*(3), 503–526.

Fishel, M., & Ramirez, L. (2005). Evidence-based parent involvement interventions with school- aged children. *School Psychology Quarterly, 20*(4), 371.

Henderson, A. T., & Mapp, K. L. (2002). *A new wave of evidence. The impact of school, family, and community connections on student achievement.* National Center for Family & Community: Connections with Schools.

Garcia-Reid, P. (2007). Examining social capital as a mechanism for improving school engagement among low income Hispanic girls. *Youth & Society, 39*(2), 164–181.

Goldring, E. B., & Shapira, R. (1993). Choice, empowerment, and involvement: What satisfies parents? *Educational Evaluation and Policy Analysis, 15*(4), 396–409.

Green, C. L., Walker, J. M., Hoover-Dempsey, K. V., & Sandler, H. M. (2007). Parents' motivations for involvement children's education: An empirical test of a theoretical model of parental involvement. *Journal of Educational Psychology, 99*(3), 532.

Gulosino, C. A., & Şişli Ciamarra, E. (2019). Donors and founders on charter school boards and their impact on financial and academic outcomes. *Education Finance and Policy, 14*(3), 441–471.

Hamlin, D. (2017). Parental involvement in high choice deindustrialized cities: A comparison of charter and public schools in Detroit. *Urban Education, 56*(6). https://doi.org/10.1177/00420859176972

Hamlin, D., & Li, A. (2019). The relationship between parent volunteering in school and school safety in disadvantaged urban neighborhoods. *Journal of School Violence, 19*(3), 36–376. https://doi.org/10.1080/15388220.2019.1700 801.

Hanafin, J., & Lynch, A. (2002). Peripheral voices: Parental involvement, social class, and educational disadvantage. *British Journal of Sociology of Education, 23*(1), 35–49.

Harris, A. L., & Robinson, K. (2016). A new framework for understanding parental involvement: Setting the stage for academic success. *RSF: The Russell Sage Foundation Journal of the Social Sciences, 2*(5), 186–201.

Henry K. L., Jr. (2019). Heretical discourses in post-Katrina charter school applications. *American Educational Research Journal, 56*(6), 2609–2643.

Hill, P., & Lake, R. (2006). *Charter school governance* [Paper presentation]. The National Conference on Charter School Research. National Center on School Choice. Vanderbilt University, Nashville, Tennessee.

Hong, S., & Ho, H. Z. (2005). Direct and indirect longitudinal effects of parental involvement on student achievement: Second-order latent growth modeling across ethnic groups. *Journal of Educational Psychology, 97*(1), 32.

Hoover-Dempsey, K. V., & Sandler, H. M. (1997). Why do parents become involved in their children's education? *Review of Educational Research, 67*(1), 3–42.

Jeynes, W. (2010). *Parental involvement and academic success.* Routledge.

Lee, J. S., & Bowen, N. K. (2006). Parent involvement, cultural capital, and the achievement gap among elementary school children. *American Educational Research Journal, 43*(2), 193–218.

Marcon, R. A. (1999). Positive relationships between parent school involvement and public school inner-city preschoolers' development and academic performance. *School Psychology Review, 28*(3), 395–412.

Marschall, M. J., & Shah, P. R. (2016). Linking the process and outcomes of parent involvement policy to the parent involvement gap. *Urban Education.* https://doi.org/10.1177/0042085916661386

Massachusetts Department of Elementary and Secondary Education (MADOE). (2010). *Education laws and regulations.* https://www.doe.mass.edu/lawsregs/stateregs.html

Nokali, N. E., Bachman, H. J., & Votruba-Drzal, E. (2010). Parent involvement and children's academic and social development in elementary school. *Child Development, 81*(3), 988–1005.

Preston, C., Goldring, E., Berends, M., & Cannata, M. (2011). *Much ado about nothing? Innovation in charter schools.* Society for Research on Educational Effectiveness.

Posey-Maddox, L. (2012). Professionalizing the PTO: Race, class, and shifting norms of parental engagement in a city public school. *American Journal of Education, 119*(2), 235–260.

Schaub, M. (2010). Parenting for cognitive development from 1950 to 2000: The institutionalization of mass education and the social construction of parenting in the United States. *Sociology of Education, 83*(1), 46–66.

Schneider, M., & Buckley, J. (2002). What do parents want from schools? Evidence from the Internet. *Educational Evaluation and Policy Analysis, 24*(2), 133–144.

Sheldon, S. B., & Epstein, J. L. (2005). Involvement counts: Family and community partnerships and mathematics achievement. *The Journal of Educational Research, 98*(4), 196–207.

Smith, J., Wohlstetter, P., Kuzin, C. A., & De Pedro, K. (2011). Parent involvement in urban charter schools: new strategies for increasing participation. *School Community Journal, 21*(1), 71–94.

Sui-Chu, E. H., & Willms, J. D. (1996). Effects of parental involvement on eighth-grade achievement. *Sociology of Education, 69*(2), 126–141.

Topor, D. R., Keane, S. P., Shelton, T. L., & Calkins, S. D. (2010). Parent involvement and student academic performance: A multiple mediational analysis. *Journal of Prevention & Intervention in the Community, 38*(3), 183–197.

Wells, A. S. (1998). Charter school reform in California: Does it meet expectations?. *Phi Delta Kappan, 80*(4), 305.

Weiler, S. C., & Vogel, L. R. (2015). Charter school barriers: Do enrollment requirements limit student access to charter schools? *Equity & Excellence in Education, 48*(1), 36–48.

Xu, Z., & Gulosino, C. A. (2006). How does teacher quality matter? The effect of teacher–parent partnership on early childhood performance in public and private schools. *Education Economics, 14*(3), 345–367.

DATA APPENDIX

Variable	Definition	Data Sources
A. Boards		
Parent on Board	A dummy variable indicating the presence of at least one donor on the charter school's board	
Founder on Board	A dummy variable indicating the presence of at least one founder on the charter school's board	Charter school annual reports; charter school applications; professional networking websites; school profiles
Staff on Board	A dummy variable indicating the presence of at least one staff member on the charter school's board	
Board Size	Total number of directors on the charter school board	
B. School Characteristics		
Percentage of Low-income Students	The percentage of students who meet any one of the following definitions of low-income: the student is eligible for free or reduced price lunch; or the student receives Transitional Aid to Families benefits; or the student is eligible for food stamps	
Percentage of Free Lunch	The percentage of charter school students eligible for free lunch	
Percentage of Reduced Lunch	The percentage of charter school students eligible for reduced-price lunch	
Percentage of African-American Students	The percentage of charter school students who are African Americans	
Percentage of Asian Students	The percentage of charter school students who are Asians/Pacific Islanders	
Percentage of Hispanic Students	The percentage of charter school students who are Hispanics	
Percentage of Native American Students	The percentage of charter school students who are American Indians/Alaska Natives	
Percentage of Female Students	The percentage of charter school students who are females	

Percentage of Non-native English Speakers	The percentage of charter school students whose first language is a language other than English	MA Charter School Profiles retrieved from: http://profiles.doe.mass.edu/
Percentage of High Needs Students	Students who belong to one or more of the following groups: students with disabilities, current or former English learners, and/or economically disadvantaged students	
Percentage with Limited English Proficiency	The percentage of charter school students whose first language is a language other than English and who are unable to perform ordinary classroom work in English	
Percentage of Special Education Students	The percentage of charter school students with Individualized Education Program (IEP)	
Percentage of Licensed Teachers	The percentage of teachers licensed in teaching assignment	
Percentage of Qualified Teachers	The percentage of core academic classes taught by teachers who are highly qualified	
Student-to-Teacher Ratio	The ratio of full-time-equivalent students to full-time-equivalent teachers	
School Age	The number of years the charter school has been in operation	

C. Academic Achievement Variables

ELA Score Index	The index score is equal to 4 times the percent of students in the advanced category plus 3 times the percent of all students in the proficient category plus 2 times the percent of students in the needs improvement category plus 1 times the percent of students in the warning category. Total points are divided by the number of students to calculate school averages.	MA Charter School Accountability Reports (MCAS), retrieved from http://profiles.doe.mass.edu/state_rep ort/mcas.aspx
Math Score Index		
Composite Performance Index (ELA)	A measure of the extent to which students are progressing toward proficiency. The CPI is a 100-point index that combines the scores of students who take standard MCAS tests (the Proficiency Index) with the scores of those who take the MCAS-Alternate Assessment (MCAS-Alt) (the MCAS-Alt Index)	
Composite Performance Index (Math)		

ENDNOTE

1. Charter school operate under performance contracts, and their renewals are primarily based on meeting their fiscal sustainability and student achievement goals (Bulkley & Wohlstetter, 2003)

CHAPTER 3

CHARTER SCHOOL GOVERNING BOARDS AND MISSED OPPORTUNITIES FOR COMMUNITY ENGAGEMENT

Elise Castillo
Trinity College

Laura E. Hernández
University of California, Berkeley

In theory, charter schools facilitate local control and democracy by empowering communities to create schools that align with local needs and preferences (Budde, 1988). Because of their autonomy from the politics and regulations established by district school boards, advocates argue that charters create spaces where community voice is heard and truly valued. However, little is known about if or how family and community stakeholders are actively engaged and represented in charter schools. Scholars have argued that charter schools' democratic potential is in tension with the market values undergirding the charter movement, including accountability, choice, competition, efficiency, and private management (Engel, 2000; Knight Abowitz & Karaba, 2010; Wells et al., 2002). Yet a limited body of scholarship investigates whether, and to what extent, charters' formal governance structure—their boards of trustees that are charged with overseeing and guiding decision making for independent or networked charters—foster local representation, democratic decision making, and community engagement in light of market pressures.

Family and Community Engagement in Charter Schools, pp. 53–71
Copyright © 2025 by Information Age Publishing
www.infoagepub.com
All rights of reproduction in any form reserved.

This chapter examines if or how charter schools' boards of trustees operate as venues for family and community engagement. This qualitative study examines the governing boards of four charter schools—two in California and two in New York, including those of distinct organizational types (e.g., independent and affiliated with charter management organizations [CMOs]) and pedagogical orientations (e.g., progressive, deeper learning). Drawing upon interview, observation, and document data, we present profiles of each school's active governing board. We focus on the demographic composition of board members (e.g., professional affiliations, areas of expertise, racial and socioeconomic background) and on how board trustees recruit new members. We also discuss the nature of public participation in board governance. We find that boards infrequently incorporated family members or other local community members, illustrating that these constituencies were little involved in charter school governance. Rather, in pursuing greater visibility and resources in local landscapes, the focal charter schools endeavored to cultivate a professional board comprising trustees with managerial acumen and connections to affluent networks. In addition, families and community members rarely participated in charter governance by attending board meetings. Hence, we argue that the focal charter school boards neglected to operate as spaces wherein local community stakeholders engaged in democratic decision making and governance. This pattern stands in contrast to claims that charters' autonomy facilitates local democracy (Budde, 1988).

SCHOOL BOARDS AND THEIR DEMOCRATIC AND COMMUNITY ENGAGEMENT POTENTIAL

Historically, public school governance has been a local affair. Given the decentralized nature of American public education, local school boards have traditionally served as school districts' governing and policymaking bodies. In addition, scholars note that local school boards have often been hubs of representative democracy, community engagement, and local governance (Kirst & Wirt, 2009; Resnick & Bryant, 2010; Tyack, 2002; Usdan, 2010). Importantly, when school boards comprise racially diverse leaders, they have, at times, been associated with minoritized communities' academic success and political empowerment (Delagardelle, 2008; Fraga & Ellis, 2009; Henig et al., 1999; Molina & Meier, 2018; Morel, 2018).

While many U.S. citizens have supported local control and educational governance (Tyack, 2002), policymakers and reformers have long debated the merits of local school boards, with some arguing that they serve as obstacles to reform. During the Progressive Era, reformers critiqued local control as rife with patronage politics. Rather than representative school

Charter Governing Boards and Community Engagement 55

boards comprising laypersons, reformers advocated for a corporate model of school governance comprising administrative "experts" who would use "business efficiency and science as guides to policy" (Tyack, 2002, p. 19). More recently, reformers have similarly critiqued local school boards as inefficient and ineffective because of their political orientations and have sought to curb boards' influence or eliminate them altogether (Chubb & Moe, 1990). For example, since the 1990s, increasing numbers of urban school districts experienced mayoral control or state takeover (Arsen & Mason, 2013; Morel, 2018; Wong & Shen, 2003).

Reformers and scholars also argue that representative school boards often neglect to fulfill their democratic potential (Maerloff, 2010). For example, because most school board elections are off-cycle with general municipal elections, some argue that their timing minimizes voter turnout and, subsequently, public engagement in school board affairs (Allen & Plank, 2005; Land, 2002). Other scholars demonstrate how a market-based public education policy context encourages school boards to engage in autocratic decision-making in the face of intense accountability pressures (Trujillo, 2013). Henig et al. (2019) further highlight the impact of marketization on local school boards, demonstrating the immense monetary influence of out-of-state donors on local school board elections as a way to weaken teachers' unions and privatize public education.

As school districts grapple with market influences on school boards' democratic and community engagement potential, one reform effort entered the scene with promises to enhance local democracy: charter schools. Publicly funded, but privately operated, charter schools, in theory, can facilitate democratic representation and governance more effectively and efficiently than traditional public schools (Budde, 1988; Rofes & Stulberg, 2004). As a privately operated school, a charter school is not governed by its home public school district's board, but rather, by a separate board of trustees, which theoretically could effectively foster community representation and collective decision-making (Wells et al., 2002).

Yet since the charter school movement's inception in 1992, its democratic goals have coincided, and often clashed with, its market-oriented goals to facilitate parental choice, exert competitive pressures on public school systems, and privatize public education (Knight Abowitz & Karaba, 2010; Wells et al., 2002). Between 2000 and 2015, the percentage of public schools with charter status increased from 2 to 7%, and charter student enrollment grew from 400,000 to 2.8 million (National Association of Charter School Authorizers, 2018). This dramatic growth was spurred on in part by market-based policies that aimed to broaden school choice and replace low-performing public schools with charters (Scott & Holme, 2016). As organizations designed to scale up rapidly, charter management organizations (CMOs) are at the forefront of charter school growth, thanks to the political and financial support of reformers animated by market values (Farrell et al., 2012; Quinn et al., 2016; Scott, 2009). In contrast, independent charter schools, or those unaffiliated with CMOs, have experienced far less growth in light of reformers' perceptions that such schools have a limited impact on marketizing public education (Quinn et al., 2016; White, 2018).

Against this backdrop, there is a small, but growing, body of scholarship examining charter school boards and their ability to foster democratic governance and representation. The limited literature indicates that charter boards do little to foster democratic representation, collective decision-making, and community engagement. For example, researchers find that charter school board members tend not to be democratically elected, but rather, strategically recruited from school founders' and existing board members' social networks (Butler et al., 2008; Lay & Bauman, 2019; Scott & Holme, 2002). Other studies demonstrate that these methods of assembling charter boards constrain democratic representation in terms of race and class: In majority African American cities such as New Orleans and Washington, D.C., African Americans are not proportionally represented on appointed charter boards (Lay & Bauman, 2019; Nelson, 2015; Squire & Davis, 2014). Finally, scholars document how charter boards' activities are only minimally transparent to the public: boards often neglect to comply with public disclosure laws and sometimes explicitly express little interest in engaging the community (Ford & Ihrke, 2019; Lay & Bauman, 2019).

Together, the existing scholarship reveals that charter school boards tend not to represent or engage local communities. This chapter extends this work by demonstrating how charters' pursuit of visibility and resources in the competitive market complicates the potential for their boards to practice democratic representation, democratic governance, and community engagement.

A CLOSER LOOK AT CHARTER BOARDS: FOUR PROFILES

Drawing from interview, observation, and document data collected between 2016 and 2018, we provide descriptive profiles of the governing boards of four urban charter schools: two independent charter schools in New York (Hudson and Liberty) and two CMOs in California (Reach and Beacon).[1] Our comparison of charter schools of distinct organizational types and locales enables us to compare and contrast their boards' approaches to family and community engagement. We found that the focal charters exhibited some promising practices for facilitating family and community engagement. Simultaneously, despite their organizational differences, the focal charters shared goals of improving their visibility and access to resources. Hence, they each strategically recruited board trustees who could contribute to these efforts. In turn, the boards focused little on involving family and community stakeholders in board governance, either as trustees themselves or as participants in board meetings.

Hudson Charter School: A Conversion Independent Charter School With Expansion Plans

Hudson Charter School, a pre-K–12 school, was founded in the mid-1990s as a traditional public school and converted to charter status shortly after New York passed its Charter School Act in 1998. Over 20 years after its founding, Hudson applied for, and received, a charter to operate a second school, Hudson II, which was in its planning stages at the time of data collection. In contrast to a CMO, where a central office oversees efforts to replicate schools rapidly, Hudson I and Hudson II comprise a "cluster" of affiliated independent charter schools, defined as having curricular and operational connections, but "no aspiration to scale as a means of influencing the broader public educational system" (Quinn et al., 2016, p. 7). Reflecting Hudson's founding mission to foster collaborative governance and distributed leadership, the school has multiple governance "layers," including a board of trustees for each school. In addition, Hudson I has a "shared school governance committee" comprising staff, parents, students, and community members who oversee the implementation of the school's progressive pedagogical mission; a PTA; and a student government. More recently, Hudson I established a fundraising board, Friends of Hudson.

Since their inceptions, both schools' boards of trustees have comprised a mix of elected and appointed members representing various stakeholder groups. At the time of data collection, Hudson I's nine-member board comprised a range of stakeholder representatives, including founding and current staff members, community members, alumni, and current teachers and parents. Comparatively, Hudson II's five-member board consisted of three staff members, one alumnus, and one community member, though they intended to expand the board to include other constituencies upon the school's opening.

Hudson's Principal Jolene Agee (a pseudonym) explained that a "constituency-based board" ensures that "we have people who really understand the [school's] mission." Both appointed and elected trustees were recruited from within the school community and from the personal and professional networks of Hudson staff and sitting trustees. As explained in its charter: "To fill board vacancies ... Hudson Charter School leverages its networks and relationships, along with those of its Board of Trustees and community-based partners and supporters." To illustrate this recruitment strategy, a board-elected alumni representative, Freddie Seiler, who serves on the boards for Hudson I, Hudson II, and Friends of Hudson, explained his recruitment:

> Roseann Street, who's on the board of Friends of Hudson, reached out and asked if I'd like to be the president of Friends of Hudson. I accepted.... Once Principal Jolene Agee found out that I was serving on the board of Friends of Hudson, she asked me if I'd like to be a part of the board of trustees.

Despite Principal Agee's assertion that the boards of Hudson I and II are not "fundraising board[s]" and "we don't have a bunch of hedge fund people who give us a lot of money," evidence suggests that Seiler was recruited not only to represent the alumni constituency, but also to connect the school with financial resources. Roseann Street, the Hudson administrator who recruited Seiler to serve on the Friends of Hudson board, explained: "Freddie does work for a financial institution, so I'm hoping that he's gonna bring some friends and we'll just meet people."

Although the boards of Hudson I and Hudson II prioritized family and community representation among trustees, the boards' racial compositions did not fully reflect that of the school community. On Hudson I's nine-member board, all but one trustee was white; and all of Hudson II's five-member board was white. In contrast, 60% of Hudson students were Latinx, while about 20% were Asian and 10% were Black. Although the majority of Hudson students were students of color, the board trustees representing this constituency—the alumni and parent representatives—each were white. This pattern reflects research demonstrating that charter school board members often do not reflect the racial demographics of their constituents (Lay & Bauman, 2019; Nelson, 2015; Squire & Davis, 2014).

In addition, based on observational data, families and community members rarely participated in board governance by attending board meetings. This was the case even though Hudson made efforts to render meetings accessible by posting meeting dates and materials to its website in advance of each meeting, in accordance with New York State's Open Meetings Law (Committee on Open Government, New York Department of State, n.d.). Also, with a few exceptions when Hudson II's board met in a small classroom, board meetings were held in the school's gymnasium, a space conducive to accommodating a large audience. Moreover, in advance of each meeting, a staff member arranged rows of folding chairs to accommodate guests and placed copies of meeting materials on each chair. Nevertheless, members of the public rarely attended board meetings, with one exception: In an annual tradition, during the board's June meeting, student groups shared performances and presentations with the board, and their parents and teachers filled the gymnasium seats. Also, Principal

Agee explained, the June meeting attracts parents with concerns about the following school year: "Maybe somebody's kid's been held over," or, "We might not be able to get the art teacher [for next year]." Yet for the most part, according to Agee, the board's parent and teacher representatives obviated the need for parent and teacher participation at meetings, as these trustees liaise between the board and their respective constituencies.

In sum, family and community members rarely participated in governance at the board trustee level. Although Hudson's boards effectively represented these constituencies by including parent, community, and alumni representatives on their trustee rosters, the racial demographics of these individuals neglected to fully reflect the racial demographics of the student population. In addition, as discussed above, Hudson provided alternative spaces for families and community members to engage in school governance, such as the shared governance committee, PTA, and student government, perhaps rendering their participation on the board trustee level less necessary. Yet as Hudson faces increasing resource needs in light of its expansion, the extent to which the school prioritizes constituency-based boards over fundraising boards remains to be seen.

Liberty Charter School: An Independent Charter School Building Its Competitive Edge

Liberty Charter School, which enrolls students in Grades 6–8, was founded in the mid-2010s by a group of primarily white parents and community members living in a racially and socioeconomically mixed neighborhood. These individuals recognized that virtually all the public middle schools in the neighborhood were academically selective, or "screened," schools. They sought to open an "unscreened" school to advance educational equity and access in the community. In addition, they envisioned a school centered on the themes of sustainability and the natural world. Liberty's founding board comprised nearly all of the 11 community members who wrote the school's charter application and subsequently opened the school; eight of these 11 were parents and/or residents of the neighborhood in which Liberty was located. However, beyond Liberty's founding year, board membership evolved away from community representatives toward business and finance professionals as the school endeavored toward mobilizing resources and building its visibility and competitive edge in a saturated charter market.

Liberty's Executive Director Justine Caruso shared that the board, in recent years, has focused on recruiting new members with "give and get" potential: the ability to make a financial contribution directly or facilitate "connections to deep pockets." Reflecting this strategy, at the time of data collection, the board chair was a retired finance professional, and the most recent additions to the 10-member board included two business and finance professionals who were recruited through Columbia Business School's nonprofit leadership program. Additionally, in an interview, one board trustee explained the need for current board members to leverage their personal networks to further recruit such individuals: "To get these people you need to be connected with these people ... you have to look at who's on the board and who is part of that network." This trustee displayed this perspective when she suggested during a board meeting that a friend of hers working at Bridgespan, a global nonprofit social impact organization, could post Liberty's board recruitment advertisement on the company's online jobs board for a $50 fee. The advertisement appeared on Bridgespan's online jobs board a few months later.

In addition, three members of the 10-member board, including one of the aforementioned Columbia Business School graduates, had CMO experience as administrators, consultants, or professional developers. As discussed in a local news article featuring Liberty, the school "tries to tap into [CMO] expertise by having representatives from a couple of the large networks sit on its board." One such Liberty board member worked for a national CMO and explained how he drew upon this experience in guiding Liberty's marketing efforts: "I definitely think some of the messaging or branding, that was a big element of [CMO] recruitment, and so I've had some conversations in the past with Justine around how to better promote Liberty and leverage Liberty's unique mission."

In comparison, family and community stakeholders were less represented on the board. At the time of data collection, two board members were current or former parents of Liberty students, and the PTA president held a non-voting seat. In addition, all but two of Liberty's board were white, whereas 70% of Liberty's student population were Black and Latinx. During board meetings, board trustees expressed their interest in increasing the board's racial and ethnic diversity. In addition, trustees discussed ideas for increasing parent representation on the board, such as recruiting parents of sixth-grade students who could serve multiyear terms and transforming the PTA president's role on the board from a non-voting to a voting member. However, despite these expressed commitments to diversity and representation, by the end of the year, the sole addition to the board was a white woman who had recently graduated from Columbia Business School.

Family and community members not only were little represented on Liberty's board, but also rarely participated in board governance by attending meetings. Like at Hudson, this was the case even though Liberty's website included information about upcoming meetings in accordance with New York State's Open Meetings Law. When non-trustees attended meetings, they were limited to teachers, administrators, or consultants who were invited to speak on a particular agenda item. Perhaps the timing of board meetings—Monday evenings—may not have been conducive to public attendance. The meeting schedule appeared to burden even the board trustees themselves: Trustees were frequently absent and three meetings in a row lacked quorum. When asked about the lack of public participation in board governance, Executive Director Caruso, like Principal Agee at Hudson, posited that there are "other channels for parents to get involved, or for others in the community to get involved," such as through the PTA. She continued, "They may want to come to the board meetings more, to have that voice heard. But I think it's being heard elsewhere." For example, she noted that parent and staff representatives sit on a search committee tasked with reviewing principal candidates for the following school year. Yet the lack of family and community participation in board meetings departs from the aim stated in Liberty's charter application to "promote parental and staff involvement in school governance," as "input from students' families and all school staff is essential to the continuous improvement of the school and the board's ability to assess and support Liberty's mission."

Despite its community roots, Liberty's board has increasingly prioritized enhancing its access to affluent networks and building its brand in a charter market where CMOs enjoy a competitive advantage given their robust resources and high visibility (Jabbar, 2015). As a result, the board has departed from incorporating family and community input toward assembling a trustee roster heavy on professionals with finance or CMO experience. Although board trustees expressed interest in recruiting more parents and people of color to the board, recruiting those with finance or CMO expertise appeared to take precedence.

Reach Public Schools: A CMO With National Repute and Acclaim

Reach Public Schools (RPS) was established in the late 1990s in Northern California by a long-time public-school educator in partnership with a Silicon Valley entrepreneur with the aim of "grow[ing] the public charter school movement by opening and operating small, high-quality charter schools in low-income neighborhoods." Under its guiding motto of "College Guaranteed," RPS has created a network of K–12 schools and since grown to become one of the largest CMOs in the state, operating over 35 schools in California while expanding its model to one Southern state. Because of its record of supporting strong achievement for its student population, who are predominantly low-income students of color, the network has garnered national attention and secured significant federal and philanthropic investment to support its operations and growth, cementing itself as a reputable and well-known CMO in the landscape.

To maintain its reputation and grow institutional presence, RPS had cultivated a governing board of 11 appointed individuals at the time of data collection. This board worked with senior leaders in the organization to direct the strategic vision and operations of its vast network. While the network was established under the leadership of a former educator, its board of trustees comprised individuals with little to no expertise in the technical core of teaching and learning—only one trustee had worked as a charter school founder and an elected member of the district school board. Instead, RPS board members had substantial experience in the business sector, with over 90% of them holding or recently retiring from positions in investment and venture capitalist firms, foundations, and major corporations. For example, six were former or current partners or Chief Executive Officers of investment firms such as TPG, Morgan Stanley, and State Farm General Insurance, while three others held senior leadership positions in Silicon Valley start-ups. Only one RPS board member was designated as an "active community volunteer," though she lived in the nearby affluent community that did not have an RPS-affiliated school.

Beyond their professional affiliations, RPS board members also shared other demographic features related to race and geographic representation. Ten of the 11 board members, including the community volunteer, were white, with only one African American male who worked as a corporate executive serving on the governing body. In addition, sitting and newly appointed board members were typically non-residents of the Northern California communities where RPS operated schools, and as noted by several board members during a 2016 governance meeting, few to no trustees were from the Southern state or the Central or Southern California regions where the network was also present. While one board member noted that he had a second home in Newport Beach, an affluent Orange County suburb, which allowed him to join board meetings from the network's Los Angeles headquarters, there was little evidence that RPS board members had roots or deep connections to the communities and residents their schools served. Moreover, its governing board comprised individuals who demographically differed from RPS students, 82% of whom qualified for free and reduced lunch and 87% of whom identified as Black or Latinx.

RPS efforts to recruit new board members suggested leaders were aware of the lack of representation on the network's board and were taking steps to reduce some of its demographic disparities. For example, a board member suggested that the governing body tap one of his African American acquaintances "who was really connected and expressed interest in wanting to help." Moreover, the RPS board had recently nominated and approved two new board members to foster more racial representation

Charter Governing Boards and Community Engagement   63

on its board of trustees. One of these new board members was an African American woman, who worked as a principal in a private school in a neighboring affluent metropolis, and the other was a Latinx male who held a position in municipal government in the same metropolitan area—a community where RPS did not operate schools. Thus, the new trustees served to racially diversify the governing body and brought some varied professional expertise to a board that had disproportionately leaned upon private sector knowledge and experience. At the same time, RPS board members continued to eschew the importance of local community representation in recruiting and selecting trustees, conceptualizing geographic representation in regional terms (e.g., Central Valley, Southern California) which could obscure the acute needs that particular communities or neighborhoods faced amid the dynamics of segregation and economic inequality.

Governance meetings themselves also had features that made them minimally conducive to local and constituent participation. For example, RPS board meetings were held quarterly on weekdays and ran during typical work hours (i.e., 9 A.M. to 3 P.M.), making attendance difficult for working constituents, particularly for those with tenuous financial circumstances like many RPS students and families. Furthermore, board meetings were held in a conference room at RPS's Northern California headquarters, which were located in an industrial park about 5 miles away from its nearest school. While the network enabled virtual participation for constituents and leaders in Southern California and in one Southern state by having live cameras at its regional offices, in-person attendance was only physically accommodated with five chairs or standing room along the outside of the large conference table where board trustees and CMO leaders convened. The location of RPS offices also required that attendees have access to personal transport, as each of their offices was located several miles off from public transportation routes. Collectively, these meeting features posed microlevel obstacles to community inclusion and participation. Thus, while RPS governance meetings were open to the public in accordance with California's Brown Act,[2] few to no members of the public or RPS students and families were present or represented at the observed board meetings.

As RPS has become a recognizable provider in the charter landscape, it has primarily relied on the guidance of trustees who exercise their private sector expertise to inform decisions about network growth and sustainability. In prioritizing these market-oriented funds of knowledge, board governance and its surrounding processes have often inhibited the inclusion of local and demographically representative voices, including those of educators and community members who are most affected by RPS's day-to-day work. While the CMO has grown increasingly aware of the need to diversify its key decision-making body, it remains to be seen if and how the network will incorporate diverse and community perspectives in this forum.

Beacon Community Schools: A CMO With Aims of Growing Its Brand

Beacon Community Schools (Beacon) opened its doors in the early 2000s in Birchwood, California, a midsized urban city.[3] For almost two decades, Beacon has focused on developing its programmatic design within its K–12 pipeline. Founded by a small group of former Teach For America (TFA) corps members and parents, the small CMO comprises three charter schools, all of which are located in low-income communities of color, under its mission of "transforming the landscape of education for historically underserved students" through its deeper learning model. In doing so, it has become a much-lauded member of the local charter community, receiving multiple awards and distinctions for high academic performance, college attendance rates, and innovative pedagogical approaches. Its leaders have also been successful in securing ample financial backing from local and national philanthropic groups, and the organization maintains a professional development arm open to all practitioners, which has brought educators together to learn about inquiry-based learning approaches. To expand upon its local reputation and in response to board member demand, Beacon has recently undertaken efforts to expand the number of schools it operates and to increase its brand recognition.

At the time of data collection, Beacon maintained a governing board of 14 appointed trustees to inform decisions related to network growth and sustainability. Demographically, the network's charter board was relatively diverse along racial lines, with half of the board members identifying as African American, Latinx, or Asian, while the remaining half identified as white. Beacon's board members also brought varied professional experiences from the private and nonprofit sectors. For example, three trustees held positions at local and national foundations, while three others were current or retired executives of corporations and financial institutions, including Wells Fargo and Clorox. Two board members were senior leaders in a nationally recognized and Birchwood-headquartered CMO, while the remaining trustees led local nonprofits and consulting firms that specialized in advancing opportunity in education, housing, and employment. Notably, about half of the board members worked or lived in Birchwood. Thus, while still cultivating a board with professional acumen—including connections to private enterprise—Beacon's trustees were more diverse along a range of demographic factors when compared to many CMOs, including RPS and others operating in the region.

Beacon's commitment to cultivating a demographically and professionally diverse board of trustees was also evident in their efforts to recruit board members to fill board vacancies. To illustrate, at a board meeting, the CMO's Executive Director described how the board sought appointees

Charter Governing Boards and Community Engagement   65

who "wore several hats" in terms of professional experience, network connections, and community roots. In turn, he discussed the nomination of a woman who was identified through their contract with Charter Board Partners, a national nonprofit dedicated to supporting charter boards by matching these governing bodies with board trustee candidates. This board candidate, who was subsequently appointed, worked with a well-known foundation, and had what the Executive Director described as the "potential to tap into national networks of people doing the work Beacon was doing." The Executive Director also noted that the prospect was from Birchwood and had school-aged children to elevate her commitment to the community.

Although the Beacon charter board had historically included diverse trustees with various community ties, community and family participation in governance meetings was rare. In accordance with California's Brown Act, the CMO held public governance meetings and made efforts to make these gatherings accessible for families and community members, including widely advertising monthly meetings and holding convenings after work hours and at school sites (i.e., large classrooms or common areas) that were easily reachable. Yet, trustees and senior Beacon leaders were almost always the only attendees at board meetings, with the exception of the occasional educator and student presentation that would begin a meeting to welcome board members or keep them appraised of innovative student learning experiences. Moreover, unlike some charters that allocate seats on their governing boards to parent or community representatives, Beacon forewent these formal positions on its board, making the perspectives of their immediate constituents rarely represented in these governing forums. Thus, while the CMO's board of trustees did include Birchwood residents, the voices of those most affected by their schools were typically absent from these decision-making spaces.

The bounded presence of constituent perspectives in Beacon's board governance was likely to be further affected by changes that appeared on the horizon. While Beacon had historically cultivated a board of trustees with diverse experiences and community connections, the CMO was aware that it was in transition from being a "founder-led organization" to a "multi-school organization," which would require changes in board composition and expertise. In turn, Beacon conducted a "governance and fundraising audit" based on 11 one-on-one interviews with sitting board members. The audit identified that the current governing board had key strengths, including mission and value-alignment, a strong sense of collegiality, and a high level of commitment among current trustees. Yet, the audit also revealed several areas of weakness. Interviewed trustees felt that the CMO board had an over-reliance on "long-service staff and Board members' memories" and engaged in poor recruitment that was not informed by the needs of a growing organization. In addition, interviewed board members identified trustees' "limited financial giving capacity" as a key deficiency in its composition, particularly in light of the CMO's forthcoming multi-million-dollar fundraising campaign. On this point, the audit report indicated, "Board members are smart and connected individuals who were selected for their skills, but are unable to make significant financial contributions to Beacon."

With these identified gaps in board leadership, Beacon's charter board embarked on steps to restructure its board recruitment and governing process to address its weaknesses. For example, sitting trustees each created "individualized fundraising action plans" focused on maximizing their financial contributions. In addition, the board revised its new trustee recruitment process, asking board prospects to indicate if they held specific expertise in "finance," "fundraising," and "facilities." Furthermore, recruits were asked to indicate if they understood "the concept of leadership giving as a Board member," and to agree to the following statement: "Each year, no later than Thanksgiving, I will make a significant gift to Beacon." While revisions to board recruitment and governance processes remained underway, these indicators suggest that Beacon may be moving in directions that could compromise the demographic and professional diversity of their board—particularly in ways that could elevate potential trustees' financial positions and networks to further Beacon's network growth goal.

DISCUSSION AND RECOMMENDATIONS

Regardless of organizational type or geographic locale, the focal charter schools each exhibited the goal of increased visibility. They pursued this goal in various ways, such as replicating schools (e.g., Hudson, Reach, and Beacon) and building its brand (e.g., Liberty and Beacon). Relatedly, the focal charters endeavored to mobilize resources to support their growth and branding goals. These patterns align with research demonstrating that charter schools increasingly perceive a need to advance their position in the competitive and saturated charter school market (Castillo, 2020; DiMartino & Jessen, 2018; Hernández, 2022; Jabbar, 2015; Lubienski et al., 2009). To enhance their organizational visibility, growth, branding, and access to resources, the focal charters strategically filled their boards of trustees with individuals possessing finance or business experience and connections to affluent networks. In doing so, the focal charters' boards only minimally engaged families and community members. Although, to varying degrees, boards recognized the need for more diversity and community representation, they rarely took meaningful steps to recruit diverse local stakeholders to serve as trustees, or to facilitate greater family and community attendance at public board meetings.

Charter Governing Boards and Community Engagement   67

In light of these patterns, we argue that the focal charter schools' boards of trustees neglected to serve as spaces where community stakeholders engaged in democratic school governance. Despite the potential of charter schools to facilitate local democracy and community engagement (Budde, 1998), we find that the broader market-based educational context exerted pressures on the focal charters to cultivate governing boards that would increase their competitive edge. Hence, our findings extend research demonstrating how the market-oriented educational landscape constrains schools' democratic potential (Engel, 2000; Hernández & Castillo, 2020; Wells et al., 2002).

To facilitate greater family and community engagement and further charter boards' democratic possibilities, we offer the following recommendations for charter school boards:

Require boards to reserve seats for parents and community representatives. Among the focal charter schools, Hudson exhibited the highest share of community representatives, as it reserved board seats for parents, staff, teachers, and community members. To ensure that a range of family and community perspectives remain represented, boards not only should allocate seats for such individuals but also allow these members voting privileges. Moreover, community representatives should be individuals living in the immediate communities served by the schools. Charter schools established more recently should also look to Hudson's example and incorporate alumni representation to their boards, when possible, while also ensuring that alumni trustees represent the current community racially and socioeconomically, as discussed below.

Ensure that board trustees represent the racial and socioeconomic characteristics of the school community. Our findings align with research demonstrating that charter school boards often neglect to represent the demographics of their communities (Lay & Bauman, 2019; Nelson, 2015; Squire & Davis, 2014). Charter boards should prioritize diversity by ensuring that new members reflect the race, class, and geographic backgrounds of the school community. Rather than recruiting from sitting trustees' networks, as was the case in the focal schools, boards can recruit more locally from within the community by advertising board vacancies with community institutions, such as museums, libraries, and local businesses and organizations. Additionally, charter school boards should engage in efforts to support and develop prospective board trustees from the local school community, particularly those who may be unfamiliar with the roles and responsibilities of charter school boards.

Transition to elected boards of trustees. In all but one school we studied (Hudson), all board trustees were appointed, having been recruited from the networks of sitting trustees. Charter schools should consider transitioning from appointed to elected boards, perhaps initially by following

Hudson's example and designating particular board positions, such as the parent representative, as elected posts.

Enhance the accessibility of public board meetings. Each of the focal schools complied with their respective state's policies regarding meeting transparency by posting announcements of upcoming board meetings and allowing members of the public to attend. However, we found that other structural barriers limited public participation. To enhance meeting accessibility, we recommend that boards meet at different times during the school year—perhaps holding half of its meetings during morning hours and half in the evening, to accommodate parents and community members with various work schedules. In addition, boards should provide refreshments and childcare during meetings to further accommodate the public. Finally, boards should meet in locations accessible to the community, such as the school site itself or alternate sites on public transportation routes; and arrange meeting spaces to comfortably seat public attendees.

Re-centering democratic values in an educational landscape deeply shaped by market tenets will require broad shifts in our political consciousness (Knight Abowitz & Stitzlein, 2018). However, the recommendations detailed above can serve as the first steps toward enhancing charter school boards' engagement with families and community members. In turn, charter schools can better fulfill the charter movement's early goals of animating local participatory democracy.

REFERENCES

Allen, A., & Plank, D. N. (2005). School board election structure and democratic representation. *Educational Policy*, *19*(3), 510–527. https://doi.org/10.1177/0895904805276144

Arsen, D., & Mason, M. L. (2013). Seeking accountability through state-appointed emergency district management. *Educational Policy*, *27*(2), 248–278. https://doi.org/10.1177/0895904813475711

Budde, R. (1988). *Education by charter: Restructuring school districts.* Regional Laboratory for Educational Improvement of the Northeast & Islands.

Butler, E. A., Smith, J., & Wohlstetter, P. (2008). *Creating and sustaining high-quality charter school governing boards.* Center on Educational Governance, University of Southern California.

Castillo, E. (2020). "Doing what it takes to keep the school open": The philanthropic networks of progressive charter schools. *Education Policy Analysis Archives*, *28*(121), 1–26. https://doi.org/10.14507/epaa.28.4452

Chubb, J. E., & Moe, T. M. (1990). *Politics, markets, and America's schools.* Brookings Institution Press.

Committee on Open Government, New York Department of State. (n.d.). Open Meetings Law. Retrieved February 14, 2017, from Open Meetings Law website: https://www.dos.ny.gov/coog/openmeetlaw.html

Charter Governing Boards and Community Engagement 69

Delagardelle, M. L. (2008). The lighthouse inquiry: Examining the role of school board leadership in the improvement of student achievement. In T. L Alsbury (Ed.), *Relevancy and revelation: The future of school board governance* (pp. 191-223). Rowman & Littlefield.

DiMartino, C., & Jessen, S. B. (2018). *Selling school: The marketing of public education.* Teachers College Press.

Engel, M. (2000). *The struggle for control of public education: Market ideology vs. Democratic values.* Temple University Press.

Farrell, C., Wohlstetter, P., & Smith, J. (2012). Charter management organizations: An emerging approach to scaling up what works. *Educational Policy, 26*(4), 499–532. https://doi.org/10.1177/0895904811417587

Ford, M. R., & Ihrke, D. M. (2019). Bridging the charter school accountability divide: Defining a role for nonprofit charter school boards. *Education and Urban Society, 51*(5), 640–658. https://doi.org/10.1177/0013124517747365

Fraga, L., & Elis, R. (2009). Interests and representation: Ethnic advocacy on California school boards. *Teachers College Record, 111*, 659–682.

Henig, J. R., Hula, R. C., Orr, M., & Pedeseleaux, D. S. (1999). *The color of school reform: Race, politics, and the challenge of urban education.* Princeton University Press.

Henig, J. R., Jacobsen, R., & Reckhow, S. (2019). *Outside money in school board elections: The nationalization of education politics.* Harvard Education Press.

Hernández, L E. (2022). Code Switching and Political Strategy: The Role of Racial Discourse in the Coalition-Building Efforts of Charter Management Organizations. *American Educational Research Journal, 59*(2), 219–251. https://doi.org/10.3102/00028312211072837

Hernández, L. E., & Castillo, E. (2020). Citizenship development and the market's impact: Examining democratic learning in charter schools in two regions. *Educational Policy.* https://doi.org/10.1177/0895904820901482

Jabbar, H. (2015). Competitive networks and school leaders' perceptions: The formation of an education marketplace in post-Katrina New Orleans. *American Educational Research Journal, 52*(6), 1093–1131. https://doi.org/10.3102/0002831215604046

Kirst, M. W., & Wirt, F. M. (2009). *The political dynamics of American education* (4th ed.). McCutchan.

Knight Abowitz, K., & Karaba, R. (2010). Charter schooling and democratic justice. *Educational Policy, 24*(3), 534–558. https://doi.org/10.1177/0895904809335109

Knight Abowitz, K., & Stitzlein, S. M. (2018). Public schools, public goods, and public work. *Phi Delta Kappan, 100*(3), 33–37. https://doi.org/10.1177/0031721718808262

Land, D. (2002). Local school boards under review: Their role and effectiveness in relation to students' academic achievement. *Review of Educational Research, 72*(2), 229–278. https://doi.org/10.3102/00346543072002229

Lay, J. C., & Bauman, A. (2019). Private governance of public schools: Representation, priorities, and compliance in New Orleans charter school boards. *Urban Affairs Review, 55*(4), 1006–1034. https://doi.org/10.1177/1078087417748783

70 E. CASTILLO and L. E. HERNÁNDEZ

Lubienski, C., Gulosino, C., & Weitzel, P. (2009). School choice and competitive incentives: Mapping the distribution of educational opportunities across local education markets. *American Journal of Education*, *115*(4), 601–647. https://doi.org/10.1086/599778

Maerloff, G. I. (2010). School boards in America: Flawed, but still significant. *Phi Delta Kappan*, *91*(6), 31–34. https://doi.org/10.1177/003172171009100609

Molina, A. L., & Meier, K. J. (2018). Demographic dreams, institutional realities: Election design and Latino representation in American education. *Politics, Groups, and Identities*, *6*(1), 77–94. https://doi.org/10.1080/21565503.2016.1182931

Morel, D. (2018). *Takeover: Race, education, and American democracy*. Oxford University Press.

National Association of Charter School Authorizers. (2018). Charter school growth report. Retrieved May 28, 2018, from http://www.qualitycharters.org/policy-research/inside-charter-school-growth/

Nelson, S. L. (2015). Gaining "choice" and losing voice. In L. Mirón, B. R. Beabout, & J. L. Boselovic (Eds.), *Only in New Orleans* (Vol. 63, pp. 237–265). https://doi.org/10.1007/978-94-6300-100-7_14

Quinn, R., Oelberger, C. R., & Meyerson, D. (2016). Getting to scale: Ideas, opportunities, and resources in the early diffusion of the charter management organization, 1999–2006. *Teachers College Record*, *118*, 1–44.

Resnick, M. A., & Bryant, A. L. (2010). School boards: Why American education needs them. *Phi Delta Kappan*, *91*(6), 11–14. https://doi.org/10.1177/003172171009100604

Rofes, E., & Stulberg, L. M. (Eds.). (2004). *The emancipatory promise of charter schools*. State University of New York Press.

Scott, J. (2009). The politics of venture philanthropy in charter school policy and advocacy. *Educational Policy*, *23*(1), 106–136. https://doi.org/10.1177/0895904808328531

Scott, J., & Holme, J. J. (2002). Public schools, private resources: The role of social networks in California charter school reform. In A. S. Wells (Ed.), *Where charter school policy fails: The problems of accountability and equity* (pp. 102–128). Teachers College Press.

Scott, J., & Holme, J. J. (2016). The political economy of market-based educational policies: Race and reform in urban school districts, 1915 to 2016. *Review of Research in Education*, *40*(1), 250–297.

Squire, J., & Davis, A. C. (2014). *Charter school boards in the nation's capital*. Thomas B. Fordham Institute and Bellweather Education Partners.

Trujillo, T. (2013). The disproportionate erosion of local control: Urban school boards, high-stakes accountability, and democracy. *Educational Policy*, *27*(2), 334–359. https://doi.org/10.1177/0895904812465118

Tyack, D. B. (2002). Forgotten players: How local school districts shaped American education. In A. M. Hightower, M. S. Knapp, J. A. Marsh, & M. W. McLaughlin (Eds.), *School districts and instructional renewal* (pp. 9–24). Teachers College Press.

Usdan, M. D. (2010). School boards: A neglected institution in an era of school reform. *Phi Delta Kappan*, *91*(6), 8–10. https://doi.org/10.1177/003172171009100603

Wells, A. S., Slayton, J., & Scott, J. (2002). Defining democracy in the neoliberal age: Charter school reform and educational consumption. *American Educational Research Journal*, *39*(2), 337–361. https://doi.org/10.3102/00028312039002337

White, T. (2018). From community schools to charter chains: New York's unequal educational landscape. In R. Sanders, D. Stovall, & T. White (Eds.), *Twenty-first century Jim Crow schools: The impact of charters on public education* (pp. 69–105). Beacon Press.

Wong, K. K., & Shen, F. X. (2003). Measuring the effectiveness of city and state take-over as a school reform strategy. *Peabody Journal of Education*, *78*(4), 89–119. https://doi.org/10.1207/S15327930PJE7804_06

ENDNOTES

1. To protect their identities, we use pseudonyms for all schools and interview participants.
2. The Brown Act of 1953 requires that California agencies and governing boards receiving public dollars hold meetings that are open to the public and provide forums for public comment. Since its establishment, the law has been interpreted to mean public access to formal governance meetings as well as communication conducted in informal or virtual forums wherein leaders convene and make organizational decisions.
3. To protect the city's identity, Birchwood is a pseudonym.

CHAPTER 4

FAMILY AND COMMUNITY ENGAGEMENT IN DIVERSE-BY-DESIGN CHARTER SCHOOLS

Priscilla Wohlstetter
Teachers College, Columbia University

Elisabeth H. Kim
California State University, Monterey Bay

INTRODUCTION

At charter schools that are Diverse-By-Design (DBD), family and community engagement is often the glue—the special sauce—that brings the school community together. DBD schools promote the values of diversity, inclusiveness, and democracy. DBD charters commonly have mission statements that seek to attract to a single school a mix of students, families, and educators from distant neighborhoods, racial groups, and socioeconomic backgrounds.

Family and community engagement is particularly important within the context of DBD schools because they serve a diverse population, often from different geographical areas and backgrounds. Thus, there is an imperative to create a school culture that is welcoming to students, parents, and educators from all backgrounds. Furthermore, research has shown that family engagement in school yields positive health outcomes in adulthood (Steiner et al., 2019) as well as gains in academic achievement (Potter & Quick, 2018; Wood & Bauman, 2017). Finally, as parents, we know that relationships children and families form in schools are important and difficult to replace.

Family and Community Engagement in Charter Schools, pp. 73–96
Copyright © 2025 by Information Age Publishing
www.infoagepub.com
All rights of reproduction in any form reserved.

This chapter reports on aspects of a larger national study of DBD schools across seven jurisdictions of the United States. We found that our DBD sample schools were more racially diverse than most charter and traditional public schools (Cordes et al., 2019). They also had increased rates of attendance and decreased rates of suspensions, particularly among Black and special education students. Finally, they exhibited higher rates of performance in English Language Arts (ELA) than in comparison schools. One important finding that emerged from this national study was the focus of all DBD schools in our sample on family and community engagement. In this chapter, we elucidate why DBD schools found it useful to attend to this issue, the strategies that were used to accomplish it, and the challenges schools faced in bringing the mission of integration in line with school operations.

RESEARCH QUESTIONS AND METHODS

In this chapter, we explore the following research questions:

1. What factors lead DBD charter schools to engage with their families and communities?
2. What strategies do DBD charter schools use to encourage family and community engagement?
3. What are some of the challenges that DBD charter schools encounter when engaging with families and communities?

This is a mixed-methods study with a sample of 28 DBD charter schools, including a mix of schools belonging to larger Charter Management Organizations (CMOs) and independent charters across the United States. The jurisdictions included three in California (Los Angeles, San Diego County, and the Bay Area); one in Denver, Colorado; and several in New York City (Brooklyn and Harlem). All the sample schools met three criteria: (1) they were in operation for at least three years as of 2016–17, (2) they were members of the Diverse Charter Schools Coalition,[1] and (3) they had an explicit commitment to diversity in their mission statements, as noted earlier.

Our research design included the collection of both qualitative and quantitative data, which afforded a more robust understanding than would be possible with either type of data alone (Creswell & Plano Clark, 2007; Greene et al., 1989; Fetters et al., 2013; Leavy, 2017).

There were two phases of qualitative data collection. During the first phase, we interviewed ($n = 70$) leaders from our sample, mainly staff at CMO home offices and the leaders of independent charter schools. In the second phase, we visited each school and focused on school operations to

Family and Community Engagement in Diverse-by-Design   75

uncover strategies for achieving DBD school missions and goals around intentional diversity. Our modes of data collection from these school visits included interviews with school principals and their leadership teams (n = 101), focus groups with teachers and teacher leadership teams (n = 40), and classroom observations in 4th, 8th, and 11th grades (n = 61). Additional data came from parent and teacher surveys administered in the sample schools. Teacher surveys were sent to all teachers in the 28 sample schools and parent surveys were sent to parents in 4th, 8th, and 11th grades. In addition, archival data from the schools were used such as sample schools' mission statements from their websites.

Interview questions were tailored to the respondents' roles in the organization spanning topics of teacher and student recruitment, the education program related to classroom integration strategies, school discipline practices, and building a community culture. We delve into the ways in which DBD schools worked to foster a sense of belonging for students, parents, and educators through family and community engagement.

Our quantitative data included student-level administrative data on racial demographics, attendance, and student test scores. (For more detailed information about the quantitative methods, please see Cordes et al., 2019). The findings from our study are compared with the existing literature on charter school family engagement in the following sections.

FINDINGS

(1) What Factors Lead DBD Charter Schools to Engage With Their Families and Communities?

There are several factors that led DBD charters to engage with their families and communities, including the school mission, the presence of diverse students that come from distant neighborhoods, and the benefits of diversity to higher achievement for students of all backgrounds.

School mission. In order to be considered "diverse by design" by the Diverse Charter Schools Coalition, schools must demonstrate a commitment to diversity in their mission statements. As such, sample schools had missions that were devoted to diversity and most, if not all, also included family and community engagement front and center in their mission statements. As seen in Table 4.1, of the sample of 12 CMOs and independent charters, 11 explicitly mentioned diversity in their mission statements. Overall, mission statements were focused on the school community of students and faculty using terms like "sense of belonging" and "warm, joyful community." Those that mentioned the external community often tied it to their curriculum in terms of community service and service-learning projects. Many schools also mentioned goals of producing "global citizens" and those who can make a positive impact on their community and world. Schools were split in terms of their focus on democratic values as an end in itself versus those who view democracy as an instrument for gaining higher student achievement and evening the playing field. In addition, almost all (98%) parents and teachers (97%) surveyed agreed that their school's mission of supporting a diverse school community is embraced by families, teachers, and school administrators. For example, as one network administrator explained, "The community is just as important as the individual…. We are only as strong as our entire community and we look out for each other and have each other's backs."

However, even when there was a demonstrated commitment to diversity in school mission statements, not all DBD charter schools attained a high level of diversity in their enrollment (Potter & Quick, 2018). This was due to factors such as residential segregation, gentrification, and changing demographics in local communities. Hence, it was incumbent upon DBD schools to recruit beyond the local community and focus on family and community engagement in order to create a sense of belonging within the school.

Diverse students from distant neighborhoods. Despite the increasing diversity of the American population, schools have become *more* segregated since the passage of *Brown v. Board of Education* well over 50 years ago (Billingham, 2019; Frankenberg et al., 2019; Orfield et al., 2012). School segregation has stemmed in large part from residential segregation in many parts of the country (Frankenberg et al., 2019; Wells, 2015). Thus, even when families sought out a DBD school for their children, they often traveled from a segregated neighborhood to get there.

As a result, family and community engagement was especially important in DBD schools as a way to welcome students and families coming from different neighborhoods and backgrounds. As an administrator at a California network explained: "People are willing to travel very long distances to get their students to our schools." A school leader at a Denver CMO spoke of students who travel over an hour to get to their school. In our research, we found that DBD charter school students attended more racially diverse schools in both Denver and California than their counterparts. Specifically, students who enrolled in a DBD charter school in Denver attended schools with a diversity index[2] that is 0.097 higher than students who do not enroll in a DBD charter school. Similarly, in California, the diversity index of DBD charter schools was 0.085 higher than comparison schools. While there appeared to be no difference in socioeconomic composition in Denver, in California, DBD charter schools were 12.4 percentage points more likely to be less than 75% low-income. In addition, almost 90% of parents surveyed reported that their child always or sometimes socializes outside of school with students from different backgrounds. An overwhelming degree

Family and Community Engagement in Diverse-by-Design 77

Table 4.1

Analysis of DBD School Mission Statements

Jurisdiction	Type and Size CMO/Independent	Schools Visited	Diversity (Abridged)	Family and Community Engagement (Abridged)
Bay Area, CA	CMO (Total # of CMO schools= 11)	6–12, 7–12, 9–12	Preparing a diverse student population … for success in a four-year college and to be thoughtful, contributing members of society; and by supporting our peers nationwide as they work to provide this same opportunity to their communities.	We are dedicated to ensuring every student can lead a fulfilled life, one with purposeful work; financial security; fulfilling personal relationships; … engagement in the community; and the physical health needed to engage in daily life …
Brooklyn, NY	CMO (Total # of CMO schools = 4)	Elementary Middle High	Prepare a diverse student body … to have a positive impact on society and a lifelong passion for learning.	… to have a positive impact on society …
Brooklyn, NY	CMO (Total # of CMO schools = 6)	Elementary	A dual language program committed to fostering academic excellence … diversity, tolerance and openness are emphasized throughout the curriculum and school life …	We recognize that our students are growing up in an increasingly "global" community…. Our entire educational program is geared towards providing students with a solid foundation to become ethical, productive citizens in this global community…. We help our students learn social and civic responsibility through the integration of community service and service learning … into their classroom studies.

(Table continued on next page)

78   P. WOHLSTETTER and E. H. KIM

Table 4.1 (Continued)

Analysis of DBD School Mission Statements

Jurisdiction	Type and Size CMO/Independent	Schools Visited	Diversity (Abridged)	Family and Community Engagement (Abridged)
Brooklyn, NY	Independent (1 campus)	Middle	Provide a hands-on, interdisciplinary education to young adolescents of all abilities and backgrounds ..., with a focus on real-world problem solving and the exploration of environmental sustainability.	[Our] students will ... excel in the core academic subjects and become engaged community members ... who are critical thinkers prepared to achieve excellence in high school and beyond.
Brooklyn, NY	Independent (2 campuses)	Elementary Middle	Students will meet or exceed the New York State standards and be prepared to excel in the 21st century by becoming independent thinkers and working productively within a diverse group of learners	... a rigorous learning community where education is embedded in meaningful real-world contexts and children are deliberately taught to see the connections between school and the world.
Denver, CO	CMO (Total # of CMO schools= 14)	6–11, Middle, High	Transform urban public education by eliminating educational inequity ... and preparing all students for success in college and the 21st century, values-driven organization, and a deliberately integrated community, serving students from all walks of life.... We appreciate each person and their story through our words, actions, and attitudes. We value their unique perspective and treat others with dignity.	We acknowledge that our actions and choices impact ourselves and our community. We take ownership of what we do and how we choose to do it.... We consistently align our words and actions.... We have a thirst for knowledge, a love of investigation, and a desire to learn about ourselves, our community, and our world.... We know that individual and collective effort are required for our community to thrive.

(Table continued on next page)

Family and Community Engagement in Diverse-by-Design 79

Table 4.1 (Continued)

Analysis of DBD School Mission Statements

Jurisdiction	Type and Size CMO/Independent	Schools Visited	Diversity (Abridged)	Family and Community Engagement (Abridged)
Los Angeles, CA	CMO (Total # of CMO schools = 5)	Elementary, Middle, TK–8	High-achieving … community-based public schools that reflect the abundant socioeconomic, racial, and cultural diversity of their surroundings … critical thinking and cognitive skills for young people from every background … helps prepare students … not only to survive but also to thrive in college, in a diverse society and in a global economy … commitment to economic and racial diversity.	Exemplify an intellectually challenging, experiential learning environment that develops each student's abilities, confidence, and sense of responsibility for themselves and their community … we work conscientiously to build strong communities both within and outside the classroom. Aided by exceptional local leadership and strong involvement from our parents … a warm, joyful community … a new generation of leaders—as trailblazers who are ready to tackle the future challenges in our world and surpass the conceived limitations of what students, communities, parents, and schools can achieve in the world.
Los Angeles, CA	CMO (Total # of CMO schools = 2)	Elementary, Middle	Truly diverse schools that hold all students to high expectations … rich academic learning experiences usually reserved for students in the most exclusive independent schools.	Providing them with the social-emotional support, inclusive community …

(Table continued on next page)

Table 4.1 (Continued)

Analysis of DBD School Mission Statements

Jurisdiction	Type and Size CMO/Independent	Schools Visited	Diversity (Abridged)	Family and Community Engagement (Abridged)
Los Angeles, CA	CMO (Total # of CMO schools = 3)	TK-4, 5–7, 8–12	Provide a socioeconomically, culturally, and racially diverse community of students … with an exceptional public education. We foster creativity and academic excellence.	Our students learn with and from each other in an experience-centered, inquiry-based learning environment. With participation from our entire community, we strive to instill in each student a dedication to improving the world we inhabit.
Los Angeles, CA	Independent (2 campuses)	K–8	Develop students who are active in their learning, aware of their interests … achieved in … primarily multi-age classrooms by creating an active and engaging learning environment based on a workshop format … opportunity for student choice within an environment of academic excellence.	Who seek to expand and explore their knowledge through dynamic collaboration with peers and teachers within an academic setting and the larger community.
Los Angeles, CA	Independent (2 campuses)	Elementary, Middle	Provide a holistic and exceptional education to a diverse student body …, cultivating in students' intellectual curiosity … and a passion for excellence."	Collaboration, respect for others …
San Diego, CA	CMO (Total # of CMO schools = 16)	Elementary Middle, High	The mission of all [our] schools, whether at the elementary, middle, or high school level, is to provide students with rigorous and relevant academic and workplace skills.	Preparing its graduates for postsecondary success and productive citizenship.

Family and Community Engagement in Diverse-by-Design   81

of teachers (91%) surveyed agreed or strongly agreed that students from different backgrounds were encouraged to have a broad circle of friends at the school. DBD schools used a variety of strategies to encourage students and families from different backgrounds to socialize inside and outside school. For example, a network in Brooklyn organizes out-of-school play-dates for classes at the local playground on the weekends.

Students and families in DBD charter schools, given their status as alternatives to neighborhood-based school-assignment, likely did not know each other prior to entering school. As such, community building was critical to ensure that DBD schools were achieving their goals of diversity and inclusivity. It was not enough to recruit a diverse student body; schools worked to ensure that they maintained that diversity over time through family and community engagement.

The benefits of diversity to higher achievement for students of all backgrounds. The literature has established that diverse schools contribute to higher achievement for all students (Card & Rothstein, 2006; Kahlenberg & Potter, 2012; Orfield, 2001; Orfield et al., 2016; Wells et al., 2016). In addition, there is a direct and positive association between family engagement and student academic achievement (Wood & Bauman, 2017). This positive relationship is particularly apparent for low-income students (Biag & Castrechini, 2016; Mediratta et al., 2009), Latinx (Biag & Castrechini, 2016; McDonald et al., 2006) and special education students (Zhang et al., 2011). Thus, when schools are welcoming to a diverse group of families and students, there are gains in student achievement for all.

Students in the schools in our sample confirmed this trend. They exhibited higher rates of achievement in ELA than their peers in other charter and traditional public schools, as seen in Table 4.1. More specifically, for each additional year of attending a DBD school in Denver, ELA scores increased by 0.046 SDs, and in California ELA proficiency rates in DBD schools were 3.5 percentage points higher. In California, DBD schools also performed slightly better in math (1.772 percentage points), although the difference was smaller than in ELA. Almost all parents (95%) surveyed agreed that the school has high expectations for students regardless of family background. Moreover, over 75% of parents agreed that school staff members often work with them to help their student do well in school. One explanation for higher ELA scores rests on the fact that most students in our sample had in effect double-ELA classes—one focused explicitly on ELA and a second on social studies/social justice topics. In addition, teachers and administrators interviewed attributed these achievement gains to the community building and anti-bias curriculum that is a priority in many DBD schools, as described below by a New York network:

> Anti-bias education, on a very basic level, is four gears working together. The first is honoring and understanding your own identity, kids understanding who they are. The second is the idea of who are the people around me, what are the identities of my community and the people around me. The third is recognizing injustice. What is the injustice that exists? The fourth is taking action. Those are the goals of anti-bias education. One of the ways that I think about it a lot is that anti-bias education is not like, "It's 2:30, let's talk about racism," but it's like how are we putting this lens on every part of our school day?

As such, DBD schools strive to infuse their values of diversity and inclusivity throughout the school day through the use of anti-bias curriculum and a focus on social justice. These practices further their work in family and community engagement as well.

Summary. We found that factors such as the school mission, a diverse student body that comes from different geographical areas, and the benefits to higher achievement for all students led DBD charters to engage with their families and communities. The DBD schools we studied were committed to family and community engagement in their mission statements and were more diverse than traditional public schools (Cordes et al., 2019). They also showed higher achievement in ELA, which is attributed in part to their focus on family and community engagement.

(2) What Strategies Do DBD Schools Use to Encourage Family and Community Engagement?

DBD schools used a number of innovative strategies to encourage family and community engagement in their schools through the recruitment of community members and the offerings of their education program. There was also a focus on building a community culture fostered by routines focused on developing a sense of belonging, mixing strategies, and authentic forms of family engagement.

Family recruitment. As mentioned above, American public schools have become more segregated, with notable increases in racial isolation for Black and Latinx students (Orfield et al., 2012). Public charter schools are even more likely to be segregated than traditional public schools (Frankenberg & Siegel-Hawley, 2013) due to marketing and recruitment strategies (Lubienski, 2007), school location (Lubienski & Dougherty, 2009) or missions to serve "at-risk" or "high-needs" students (Eckes & Trotter, 2007). In our sample, we found that DBD schools were successful in recruiting a more diverse student body and that they developed sophisticated strategies for recruiting families to their schools.

Family and Community Engagement in Diverse-by-Design   83

For example, they employed a variety of different practices to reach families such as neighborhood canvassing, visits to feeder schools, hosting events at the school, outreach by diverse parents, attending community events, and direct contact via social media, phone, or email. Sample schools also used data to decide which recruitment strategies to deploy and which groups to target. Also, schools had found that the best way to recruit a diverse population could be by word of mouth or through other families. A California network explained: "What we have found is that people often come in groups. Their most reliable source of application is family to family."

Importantly, nine out of the 12 operators also mentioned that they were concerned not just with *recruiting* a diverse population but also *retaining* that population as described below:

> Unless we ensure that families feel like this is the place where they can be welcomed, and they can feel a sense of belonging, we won't attract the students, and often not retain many students. If we get kids in the door, but they don't feel like they belong, they don't feel like they are valued here and they won't stay with us.

It was especially in the area of student retention where the family and community engagement piece was most important.

Recruitment of diverse staff. Research suggests diverse teachers contribute to improved student outcomes for diverse students (Dee, 2004; Egalite et al., 2015; Ehrenberg et al., 1995; Sohn, 2009). When a Black male student has just one Black teacher in Grades 3–5, the probability of dropping out of high school decreases significantly. Further, the experience contributes to an increase in the likelihood of *both* sexes aspiring to attend a four-year college (Gershenson et al., 2017). Moreover, increasing the diversity of the teacher workforce has been shown to benefit all students, as diverse teachers bring a varied set of experiences and perspectives into the classroom (Irizarry, 2007).

As such, just as DBD schools prioritized recruiting a diverse student body, they have also begun to do the same for faculty and staff. Interviewees often mentioned the need to recruit faculties that were representative of the students and families in their schools. They also cited the importance of the exposure of students to teachers and administrators from different backgrounds. As a New York network noted, "There's a lot of research about how important it is to make sure that the faculty and the principals are representative of the student population." A teacher at a California network reported recruitment efforts at Historically Black Colleges and Universities (HBCUs): "We tell them to go out to Spelman and Howard and state universities and other top tier places and get us faculty of color."

84 P. WOHLSTETTER and E. H. KIM

They also partnered with postsecondary institutions for teacher training and professional development purposes. A New York based network was working with the Yale Center for Emotional Intelligence to bring social-emotional learning to its schools. Another New York based network had a partnership with New York University to recruit student teachers. They worked as co-teachers with more experienced faculty at the schools and received regular training in DBD practices. Many of the student teachers became teachers within the network upon graduation. As mentioned earlier, some schools and networks partnered with HBCUs in order to recruit more diverse faculty and staff as well.

To work toward teacher diversity goals, the schools in our study engaged in strategic efforts to recruit and retain diverse teachers. This included "grow your own" approaches used by three of the study schools, in which charter schools partnered with a university to credential teacher candidates recruited from colleges serving predominantly students of color rather than relying on existing credentialing programs to produce the diverse candidates sought by the schools. Four study schools described how important it was to build on the personal networks of teachers they already had on staff, with some providing financial incentives for teachers to refer candidates.

There are clear benefits to student achievement and school climate when students see school staff who share their cultural characteristics. As schools of choice, a diverse faculty also served as a way of signaling to potential families that families like theirs were welcomed and valued in the school community. At least at the point of recruiting families, having a faculty and staff that approximated the makeup of the student body served as a way to begin trust building and communicating their commitment to diversity.

Engagement in the education program. DBD schools also incorporated family and community engagement in their education program as evident in the following mission of a Brooklyn network.

> Our entire educational program is geared towards providing students with a solid foundation to become ethical, productive citizens in this global community. We help our students learn social and civic responsibility through the integration of community service and service learning into their classroom studies, and diversity, tolerance and openness are emphasized throughout the curriculum and school life.

All the schools we studied achieved indicated their use of culturally responsive pedagogy (CRP) and nine also did so through Project Based Learning (PBL) in their classrooms. They used these curricular models in an attempt to include students of different abilities and backgrounds more effectively within the classroom. Proponents of CRP suggest it is a way for schools to acknowledge the home-community culture of the students (Gay, 2000). Through sensitivity to cultural nuances, schools are better able to

Family and Community Engagement in Diverse-by-Design 85

integrate these cultural experiences, values, and understandings into the teaching and learning environment (Brown-Jeffy & Cooper, 2011). Similarly, PBL is a comprehensive approach to classroom teaching and learning that is designed to engage students in the investigation of authentic problems (Blumenfeld et al., 2011).

Almost all schools used a combination of the two models emphasizing an integrated anti-bias approach to learning, drawing from student experiences and challenging culturally dominant narratives. Anti-bias lessons were often anchored in interdisciplinary projects with a social justice approach. Building off of students' lived experiences gave them confidence and expertise to engage with content. Moreover, it potentially allowed for all students to find success and see a positive role for themselves in society.

All schools in the sample were engaged in explicit instruction around identity and bias with students. Eleven of the operators taught these issues primarily through advisory periods, while other schools prioritized embedding explorations of diverse identities throughout all content and curriculum. Further, nearly all sample schools described beginning instruction around identity and bias with their youngest students. In addition, nearly all schools in the sample have made some efforts at representing diverse identities, perspectives, and backgrounds in school texts and curriculum.

Several schools within the sample used investigations of the surrounding community to engage their students. This approach to culturally relevant learning was based on leveraging student's interests in their surroundings, oftentimes with interdisciplinary projects that culminated in action or advocacy. For example, a California-based network incorporated community building in their "project work" curriculum in age-appropriate ways. Younger students helped design playground and recess time and developed norms for behavior. Older students engaged in internships in the community and presented their work at the town courthouse for which community members were invited. They also sold their work in art galleries in the community and donated the proceeds to local organizations. Similarly, a New York independent charter focused on environmental conservation connected with the local community through their fieldwork. For example, a group of eighth graders studied food insecurity and nutrition. They researched options in the area and made a map of where local residents could use food stamps to buy fresh vegetables, which was then distributed through local community organizations. As a school leader explained, "It's a really great learning experience for kids. Sometimes, the 'ah-ha moment' comes in when they're presenting to community experts." Thus, learning was not only happening *in* the community but *with* the community as well.

Building a community culture. DBD schools reinforced community by building a school culture that kept community at the forefront. Inclusive school cultures with strong engagement practices have been found to contribute to high levels of relational trust with families, which also leads to improved student achievement (Bryk et al., 2010; Francis et al., 2016; Froiland & Davison, 2014; Mapp & Kuttner, 2008). An administrator at a Colorado network explained: "This is very much about community. Not just the community around the school, but the network of how all the schools support each other, and that is very profound as well."

This sense of community was accomplished through morning meetings and school spirit activities as well as heterogeneous grouping within classrooms. Sample schools stressed that it was not enough to enroll a diverse population of students, but routines were necessary to focus on community building to ensure that the school was authentically integrated. A network leader explained: "We have to make sure that on top of integration by the numbers, integration is true throughout the school. That's where that community piece really comes in. It's in all the little things and it's in the routines."

After-school programs and clubs provided students with the opportunity to take on leadership roles and work with students with similar interests from different classes and grades. Studies have shown that schools that are more inclusive of students' voices and needs demonstrate positive outcomes in terms of graduation rates, college readiness and going, school attendance and test scores (Potochnik et al., 2016). For example, in one Brooklyn sample school students were encouraged to take the initiative to start their own clubs. A White student started a hip-hop group and a Black student started an after-school fencing club. In another network, fifth-grade students were trained as mentors for younger students through a popular "Community Builder" program. Students at a third sample school were given the opportunity to participate in a student-led conference on advocacy for diversity and integration in their local schools. This focus on both the academic and non-academic lives of their students suggests another way in which DBD schools build bridges with their surrounding communities.

Research has demonstrated that a sense of belonging is positively related to academic achievement, motivation, self-concept, self-efficacy, and behavioral outcomes (Korpershoek et al., 2018). All DBD sample schools used a variety of strategies, such as advisory or mentor groups, mixing grades, skills and student backgrounds within groups and classrooms as a way to build community and a sense of belonging in school. These groups provided a "home base" or feeling of "family" at school so that no one went "unnoticed." At a California-based network, they were very intentional about the composition of the mentor groups so that they were "diverse just

Family and Community Engagement in Diverse-by-Design   87

like [their] school." "My advisory group was the first family I shared my college acceptances with" was a refrain we heard across all seven jurisdictions. All but one of the sample schools used mentoring/advisory groups to create "school families" for students. This was accomplished by keeping students and faculty together during the entire education school program—elementary or middle or high schools. They also built dedicated time into their weekly schedule for community building. A teacher explained:

> Every week the mentor groups have a community circle where they sat down together. The intent is to have a space for kids to share, hear from each other, build empathy and build relationships with each other. When kids have strong relationships with each other, they build empathy.

A key part of these groupings was to build relationships within the school community. Similarly, an administrator at a California network explained:

> We work to coach teachers in setting a foundation in their classrooms and also in what is a non-instructional part of our model, which is our advisory program. [Teachers in advisory] are advocates in terms of academic supports. They are family liaisons with a strong focus on communication. This has helped set an effective stage for building meaningful relationships among students.

Research has also shown that parent classes, events and activities contribute to positive outcomes for families and students (Auerbach & Collier, 2012; O'Donnell et al., 2008; Portwood et al., 2015). As such, the schools we studied offered many opportunities for families to participate in the community. DBD schools held sports, arts and music nights for families with the goal of more deeply exploring their mission of equity and diversity. They also held book clubs and cooking classes featuring families' diverse cultures. For example, a New York based network implemented weekly short-term courses for families such as "Chef of the Night" where a parent taught others to make their favorite recipe and then the group shared the meal together. As one school leader explained, "What we've tried to do is break apart this idea of what family engagement looks like. We're not trying to get everyone in the community there but we create programming that's actually very limited in the number of people that can come." Thus, families had the opportunity to get to know one another on a smaller, more intimate basis. Building intentional programming for families was evidence of these schools' commitment to engaging with families and community.

DBD schools have also developed their own community traditions that families looked forward to every year. For example, an independent charter in California held a popular event based on the folktale "Stone Soup". Everyone in the school community (even kindergarteners) participated in the cooking. The surrounding community was invited to share in the meal and many times local police officers and firefighters attended as well. An administrator explained, "It's a day of the whole community coming together to appreciate. Teachers and students get to see each other in a different light."

This kind of authentic engagement leads to greater trust and stronger relationships with school faculty and staff. As such, over 70% of families surveyed in all schools agreed that they trusted and felt connected to their child's school and over 80% reported that the school often or sometimes provided opportunities for families to interact and form relationships with one another. Similarly, 84% of parents surveyed reported that their child's school often or sometimes actively seeks input from families when making decisions about school policies, practices, and programs. As seen in the following excerpt of a mission statement from a California based CMO, family engagement is integral to their mission:

> Aided by exceptional local leadership and strong involvement from our parents, our student-centered learning model has been demonstrated to boost critical thinking and cognitive skills for young people from every background.... We are preparing our students to emerge as a new generation of leaders—as trailblazers who are ready to tackle the future challenges in our world and surpass the conceived limitations of what students, communities, parents, and schools can achieve in the world.

When a school includes family and community engagement in their mission, it demonstrates a commitment which contributes to the strong relationships found in sample schools.

Further, seven schools cited the need for a dedicated person to work on family and community engagement in order for it to be truly effective. They had actually taken the step to develop a position like director of student recruitment and family engagement or director of community development at their schools. It was found to be particularly effective when this person had a close connection with the community so they were able to engage with a diverse set of families.

Summary. DBD schools used a number of innovative strategies to encourage family and community engagement in their schools. They recognized the importance of recruiting and retaining diverse students, faculty, and staff. In addition, they offered educational programs such as CRP and PBL in order to better reach a diverse student body. Schools strove to build a community culture through the use of routines focused on developing a sense of belonging, innovative mixing strategies and authentic activities and events for parents.

(3) Engagement Challenges in DBD Schools

Despite the emphasis on family and community engagement in all sample schools, there were still a number of challenges that DBD schools faced. These include distance, homophily, engaging more effectively with families, and monitoring progress to inform decision making.

Distance. As mentioned earlier, due to the fact that DBD schools recruited a diverse student body, and are not bound by traditional geographic school assignment policies, students often travel long distances to get to school. While this practice is beneficial for the schools' diversity goals (Potter & Quick, 2018), distance can present challenges for family and community engagement. For example, most if not all schools reported that students and families were often unable to participate in afterschool and weekend activities. A teacher at a California network shared that low-income, mostly Latinx students often missed after school "office hours" because they lived farther away. Similarly, an administrator at a New York independent charter mentioned that it was sometimes difficult to get students to participate in their afterschool program because transportation challenges meant that they were unable to spend additional time at school. She explained:

> The community building is there in the class work but staying for extracurricular activities is my challenge. I think they are missing out on the opportunity to really get to know their peers outside of the classroom doing something they enjoy together.

Some sample schools were beginning to develop strategies to address these challenges but were still in the early stages. As a teacher at a California network explained, "We're diverse by design so that also means that we're a commuting school for everyone. No one really walks to school here. So, you have to do a huge amount to build the community which is automatically there in some schools where people aren't having to drive for a long time in traffic to get to." The very nature of diverse by design often requires that students are recruited from outside of the surrounding geographic community. As such, family and community engagement become even more important.

Homophily. People tend to self-segregate or engage in homophily even in diverse schools (Lewis & Diamond, 2015) such as those studied here. This is particularly true at the high school level (Wood & Bauman, 2017). Despite working on community building extensively, three sample schools still reported that students (particularly in the upper grades) were self-segregating at lunchtime, afterschool, and on weekends. Consequently, they stressed the importance of setting up systems and structures to ensure that the mixing strategies used *within* the classroom were practiced *outside* of the classroom as well. For example, teachers and administrators at a California network noticed that students were re-segregating during afterschool activities, so the educators actively encouraged students to branch out and try new activities. Mostly Latinx males were participating in soccer club but then began to try other options such as STEM and debate clubs. However, a teacher in the same network also mentioned that special interest groups like the Black Student Union could be very beneficial for marginalized groups who might not feel their voice is heard in the larger school environment. While these groups might not be racially diverse, they can create a sense of belonging, thus improving student retention, and giving students more opportunities to for cross-group friendships. Thus, a balance may be needed in order to build an inclusive community in a diverse environment.

In addition, community engagement must extend beyond the school walls into families' homes and neighborhoods. As depicted in the following quote, family engagement is critical in forming a bridge between what happens inside and outside the school community as an administrator at an independent charter in California noted:

> You might sit together in the classroom but if those same kids aren't coming over to your house for a birthday party or the parents aren't socializing like you would at your neighborhood school, then I don't feel like the [integration] work is done.

Thus, the schools often try to foster engagement that might not be happening in largely segregated communities.

Diverse families, diverse strategies. Teachers and administrators often shared that they felt that they had to work harder at community building than a neighborhood school might. A recent literature review (Wood & Bauman, 2017) on family and community engagement identified cultural competency as essential in schools with diverse populations. While most DBD schools studied were engaging in some form of anti-bias or cultural competency training, they still struggled to reach all families, particularly those who were low-income and of color. Due to the fact that DBD schools serve a more diverse population of students and families than is typical in their districts, teachers and administrators found that it was necessary to adapt more intentional forms of family and community engagement in order to be most effective in reaching people from different backgrounds. They also had to ensure that they were always acting in line with their values of diversity and inclusion.

For example, almost all schools struggled with low attendance, particularly for low-income families of color at family and fundraising events. Due in part to their monitoring efforts, they learned more about the causes for

Family and Community Engagement in Diverse-by-Design   91

low attendance, such as distance, scheduling issues and homophily. As they got to know their families better, they started to plan events that would be inclusive to more families, especially those who live at a distance or were low-income. For example, low-income families at a California network felt uncomfortable attending a gala or benefit even though they wanted to support the school. An administrator explained: "The word gala just turns people off. It seems elitist. How do we make these events more inclusive because we have families who are living below the poverty line?" At the time of this study, they were beginning to develop more approachable and inclusive forms of fund-raising.

Another California network noticed that there was low attendance, particularly for Latinx families at their events. Thus, they developed a parent group specifically for Latinx families, which has been very effective as this school leader explained: "Some of our Spanish speaking families have really taken the lead on organizing a specific group for Latinx families. They bring people in so they can understand what's happening at the school and take part in project work." Once brought in, Latinx families begin to interact with families from other backgrounds as well. The network also relied on parents to do outreach about events because they have found it to be more effective. This practice is consistent with the research on the empowering effects of parent networks in schools, particularly for low-income parents of color (Alameda-Lawson, 2014; McDonald et al., 2006; Mediratta et al., 2009; Potochnik et al., 2016).

In addition to moving beyond traditional forms of family and community engagement, DBD schools recognized that they needed to have the same discussions about equity with families that they were having with students and staff. At a New York network, an administrator explained, "We had a multicultural potluck but we're not having discussions with the parents, which is a goal of mine with the Parent Association; to have very real discussions because it starts with the adults." These discussions are important because they help reinforce the values that DBD schools are trying to promote.

Monitoring progress. A recent literature review (Wood & Bauman, 2017) identified data use to determine and act upon priorities as one of four foundational elements of partner collaboration with families and communities. All but one of the sample schools were in fact using data to track engagement efforts but did not always have the systems and structures in place to act on what they found in order to inform decision making. Many schools held regular focus groups, conducted one-on-one meetings, and collected surveys from key stakeholders. For example, an advisory teacher at a California network determined that many of her low-performing students were unable to attend afterschool office hours because they had family childcare commitments. In addition, they were unable to

P. WOHLSTETTER and E. H. KIM

use the school issued laptops to complete homework because they did not have internet access at home. She voiced that while she had identified this extremely valuable information about her students; she was unsure who to share it with or how to act on it.

Sample schools were beginning to adapt their practices based on what they learned. For example, another California network collected regular surveys from students that included questions about their sense of belonging. Teachers noted that girls reported a stronger sense of belonging than boys at the school did. They posited that the boys might not be as accustomed to sharing their feelings during community circles. Consequently, they began to discuss how they might adapt the practice to be more inclusive during professional development sessions. Similarly, a New York network learned through focus groups with families that the days they were holding events were in conflict with some religious and cultural traditions. As a result, they began to alternate the days of future events so that they were more in line with all families' needs.

Summary. Despite a focus on family and community engagement by all sample schools, DBD schools encountered a number of challenges. This included distance, homophily, engaging more effectively with families, and monitoring progress to inform decision making. They have begun to develop innovative strategies to address these issues, but there is still more work to be done in the future.

CONCLUSION

Family and community engagement contributed to a sense of belonging in DBD charter schools among different stakeholder groups. There was a strong focus on relationships, inclusiveness and equity. As an administrator at a Colorado network stated:

> What is foundational to our model is a huge emphasis on relationships. I'd say it's a linchpin of how we work to keep our schools integrated, connecting people to one another in a meaningful way and really knowing one another.

DBD charters all possess some level of student body diversity, but this is insufficient in creating equal opportunities. It is clear that the schools see creating bonds across lines of difference as central to fully realizing their integration efforts.

This research reveals implications for charter schools and traditional public schools and more generally for family and community engagement practices. In order to be truly *integrated*, DBD schools must focus not just on recruiting a diverse student body but also on retaining students and

Family and Community Engagement in Diverse-by-Design   93

families from underrepresented backgrounds and ensuring they receive an educational experience that is exceptional. Thus, the goal is not just one of student numerical diversity but about inclusion and equity of educational opportunity as well (Phelan & Teitel, 2019). Integration is also a job for faculty and staff. Equity must be infused throughout the education program, student discipline, and family and community engagement practices.

DBD schools have had to make difficult decisions about the extent of their commitment to their values, which often become quite visible in family and community engagement practices. An administrator at a New York network shared that it's essential that DBD schools do the "hard work" to ensure integration and equity. It has to be infused throughout the school day within the education program and permeate the school walls so that these values are present in the community and families' homes. The administrator stated:

> We could have taken a beautiful Benetton ad photo but, unless we're really working every day to undo biases and unless we're working every day to actually be intentional about building community within that space, you end up just perpetuating the same stereotypes that exist outside of the school walls.

Thus, community building is key to ensuring that DBD schools live up to their values.

As such, it is critical that DBD schools be intentional about their choices when engaging with families and communities so that everyone feels a sense of belonging. In addition, DBD schools must collect data regularly through informal and formal means and develop systems and structures to use that data to inform decision making. In this way, they will be more intentional about family and community engagement and plan events that are more well aligned with different families' needs.

REFERENCES

Alameda-Lawson, T. (2014). A pilot study of collective parent engagement and children's academic achievement. *Children and Schools, 36*(4), 199–209.

Auerbach, S., & Collier, S. (2012). Bring high stakes from the classroom to the parent center: Lessons from an intervention program for immigrant families. *Teachers College Record, 114*(3), 1–40.

Biag, M., & Castrechini, S. (2016). Coordinated strategies to help the whole child: Examining the contributions of full-service community schools. *Journal of Education for Students Placed at Risk, 21*(3), 157–173.

Billingham, C. M. (2019). Within-District Racial Segregation and the Elusiveness of White Student Return to Urban Public Schools. *Urban Education*, *54*(2), 151–181.

Blumenfeld, P. C., Soloway, E., Marx, R. W., Krajcik, J. S., Guzdial, M. & Palincsar, A. (1991). Motivating Project-Based Learning: Sustaining the Doing, Supporting the Learning, *Educational Psychologist*, *26*(3-4), 369–398.

Brown-Jeffy, S. & Cooper, J. (2011). Toward a conceptual framework of culturally relevant pedagogy: An overview of the conceptual and theoretical literature. *Teacher Education Quarterly*, *38*, 65–84.

Bryk, A. S., Sebring, P. B., Allensworth, E., & Luppescu, S. (2010). *Organizing schools for improvement: Lessons from Chicago*. University of Chicago Press.

Card, D., & Rothstein, J. (2007). Racial segregation and the black-white test score gap. *Journal of Public Economics*, *91*(11-12), 2158–2184.

Cordes, S., Wohlstetter, P., & Smith, J. (2019). *The impact and implementation of diverse by design charter schools* [Paper Presentation] APPAM Fall Research Conference, Denver, CO. November 7–9, 2019.

Creswell, J. W., & Plano Clark, V. L. (2007). *Designing and conducting mixed methods research*. SAGE.

Dee, T. (2004). Teachers, race, and student achievement in a randomized experiment. *Review of Economics and Statistics*, *86*(1), 195–210.

Eckes, S., & Trotter, A. (2007). Are charter schools using recruitment strategies to increase student body diversity? *Education and Urban Society*. *40*(1), 62–90.

Egalite, A. J., Kisida, B., & Winters, M. A. (2015). Representation in the classroom: The effect of own-race teachers on student achievement. *Economics of Education Review*, *45*, 44–52.

Ehrenberg, R. G., Goldhaber, D., & Brewer, D. J. (1995). Do teachers' race, gender, and ethnicity matter? Evidence from the National Educational Longitudinal Study of 1988. *Industrial and Labor Relations Review*, *48*(3), 547–561.

Frankenberg, E., Ee, J., Ayscue, J., & Orfield, G. (2019). Harming our common future: America's segregated schools 65 years after Brown. Civil Rights Project/Proyecto Derechos Civiles and Center for Education and Civil Rights.

Fetters, M. D., Curry, L. A., & Creswell, J. W. (2013). Achieving integration in mixed methods designs—principles and practices. *Health Services Research*, *48*(6 Pt 2), 2134–2156.

Francis, G. G., Blue-Banning, M., Turnbull, A. P., Hill, C., Haines, S. J., & Gross, J. S. (2016). Culture in inclusive schools: Parental perspectives on trusting family-professional partnerships. *Education & Training in Autism & Developmental Disabilities*, *51*(3), 281–293.

Frankenberg, E., & Siegel-Hawley, G. (2013). A segregating choice? An overview of charter school policy, enrollment trends, and segregation. In G. Orfield, E. Frankenberg, & Associates (Eds.), *Educational delusions?: Why choice can deepen inequality and how to make schools fair* (pp. 129–144). University of California Press.

Froiland, J. M., & Davison, M. L. (2014). Parental expectations and school relationships as contributors to adolescents' positive outcomes. *Social Psychology of Education*, *17*(1), 1–17.

Gay, G. (2000). *Culturally responsive teaching*. Teachers College Press.

Gershenson, S., Cassandra, S., Hart, M. D., Lindsay, C. A., & Papageorge, N. W. (2017). *The long-run impacts of same-race teachers.* IZA Institute of Labor Economics Discussion Paper Series No. 10630.

Greene, J. C., Caracelli, V. J., & Graham, W. F. (1989). Toward a conceptual framework for mixed-method evaluation designs. *Educational Evaluation And Policy Analysis, 11*(3), 255–274.

Irizarry, J. (2007). Ethnic and urban intersections in the classroom: Latino students, hybrid identities, and culturally responsive pedagogy. *Multicultural Perspectives, 9*, 21–28.

Kahlenberg, R., & Potter, H. (2012). *Diverse charter schools: Can racial and socioeconomic integration promote better outcomes for students?* The Century Foundation.

Korpershoek, H., Canrinus, E. T., Fokkens-Bruinsmam M. & de Boer, H. (2018). The relationships between school belonging and students' motivational, social-emotional, behavioural, and academic outcomes in secondary education: a meta-analytic review. *Research Papers in Education, 35*(6), 641–680. https://doi.org/10.1080/02671522.2019.1615116

Leavy, P. (2017). *Research design: Quantitative, qualitative, mixed methods, arts-based, and community-based participatory research approaches.* Guilford.

Lewis, A. E. & Diamond, J. B. (2015). Despite the best intentions: How racial inequality thrives in good schools In *Transgressing boundaries: Studies in Black politics and Black communities.* Oxford University Press.

Lubienski, C. (2007). Marketing schools: Consumer goods and competitive incentives for consumer information. *Education and Urban Society, 40*(1), 118–141.

Lubienski, C., & Dougherty, J. (2009). Mapping educational opportunity: Spatial analysis and school choices. *American Journal of Education, 115*, 485–491.

Mapp, K. L., & Kuttner, P. J. (2008). *Partners in education: A dual capacity-building framework for family-school partnerships.* SEDL.

McDonald, L., Moberg, D. P., Brown, R., Rodriguez-Espiricueta, I., Flores, N., & Burke, I. (2006). After-school multi-family groups: A randomized controlled trial involving low-income, urban, Latino children. *Children & Schools, 28*(1), 25–34.

Mediratta, K., Shah, S., & McAlister, S. (2009). *Building partnerships to reinvent school culture.* Annenberg Institute for School Reform.

O'Donnell, J., Kirkner, S. L., & Meyer-Adams, N. (2008). Low-income urban consumers' perceptions of community school outreach practices, desired services and outcomes, *The School Community Journal, 18*(2), 147–164.

Orfield, G. (2001). *Schools more separate: Consequences of a decade of resegregation.* Harvard Civil Rights Project.

Orfield, G., Kucsera, J., & Siegel-Hawley, G. (2012). *E Pluribus ... Separation deepening double segregation for more students.* Civil Rights Project/Proyecto Derechos Civiles, UCLA.

Orfield, G., Ee, J, Frankenberg, E., & Siegel-Hawley, G. (2016). Brown at 62: School segregation by race, poverty and state. Civil Rights Project/Proyecto Derechos Civiles, UCLA.

Phelan, L. W., & Teitel, L. (2019). *Beyond diversity to equitable, inclusive schools.* DC Policy Center. https://www.dcpolicycenter.org/publications/beyond-diversity-to-equitable-inclusive-schools/

Portwood, S. G., Brooks-Nelson, E., & Schoeneberger, J. (2015). Data and evaluation strategies to support parent engagement programs: Learning from an evaluation of Parent University. *Children & Schools, 37*(3), 145–153.

Potochnik T., Romans, A. N., & Thompson, J. (2016). *We made a promise: School-community collaboration, leadership, and transformation at Promesa Boyle Heights.* Annenberg Institute for School Reform.

Potter, H., & Quick, K. (2018). *Diverse by design charter schools.* Century Foundation.

Sohn, K. (2009). Teacher turnover: An issue of workgroup racial diversity. *Education Policy Analysis Archives, [S.l.], 17*(11), 1068–2341.

Steiner, R. J., Sheremenko, G, Lesesne, C, Dittus, P. J., Sieving, R. E., & Ethier, K. A. (2019). Adolescent connectedness and adult health outcomes. *Pediatrics, 144*(1). https://doi.org/10.1542/peds.2018-3766

Wells, A. S. (2015). *Diverse housing, diverse schooling how policy can stabilize racial demographic change in cities and suburbs.* National Education Policy Center brief.

Wells, A. S., Fox, L., & Cordova-Covo, D. (2016). *How racially diverse schools and classrooms can benefit all students.* Century Foundation Report.

Wood, L., & Bauman, E. (2017). *How family, school, and community engagement can improve student achievement and influence school reform.* Literature Review. American Institutes for Research, Nellie Mae Education Foundation.

Zhang, D., Hsien-Yuan, H., Oi-man, K., Benz, M., & Bowman-Perrott, L. (2011). The impact of basic-level parent engagements on student achievement: Patterns associate with race/ethnicity and socio-economic status (SES). *Journal of Disability Policy Studies, 22*(1), 28–39.

ENDNOTES

1. The Diverse Charter Schools Coalition, which was created in 2014, is an advocate for charter schools whom the coalition judges to be diverse by design, based on a review of documents from the nominated charter school including mission statement, diversity data, goals and strategies (e.g. student enrollment preferences and family outreach strategies).

2. The diversity index is constructed as a modified Herfindahl index and can be interpreted as the probability that any two students randomly selected from the school will be of different races, thus a higher number indicates more racial diversity. In order to explore socioeconomic diversity, we examined both the percent Free and Reduced Price Lunch eligible (FRPL) and the probability that a school is less than 75% FRPL. We chose the threshold of 75% because the majority of our DBD charter schools are located in relatively high poverty school districts. In order to explore other dimensions of diversity, we also examined the percent of English language learners.

CHAPTER 5

CONSTRAINED COLLABORATION BETWEEN CO-LOCATED CHARTER AND DISTRICT SCHOOLS

Brian Robert Beabout and Shanté Williams
The University of New Orleans

INTRODUCTION

Collaboration and networks have been a promising avenue of research for school improvement for over 20 years (Datnow, 2011; Hopkins, 2007; Hargreaves, 1994). The implied theory of action in much of this research has been that collaboration can provide the proper doses of both *support* and *pressure* needed to sustain educational change despite ubiquitous challenges (Fullan, 2000). Collaborative relationships can provide additional resources, expertise, and political stability for schools engaging in longer term improvement activities (Beabout, 2010; Corcoran & Lawrence, 2003).

Promisingly, collaborative strategies for school improvement have become a fixture in most Western school systems, with professional learning communities, school networks, and other forms of collaboration becoming common (Bodilly et al., 2004; Bryk et al., 1999). Important theoretical groundwork in the area of collaboration in schools was laid by Andy Hargreaves (1994) with the differentiation of more and less productive forms of professional collaboration. The less productive forms, dubbed *contrived collegiality*, included collaboration that was fixed in time and place,

---

Family and Community Engagement in Charter Schools, pp. 97–119
Copyright © 2025 by Information Age Publishing
www.infoagepub.com
All rights of reproduction in any form reserved.

mandatory, implementation-oriented (rather than problem-seeking), and administratively governed. On the other hand, he also identified more beneficial *collaborative cultures* in which helpful interactions were spontaneous, development-oriented, flexible and unpredictable in form and function.

While this scholarship on collaborative approaches to school improvement has evolved significantly in the last 20 years, significant barriers to operationalizing it in schools remain. That is, where collaborative structures are found in schools, they are just as likely to be examples of contrived collegiality rather than outgrowths of truly collaborative cultures. First, among these challenges, is the need to create collaborative cultures out of the more individual cultures currently in place in many schools. Administrators undoubtedly play a key role in changing school culture, but doing this in ways that do not create contrived collegiality is challenging. School leaders do not often have strong collaborative skills, the external environment surrounding schools has become increasingly competitive, and there remains a long-identified *intensification* in the work of schools- as educators perceive insufficient time for anything other than teaching (Hargreaves, 1994; Meier, 2000). Schools might collaborate with businesses, community-based organizations, universities, reform-support organizations, or philanthropic groups (Beabout, 2010; Warren & Mapp, 2011).

One particularly useful source of partners is other schools. They understand intimately the challenges of educating students, possess significant expertise in the technical core of teaching and learning, and can generate the sort of inter-organizational trust that can be hard for non-educators to achieve (Bryk & Schneider, 2003; Levin & Fullan, 2008). This chapter describes school-school collaboration in a context of two schools being co-located on the same campus.

In 2009, a somewhat novel reform effort saw four low-performing public schools in New Orleans divided in half. The lower grades were converted into charter schools with separate administrations, uniforms, and teaching staffs. The upper grades remained part of the recently expanded state-run takeover district. The four original schools had been removed from New Orleans Public Schools control in 2005, as the state largely took over the district (Beabout, 2010; Harris, 2020). While academic results of this policy were disappointing (only one of the four takeover schools will be in operation in fall 2022), little is understood about co-location when two schools inhabit the same space, including sharing students from many of the same families (Cordes, 2018; Hall, 2021). In an organizational context that would seem to promote school collaboration, we asked *what was the nature of leader collaboration between co-located pairs of district-run and charter schools?*

CHARTER AND DISTRICT SCHOOL INTERACTIONS

Much of the existing literature on the interactions between district and charter schools is focused on the academic impacts to school districts when charter schools open. In essence, these are typically not studies of *collaboration* between schools, but examinations of the impacts of *competition* on district schools often using econometric approaches (Hicks & Lens, 2021). Gao and Semykina (2021) found that the addition of charter schools in a local education market (LEM) lowered the qualifications of teachers in nearby public schools, while at the same time leading to improvements in math achievement for some groups of students. In a longitudinal study (2009–2015) of the impact of charter school presence on the achievement of district-run schools, Han and Keefe (2020) found a small negative effect of charters on the performance of local school districts. Similarly, in a study focusing exclusively on the academic performance of co-located schools in New York City, while results were neutral overall, scenarios in which charter schools were co-located with district schools exhibited a negative impact on middle school math and ELA achievement in the district-run schools (Baumgartner, 2012). The author explains, however, that this might be more related to the rancorous debates about charter school co-location and an attendant negative effect on school climate, rather than on the dynamics of co-location itself. Also reporting on data from New York City, but coming to a different conclusion, Cordes (2018) found that the presence of charter schools was associated with slightly higher math and ELA achievement in district-run schools- attributed largely high instructional spending after charter school competition. Interestingly, for this discussion, these positive academic effects for district schools were strongest when charter schools were co-located with district schools, rather than simply located nearby. This rather mixed evidence on the effect of charter schools on school district achievement does not provide much evidence as to *how* charter schools impact district schools. The present chapter aims to look inside this black box of charter-district school interactions, and to access their direct interactions, rather than examinations of how the changing school ecosystem might affect districts.

Another line of research examining the interactions between charter and district-run schools looks at competition for students (and thus fiscal resources) as charter schools enter a LEM. Jabbar (2015), in a paper aptly titled, "Every Kid is Money," found that charter school principals in New Orleans were very attuned to market pressures, and that their responses to such pressures often varied depending on a school's position in the market, with some schools concentrating on school improvement activities while others enhanced marketing and aimed to attract higher-performing students. A larger-scale study examining spending patterns in Michigan school districts facing competition for students from charter schools similarly failed to identify any salient patterns in how districts responded to charter school pressures (Arsen & Ni, 2012). Additional evidence suggests that charter presence in New York districts increased the costs and short-term efficiency of local school districts primarily by siphoning off middle-class students and increasing the concentration of poor students left in district schools (Buerger & Bifulco, 2019). Again, this line of research suggests that there may be some interactions between district schools and charters schools vis-à-vis their shared educational ecosystem. Direct interactions or any forms of collaboration are generally unreported.

METHODS AND EVIDENCE

The study employs an intrinsic case study design (Stake, 1995). Rather than being representative of a larger phenomenon, this case of transformation schools in New Orleans is explored simply in its singularity. This single case examines the implementation of the transformation school model of four New Orleans campuses from 2009–2013. Six of the eight transformation school principals participated in this study, including all four charter school principals and two from the state-run Recovery School District (RSD).

Individual, semi-structured interviews (Seidman, 1998) were conducted with each participant. Public data was analyzed to provide additional context to the interview transcripts, including school performance scores, enrollment counts, and grades served for the 2009–2016 school years. Additional document data was collected from charter application documents and media reports.

CONTEXT OF THE STUDY

In 2003, the Louisiana Legislature established the Recovery School District, expanding the state's school charter laws and granting its Board of Elementary and Secondary Education the power to assume control of "academically unacceptable" schools from their locally elected school boards. In New Orleans, the state's largest district at the time, more than 60% of public-school students attended schools whose performance scores had earned that label. By the summer of 2005, five of Orleans Parish Schools' lowest performing schools had been taken over by the statewide RSD and transferred to independent charter operators.

Constrained Collaboration   101

In August 2005, the landfall of Hurricane Katrina and subsequent flooding temporarily halted the operation of public education in the city of New Orleans. In the interim, state lawmakers saw the city's damaged schools and displaced population as an opportunity for a new start for the city's chronically underperforming and massively under-resourced public school system. New legislation was approved to accelerate the efforts of the Recovery School District towards a vision of whole-city reform. The RSD's reach was expanded to allow the district to takeover any school that was operating below the state average, beginning what would become a decade-long transition to a 100% charter school district.

In this context, local nonprofits emerged (or evolved) to engage in the process of widespread school reform. In 2006, one local nonprofit organization, New Schools for New Orleans, established a charter incubator to recruit, prepare, and support school leaders through founding new charter schools (Ableidinger & Steiner, 2011; Maxwell, 2008). The organization provided a one-year fellowship to each leader, including salary, office space, and professional development as they completed the charter application process (Maxwell, 2008). The first class of NSNO-incubated charter schools were approved as new starts—beginning with one grade and expanding as their students progressed. By 2007, however, our conversations with district officials indicate that the educational landscape had shifted, and new start charter schools were no longer desired by RSD superintendent Paul Vallas. New start charter schools typically preferred to open with three of four grades only and this led to a glut of seats available in some grades, and potential financial troubles if schools did not reach enrollment targets. More rapid whole-school takeovers were preferred by the district, but not preferred by charter operators because of the inherent challenges of taking over a large K–8 campus with tremendous, short-term performance expectations. Thus, the transformation model emerged as something of a compromise between the Recovery School District and the charter operators. In the fall of 2009, the district-run campuses of Gregory, Wicker, Drew, and Carver Elementary each were joined by a charter school, co-located on the same campus, and serving the lower grades with an expectation that one grade per year would be transferred from the district school to the charter school until the entire campus was run by the charter school, and the district school would cease to operate. It should be noted that such co-location was not common within the New Orleans Public Schools, perhaps limited to these four campuses. Unlike in other cities where this practice is more common, educators and families would not have had experience with such an arrangement with two schools serving one physical campus. Our exploration of the interactions between these eight school leaders is described in the findings below.

FINDINGS

Our findings from school leader interviews regarding charter-district school co-location are listed below. They are organized around two primary categories. The first describes challenging contexts for collaboration as described by participants. Our discussions flowed consistently towards the district-level contexts in which both schools operated, and the challenges were created for a true collaborative culture between co-located campuses. The second category describes the constrained collaboration our principals described. This was a collaboration that was mechanical, polite, and took place only as needed. This is somewhere in between Hargeaves's (1994) poles of *contrived collegiality* and *collaborative cultures* in that earnest exchanges took place, but they tended to avoid collaboration on matters of teaching and learning- instead focusing on managerial and facilities concerns. Prior to the dealing with the challenging context and the constrained collaboration, they gave rise to a brief summary of the schools themselves

A Statistical Snapshot

As shown in Table 5.1, what began as four RSD-run schools in the 2008–09 school year became eight schools in the 2009–10 school year, as the lower grades of the RSD school were handed over to the charter operator, who ran three or four grades in their first year, and then added grades each year. Demographically, the matched pairs of district-charter schools were nearly identical with each other, with more than 90% of the students identifying as African American and more than 90% of families qualifying for free and reduced-price lunch (FRL).

As all of the district-run schools began as K–8 or PK–8 schools, the original timeline for the charter school to "takeover" their partner was five or six years. This did not happen, however, as the table indicates. All of the district schools, which would have expected to operate (albeit with fewer and fewer students) until 2013 or 2014, were closed by 2011. This accelerated takeover occurred after the schools were already open and the RSD wanted to quickly close their district-run schools and avoid having small, poorly performing schools in their books. This faster than anticipated growth certainly contributed to the academic struggles which the charter schools faced. As of this writing, two of the four charters had been closed for poor academic performance, with a third to close after the 2022–2023 school year after its charter was relinquished due to declining enrollments (Fazio, 2023).

Constrained Collaboration   103

Table 5.1

Enrollments and Student Body Composition

School Name		2008-09	2009-10	2010-11	2011-12	2012-13
Success Academy	Enrollment		238	330	380	410
	Grades Served		PK-3	K-4	K-5	K-6
	% African American		98.7	99.1	98.7	97.1
	% FRL		96.7	97.9	95.3	97.3
Wicker (RSD)	Enrollment	292	245			
	Grades Served	K-8	5-8	closed Summer 2010		
	% African American	98.6	99.6			
	% FRL	91.1	94.3			
Pride Charter	Enrollment		132	194	248	323
	Grades Served		PK-2	K-3	K-4	PK-5
	% African American		97.0	98.5	97.6	96.0
	% Free/Reduced Lunch		95.4	96.9	96.8	96.0
Gregory (RSD)	Enrollment	471	289	281		
	Grades Served	PK-8	4-8	5-8	closed Summer 2011	
	% African American	98.1	99.0	89.3		
	% FRL	82.3	92.1	76.8		
Arise Charter	Enrollment		198	241	311	387
	Grades Served		PK-2	PK-3	PK-4	PK-5
	% African American		99.5	97.5	97.4	98.2
	% Free/Reduced Lunch		98.0	100	98.1	98.4
Drew (RSD)	Enrollment	515	317	291		
	Grades Served	PK-8	4-8	5-8	closed summer 2011	
	% African American	98.8	99.4	100		
	% FRL	89.9	94.6	90.0		
Mays Charter	Enrollment		140	198	313	340
	Grades Served		PK-2	PK-3	PK-4	K-5
	% African American		99.3	99.5	99.7	99.1

(Table continued on next page)

Table 5.1 (Continued)

Enrollments and Student Body Composition

School Name		2008-09	2009-10	2010-11	2011-12	2012-13
	% Free/Reduced Lunch		98.6	98.5	77.6	99.1
Carver (RSD)	Enrollment	544	257	180		
	Grades Served	PK-8	4-8	5-8	closed summer 2011	
	% African American	98.9	100	100		
	% FRL	94.7	96.5	93.4		

Challenging Contexts for Collaboration

As seen in other research on New Orleans' reforms (Beabout & Perry, 2016; Buras, 2010; Harris, 2015), the abrupt dismissal of pre-Katrina staff and the recruitment of new teachers and school leaders was common in the eight schools examined here. From a purely structural perspective, the transformational model used in the Recovery School District, led by high-profile Chicago-imported reformer Paul Vallas, brought in a second administrative team to each of the four transformation campuses. Our evidence suggests, unsurprisingly, that the backgrounds, training, and expectations of these school principals influenced their experience, the forms of collaboration believed to be possible or desirable and ultimately, the success of the model itself. The charter principals were asked to make rapid improvements to student achievement, scale up quickly, and operate in a wildly turbulent landscape, making sustained improvement challenging (Beabout, 2012; Gross, 2004). Our data suggests the following characteristics of these newly organized schools: *Reform-oriented school leadership, inexperienced charter principals*, and *charter principals with an independent streak*.

Reform-oriented school leadership. Each of the four transformation charter school principals were recruited from out of town and had connections to the dominant educational reform organizations in the city at the time: *KIPP, Teach for America*, and *New Leaders for New Schools*. In fact, two of the RSD principals who came in at the time of the transformation had connections with these organizations as well. This reform-oriented background, which was also common in many of the other charters in the city, has some identifiable impacts on the operation of the transformation model. This orientation could be characterized by a generally deficit view of existing schools in the city, a belief in test scores as the appropriate metric for judging successful schools, and a belief in school choice as a mechanism for system level improvement.

Within this mindset, charter leaders sought to establish schools distinct from those of the traditional RSD schools that they would be replacing. However, these leaders had to do so while still sharing facilities with and serving intact student populations inherited from the preexisting RSD schools. These remnants of the preexisting RSD schools were largely seen as challenges to overcome. One of the new charter principals interviewed explained how the introduction of the transformation schools model changed their approach to building school culture, noting, "You have to do a re-culturation. That's the addition [to other new start charter schools]. Instead of just laying out your culture, you have to do some re-culture, because there's already been a culture." Removing what was seen, rightly or wrongly, as *bad* school culture from their students was seen as extra work for transformation charter school leaders, but work that was absolutely necessary if their vision was to be implemented.

This aligns with a view in which schools were places to be replaced and rebuilt according to a pre-devised plan, rather than improved over time. As one charter principal noted, "I don't think anybody was very proud of this [RSD school]. And I don't think that this was really anybody's choice to go to school here." We have no evidence that this view was based on information from parents, and indeed many residents have described their schooling in the pre-Katrina system with great pride, despite demonstrable low academic results (Mitchell, 2015). Nonetheless, we see this view as emblematic of the reform-orientation that was common amongst the charter principals in this study. This preference for replacement, rather than improvement, and the dismissive approach toward veteran educators this entails has been referred to as "shock therapy" (Walker Johnson, 2012) and the "shock doctrine" (Klein, 2007) by others writing about modern urban school reform. Change is seen as a wholesale revolution rather than an incremental evolution in this view.

The reform-orientation of the charter principals likely complicated collaboration with long-time educators in the city, which included two of the RSD principals in our study. As one charter leader described this principal-principal relationship, "she's a veteran principal and they're up against a new principal, this out-of-towner. So. it was already the, 'I don't like you, and I don't plan on liking you' mentality." It should be noted this contentious relationship between these two principals was only evident on one transformation campus. It does suggest, however, that the reform-orientation of the hand-selected charter school leadership seen here has the potential to make collaborative relationships difficult with long-time educators who were clearly marginalized during the reconstitution of public schools (Stelly, 2007). These educators were part of the old system and would be unsympathetic to the *out with the old* rhetoric of the ascendant reform movement.

In perhaps a savvy move on the part of RSD superintendent Paul Vallas, two of the RSD-run school principals also had reform-oriented backgrounds, in addition to all four of the charter principals. One RSD principal had worked at a charter school network and having been part of a start-up school previously:

> Well, I was recruited to come to New Orleans from KIPP Academy in Memphis TN. I'm from here—worked in New Orleans schools- in fact had helped start one of the first KIPP schools ... *the* first KIPP school in New Orleans.

In this case of reform oriented, co-located principals, a shared set of beliefs and shared professional backgrounds likely helped their relationship. One RSD principal, in reflecting on a common background with his partner principal, noted that "we both have KIPP backgrounds. So, the same philosophies, shared visions." The reform-backgrounds of two the charter principals provided them with connections to national reform networks and most had teaching experience in schools with successful track records in raising student achievement for low-income students of color. As one charter principal noted, "these are just things that we've brought in from the high-performing charter world, that [the RSD principals] had just never really seen." The implication here being that these connections and experiences are typically not available to a principal in a district-run New Orleans Public School. The connections to the reform community brought potentially valuable connections to external support networks, but also increased expectations for rapid school improvement and furthered the divide between Black New Orleanians and the new regime of school leadership (Cook, 2010).

From the perspective of the district, bringing in new school leadership provided an opportunity to hire someone who accepts the climate of accountability for academic performance that, for better or worse, clearly dominates the political landscape of urban education (Anagnostopoulos et al., 2013). One charter principal indicated his adherence to this accountability infrastructure, stating unequivocally, "And if ... our school's not performing, they need to close us down...I mean, I'm going to fire myself if ... [we can't reach my] serious goals." Certainly, a superintendent with an accountability focus like Paul Vallas would appreciate a principal who shared his views on this matter. Interestingly, while this quotation was from a leader at a transformation charter school still in operation, two of the charter schools have since been closed due to poor academic performance, both of which exerted some unsuccessful efforts to remain open once the charter authorizer decided to close them (Dreilinger, 2012). Overall, this

Constrained Collaboration 107

strong espoused adherence to the brand of reform supported by Vallas certainly may have been a contextual barrier to strong collaboration between co-located charter and district principals.

Interestingly, one of the transformation charter principals grew up locally and found that her local connections benefited her tremendously in building rapport with families. For example, she noted, "I had a brother ... and he was ... a bit of a football star in high school. So, I would like [say] 'Hey, I'm Devon's big sister!' You know, and get them involved in that way." Despite being a charter school principal and in somewhat contentious relationships with her co-located principal, this leader found a way to overcome some of that stigma by articulating her local connections. Such connections highlight the bond between the principal and the local community, and certainly help to moderate the perception that the charter school leaders are dismissive of local community concerns. The need for school reformers to leverage the work of local educators who represent the community itself has become increasingly recognized by the reform community (Khalifa, 2012; Padamsee & Crowe, 2017).

Inexperienced charter principals. The second factor which created a context where collaboration was difficult was the general experience of the charter school principals. The reform-oriented leaders that were brought in to oversee the RSD's transformation school project were extremely inexperienced, and there is some reason to believe this impacted their context for collaboration. Of the eight principals (4 charter, 4 Recovery School District) that led the eight schools we studied; six principals (75%) had no previous principalship experience. In a 2017 interview, one of the architects of the transformation model in New Orleans also cited principal inexperience as a key issue in the mixed success of the model. Other than the paid incubation year provided by New Schools for New Orleans, only 1 of the 4 charter principals had formal leadership preparation. And this lack of preparation was recognized as a challenge by the charter leaders themselves. As one charter principal put it bluntly, "I can honestly say that as a principal ... I was self-taught ... I had no experience." Another RSD transformation principal indicated, "mind you that I was a KIPP *teacher*, so I had no administrative experience." This inexperience had concrete impacts on their work. This same RSD principal noted the challenges he had in managing staff:

> In the very first year, I didn't know all of the processes for getting rid of ineffective teachers. I must say, that becoming transformation helped me out. I had some ineffective teachers I needed to get rid of. And many of them were in the lower grades ... so, it made it very easy ...

In this case, cutting the school in half served as a way to remove of teachers that the inexperienced principal did not know how to dismiss. They were technically dismissed form the district and had to apply to the charter school and be re-interviewed by the charter principal who could make a hiring decision themselves. No charter principals discussed conferring with their district partners on re-hiring decisions. And given the previously described reform-orientation of the charter principals, and their sense that they were supposed to be better than their counterparts, one can see this combination on inexperience and expected superiority would create a context of limited collaboration.

Significant amounts of learning on the job seemed the only likely path for these charter principals. With the overwhelming pressure for rapid test score growth and an expectation that the hundreds of thousands of dollars in start-up funds would bear fruit and justify the transformation model, admitting the need for help may have been difficult. These novice principals after all had been framed by reformers as *the solution* to poor district performance. How could they come asking for help? Ironically, the risk to one's professional image and the threat of exposing one's vulnerabilities may have worked against help-seeking for these novice principals (Nir, 2009).

Inexperience may have led to some regrettable management decisions. Several of the charter schools were pressured into accelerating their growth and taking on more new grades sooner than originally planned. One of them noted that their acquiescence might have been due to their inexperience: "being a new principal, I was thinking with my heart." While wanting to serve more students in the school, this accelerated growth brought more academically struggling students into the school, all of whom were in the testing grades (third and above) and needed additional supports the schools did not have on hand. This accelerated school growth (heavily pressured by Paul Vallas) was described as a significant contributor to poor school performance on accountability metrics, and ultimately the threat of closure faced by the schools.

Charter principals with an independent streak. A third factor which created a context unsupportive of collaboration was an exceptional level of independence observed among the charter principals we studied. These novice principals also displayed a sense of independence that perhaps would have made them unlikely candidates for school leadership positions in a traditionally structured school district where principals are more middle managers than they are CEOs. Part of this independent streak may have come simply from the manner in which these charter schools were created. While receiving a salary and office space with New Schools for New Orleans, these principals, while supported, did the majority of the work on the school themselves. As one charter principal described, "you're

Constrained Collaboration 109

writing charter [applications] ... you're building this school, and like, some people talk about, *'the school started on my computer.'* " Given this high level of independence in their work to found a school, it is easy to see how an independent streak might carry through into their work as a principals.

Even in the autonomy-focused world of charter schools, charter principals in this study set themselves apart. While much of the charter expansion in New Orleans post-2015 has taken the form of replication and growth of existing charter schools into multi-site charter management organizations (CMOs), even that amount of bureaucracy felt stifling to some:

> I specifically didn't want to be a part of a CMO, I wanted to do it ... I wanted it to be in-house—so that every decision made is made on this site for this site ... and I also, I think, a little bit easier to innovate.

From this perspective, the principal wanted to preserve maximum decision-making authority and autonomy for themselves and their school. This was seen as non-negotiable if they were to meet the accountability demands their schools would face and achieve their personal vision of a student-centered school. Given this preference for independence, one that was perhaps selected for as these charter leaders were recruited, it shouldn't come as a large surprise that the paired RSD and charter schools showed limited efforts at collaboration (see *constrained collaboration* discussion below). One charter school leader indicated that they may not have even accepted their position if collaboration between the schools had been mandated:

> Had there been some sort of requirement for collaboration, that would have thrown a little monkey wrench into it. Because again, I just wasn't up to it, that's not what I signed up for, I signed up to run a charter school, and that's what they're allowing me to do.

Despite undoubtedly having more autonomy than a typical district principal, transformation charter principals were still dependent on a number of external entities for support, all of which came with some strings attached. These charters needed the local district for facilities, the RSD for funding, the nonprofit reform community for political support, philanthropic support for start-up costs, and the state board of education for authorization and reauthorization. Given the densely nested political systems surrounding schools in the immediate post-Katrina period, there were certainly limits to the autonomy that would be possible. Expecting support from all of these entities but then not expecting that support to come with strings attached is perhaps a bit naïve. Scholars may need to think in more nuanced ways about charter school autonomy. Such work is exemplified in a recent unpublished doctoral dissertation by Sharon Latten-Clark (2002), who interviewed ten New Orleans charter school principals and found that autonomy over curriculum, school operations, and finances were most important to their satisfaction and willingness to stay in the job of principal. Charter schools are autonomous from some district-level decisions, but even more reliant than district schools for help with facilities, startup costs, and political support. Autonomy might more accurately be seen as a multifaceted *autonomy-from-what* rather than a simple binary autonomy-dependence.

In the end, what we learned from study participants was that both the context of transformation schools and the individual characteristics of the leaders selected were not highly amenable to school-school collaboration, even in a high-contact scenario, such as co-location. The competitive nature of the post-Katrina reforms and the external pressures almost mandating that charter schools out-perform district schools served to create an environment in which productive collaboration was unlikely, even if individual leaders had been interested.

Theme 2: Constrained Collaboration in Turnaround Schools

When the four district-run schools were cut in half for the beginning of the 2009–10 school year, the result was eight smaller schools and eight separate staffs and administrative teams. Each school shared a building with another school and had to coordinate the use of shared spaces like main offices, parking lots, and the cafeteria. Given little expectation or guidance from the district on how or why to collaborate on instructional matters, we found very few examples of administrative collaboration regarding teaching, learning, or leadership, despite abundant literature supporting the value of collaboration to school improvement (Hargreaves, 1994; Hopkins, 2007; Leithwood et al., 1999). What we saw here might be termed *constrained collaboration* in that there was authentic interaction among school leaders, but it was limited to more mundane managerial aspects of their work (hallways and lunchtime), not the educational core of teaching and learning. We see this as a missed opportunity to improve student outcomes at both types of schools, where this was sorely needed.

Cordial, Not Collaborative

Our data suggests that while administrative collaboration was certainly *constrained*, it did nevertheless exist. In most cases, the co-located principals had positive regard for one another and described cordial relations. As one charter principal described his RSD partner: "He's a really good guy. He's

Constrained Collaboration   111

a good guy." This repetition almost indicating a professional distance, as if there wasn't much else to say other than these pleasantries. Another charter principal described their RSD counterpart similarly [pseudonyms used]:

> James is a great guy, Mr. Franklin, he's a great guy. But we really don't, ... work together other than to kind of make sure that everybody has their space. I mean, we get along great, we're good friends, but you know, we don't really work together much ... it's not like we're like *collaborating* on many things at all.

Again, we see here a relationship that was neither positive nor negative, simply *good*. Principals described their partners in ways that were professional and cordial, but not collaborative, learning-focused, or team-oriented. This was somewhat surprising given that the schools both served similar student populations, even siblings in many cases, and faced immense pressure to rapidly improve student achievement. One explanation for this lack of collaboration may be the competitive educational environment in New Orleans at the time (Jabbar, 2015). These leaders may have been so concerned with public accountability pressures, and the inevitable comparisons made between charters and district-run schools, that authentic collaboration on instructional matters simply did not seem feasible. In some sense, the external environment had tainted these relationships with competition and without some counteracting force, learning focused collaboration did not happen.

Despite serving similar students and their geographic proximity to one another, these constrained relationships may also have been a result of the somewhat different roles the paired principals had. While the charter schools had the backing of the reform coalition and significant philanthropic support, the district schools were expected to be taken over and closed. An implicit assumption of the model is that the district schools would not improve. In a sense, the charter principals were enacting a slow-motion takeover of their partner school. And the principals had a clear sense of this distinction. As one charter principal indicated, "the principal at [the RSD school] was brought on knowing full well the job that he was going to be doing. Sometimes I call it, 'Captaining the sinking ship.'" While charter principals had the role and expectations of a school turnaround specialist, the RSD principals were implicitly expected to quietly maintain order at the RSD school, and raise achievement if they could, but ultimately their school would be closed down in several years regardless of school performance. It is important to reiterate here that all eight RSD principals and the charter principals were newly hired at their schools when this model was implemented in 2009. The RSD principals, in effect, knew what

112 R. B. BEABOUT and S. WILLIAMS

they had signed up for. Without this move, we likely would have uncovered significantly more hostile relations between principals.

Instead, we saw cordial, but not collaborative, relations, and even a bit of sympathy for the difficult role of the RSD principal. As expressed by one charter principal: "he's taken on this role with great spirit, as far as teamwork and wanting to make it happen. And it's been really easy working with him on issues." The issues that they worked on together were overwhelmingly related to sharing the building in an orderly fashion. While this fell short of the sort of collaboration that might improve instructional capacity in the schools, there was clearly significant amounts of negotiation regarding facilities use, as described next.

Clearly Defining Separateness

In stark contrast to the lack of authentic collaboration on instructional matters, the principals described a great deal of collaboration over the use of their shared school facilities, especially during the beginning of their co-location in the fall of 2009. Interestingly, this was an area of collaboration that was officially sanctioned and supported by the district. A pre-opening meeting occurred with representatives of the district and the administrators from the two partnered schools:

> [The RSD] put together a template of questions that they thought we needed to answer. The first part was sort of laying the groundwork for the relationship. How often would we meet? When we met, whose office would we meet in? Who would set the agenda? Really just sort of establishing the relationship and the working relationship. And part two of the template was deciding things like, how would we divide the buildings up? Where would [my school] end up? What would the bell schedule look like? How do we distribute keys? How do we divide the parking lot?

Clearly, the two paired schools needed a basic working relationship, and a firm understanding of the expectations for sharing a facility. These meetings resulted in an approved document that strictly governed the use of space. As one charter principal noted, "we had a really tight MOU (memorandum of understanding) ... everybody cooperates as far as that goes. They use that stairwell; we use that stairwell." At the conclusion of data collection, our research team even joked that this study had become mostly about stairwells and parking lots—noting the scarcity of instructionally focused collaboration. There were the basic building blocks of cordial relationships and some professional trust built up from sharing facilities, but teaching and learning only rarely became the subject of school leaders' collaborative exchanges. We consider the structuring of collaboration with

Constrained Collaboration   113

regards to school facilities provided by the district to be significant. Where collaboration was expected and supported, it happened. Study participants reported few issues in sharing their facilities. As is described in the following section, none of this structure was in place for instructional collaboration.

Hints of Instructional Collaboration

Despite interactions that most often focused on facilities concerns, there were moments in which participating principals would show a desire for more substantial collaboration, or even took small steps to build instructional expertise across schools. One charter school leader even noticed some desire for collaboration from his RSD counterpart, but did not reciprocate because it was beyond what he saw as his role: "I would even venture to say that [my RSD partners] were more attracted to the idea of more collaboration. They were very ... willing to talk more collaboration maybe than I was actually envisioning." This suggests that the way the transformation model was envisioned by the charter principals did not include a significant emphasis on school-school instructional collaboration. It simply was not a part of the model, as they understood it, and as novice leaders facing massive pressure for rapid test score improvement, they likely experienced what organizational theorists have termed *threat rigidity* (Olsen & Sexton, 2015). At a time when external threats to the schools were high (possible closure, annual performance rankings in the media, possible loss of students and their funding) they may have become less able to creatively problem solve, and more likely to double-down on existing strategies. When external threats are high, there is little allowance for any performance declines, even those that might be necessary for longer-term improvement.

After a time, however, this same charter principal came to view collaboration as a potentially positive addition to his school: "I think increased collaboration could have a positive effect on the whole school, but it's neither mandated nor is it happening independently." Here we see a potential role for district guidance that was not forthcoming or a role for more experienced or more naturally collaborative leaders who might have taken advantage of this built-in partnership. Perhaps unsurprisingly, many of the families involved in the transformation of schools had students attending both the traditional district-run school and the new charter simultaneously. The families naturally began making comparisons between schools. As one RSD principal noted hearing form his school families, "They'd go over to Carver and say, 'Well, why don't y'all do this thing that they're doing over at Mays Prep?" While none of the schools had well-established parents'

114   R. B. BEABOUT and S. WILLIAMS

groups, an influential body of family members might have been able to ignite the sharing of promising practices between pairs of schools.

Both schools were also faced with the need to develop large numbers of novice teachers, so it came as little surprise that teacher professional development was a shared concern. As one principal noted, "we've been really good about sharing professional development documents with one another." But it was clear that this interaction didn't go much beyond the sharing of documents.

In one case, two principals discussed a problem with substitute teachers they were having with one principal offering advice to the other:

> Just the other day we were talking about how he had just decided to no longer hire substitutes in his building, but rather have his own staff cover and we were talking about advantages and disadvantages and how that was working out for him.

While here was a more authentically collaborative exchange, with shared classroom-level problems being discussed and attempted solutions evaluated, we see the topic is again managerial (substitute teacher assignment) rather than instructional.

Instances of Strained Relationships

While the relationships between charter and district principals at the four transformation school sites were not wholly collaborative, they were generally cordial and cooperative. However, our data does indicate some measure of strain in the relationships between the principals and faculties of these transformation school pairs. Oftentimes this was in relation to the sharing of facilities discussed earlier. For some leaders, their lack of control of shared facilities was a source of frustration. One charter leader shared in frustration, "There's manuals about laws and you're not supposed to just walk in schools, right? You can just walk in this school anytime you want. [Yes] doors are left open." Another charter leader expressed similar frustrations over their school's shared front office. She described the stark differences in dealing with students' families. However, for parents and students, the distinction between the co-located schools may have seemed more of an abstraction than tangible reality. One principal recounted having to repeatedly explain to parents that, "Yes, it's a new school, but we're in the same building. Yes, this is a new principal, but we're in the same building."

One a larger level we witnessed one co-located campus pair where the conflicts were not about facilities issues, but seemingly stemmed from an

Constrained Collaboration 115

RSD principal who was not supportive of the transformation model to begin with. A charter leader notes this strained relationship between the two schools:

> That first year was interesting, because the [RSD] principal was very vocal ... about their feelings and the staff kind of took on the same [attitude].... So even though we were working on the same campuses, the teachers wouldn't speak to me.

There are signs that these strained relationships may be attributed to the transformation model itself. In one charter leader's words: "It felt as if we were taking something from them.... We were invading their space, their territory." Given the design of the transformation model, this assessment is understandable. There was no evident support from the district in working through these challenging relationships, as the co-location was simply viewed as a temporary imperfect situation to remedy by closing the RSD schools as soon as was practical.

An RSD principal from a different campus explained the possible slowly evolving effects of a new school entering a campus: "While it may be fresh to teachers in the beginning, once it's settled that there's a school in our building, there begins to be ... some thoughts of it being unfair." In this case, the sets of co-located schools- one charter and one district-run, were held to the same academic accountability standards but differed immensely in their access to philanthropic dollars, in the level of respect given to them by the district, and in the amount of autonomy granted to the leader. As might be expected if siblings were treated unequally in a household, some pairs of schools certainly experienced conflict, though evidence suggests this was not the primary dynamic in three of the four campuses studied.

CONCLUSION

Our examination of the unique transformation schools reform effort on four K–8 campuses in post-Katrina New Orleans has been presented above. We sought to answer the question: *what was the nature of leader collaboration between co-located pairs of district-run and charter schools?* The evidence suggests, somewhat ironically, that collaboration between paired schools was often done with a spirit of ensuring the two schools remained separate, rather than worked together. Almost no examples of collaboration on instructional matters were described, despite schools serving similar populations of students and struggling with poor accountability ratings from the state. We saw evidence of collaboration related to sharing facilities, and occasionally some level of conflict between schools, but mostly we saw polite interactions and people minding their own business. Collaboration between school leaders to improve the effectiveness of teaching and learning in their schools was generally absent.

There is a sense that there were missed opportunities to make this reform model work more effectively for all students and educators involved. One missed opportunity was for principal mentoring if experienced and new principals were paired on the same campus. One could imagine a successful, late career principal engaging in a transformation relationship with a novice and slowly handing the school over within a couple of years. The pair could be selected together and serve as a long-term mentoring relationship in which the veteran principal spent time coaching and working with the less experienced one as an explicit job component. While this often happens when new administrators take on assistant principal roles, a transformation model would offer a more significant role for the new leader, and perhaps a rewarding end to the career of the mentor principal.

Another missed opportunity was for the two schools to work together on issues of instructional importance. Both sets of schools struggled with new teacher induction, starting up special education systems and student referrals, and delivering effective academic interventions. If the context around the schools was less competitive, and district officials set minimum expectations about instructional collaboration, then students would likely have benefitted. A talented reading interventionist on one side of the school could train novice colleagues on the other side in effective methods. Similarly, a middle school science teacher learning the new state standards might have had a larger pool of colleagues to seek help from, or a more natural mentor, if the two schools explicitly fostered collaboration. But there was no evidence of this.

Schools engage with many external entities, and much has been written about these relationships. Only a tiny sliver of this community engagement literature is focused on school-school collaboration (Armstrong et al., 2021). New Orleans' transformation was not an overall success in terms of student achievement and school stability. But it does provide a window into arrangements that might be better leveraged in other situations to promote school improvement.

REFERENCES

Anagnostopoulos, D., Rutledge, S., & Jacobsen, R. (Eds.). (2013). *The infrastructure of accountability: Data use and the transformation of American education*. Hasrvard Education Press.

Armstrong, P. W., Brown, C., & Chapman, C. J. (2021). School-to-school collaboration in England: A configurative review of the empirical evidence. *Review of Education, 9*(1), 319–351. https://doi.org/10.1002/rev3.3248

Constrained Collaboration   117

Arsen, D., & Ni, Y. (2012). The effects of charter school competition on school district resource allocation. *Educational Administration Quarterly, 48*(1), 3–38.

Baumgartner, S. E. (2012). *Scheduling conflicts: Measuring the academic impact of co-location on grades 3–8 traditional public and charter schools in New York City, 2006–2010* [Master's thesis, Georgetown University] https://repository.library.georgetown.edu/handle/10822/557791

Beabout, B. R. (2010). Leadership for change in the educational wild west of post-Katrina New Orleans. *Journal of Educational Change, 11*(4), 403–424.

Beabout, B. R. (2012). Turbulence, perturbance, and educational change. *Complicity: An International Journal of Complexity and Education, 9*(2), 23–37.

Beabout, B. R., & Perry, A. M. (2016). Reconciling educational achievement and local self-determination: School debates in post-Katrina New Orleans. In J. Bower & P. L. Thomas (Eds.), *De-testing and de-grading schools: Authentic alternatives to accountability and standardization* (Revised ed., pp. 105–125). Peter Lang.

Bodilly, S. J., Chun, J., Ikemoto, G. S., & Stockly, S. (2004). Challenges and Potential of a collaborative approach to education reform. RAND Corporation. https://www.rand.org/pubs/monographs/MG216.html

Bryk, A., Camburn, E., & Louis, K. S. (1999, December). Professional community in Chicago elementary schools: Facilitating factors and organizational consequences. *Educational Administration Quarterly, 35*, 751–781.

Bryk, A. S., & Schneider, B. (2003). Trust in schools: A core resource for school reform. *Educational Leadership, 60*(6), 40–45.

Buerger, C., & Bifulco, R. (2019). *The effect of charter schools on districts' student composition, costs, and efficiency: The case of New York State.* Economics of Education Review. https://doi.org/10.1016/j.econedurev.2019.01.003

Buras, K. L. (2010). *Pedagogy, policy, and the privatized city: Stories of dispossession and defiance from New Orleans.* Teachers College Press.

Datnow, A. (2011). Collaboration and contrived collegiality: Revisiting Hargreaves in the age of accountability. *The Journal of Educational Change, 12*(2), 147–158.

Cook, D. A. (2010). Disrupted but not destroyed: Fictive-kinship networks among Black educators in Post-Katrina New Orleans. *Southern Anthropologist, 35*(2), 1–25.

Corcoran, T., & Lawrence, N. (2003). *Changing district culture and capacity: The impact of the Merck institute for science education partnership.* University of Pennsylvania.

Cordes, S. A. (2018). In pursuit of the common good: The spillover effects of charter schools on public school students in New York City. *Education Finance and Policy, 13*(4), 484–512.

Dreilinger, D. (2012, December 4). *New Orleans' Benjamin E. Mays Preparatory School makes case to stay open.* Retrieved October 20, 2017, from http://www.nola.com/

Fazio, M. (2023, February 10). *2 New Orleans schools, Mildred Osborne Charter and Akili Academy, will merge next year.* Retrieved March 24, 2023, from http://www.nola.com

Fullan, M. (2000). The three stories of education reform. *Phi Delta Kappan, 81*(8), 581–584.

Gao, N., & Semykina, A. (2021). Competition effects of charter schools: New evidence from North Carolina. *Journal of School Choice, 15*(3), 393–416.

Hall, C. (2021). *District and charter school principals' perceptions of the challenges of co-location* [Doctoral dissertation, Concordia University]. Chicago, IL.

Han, E. S., & Keefe, J. (2020) The impact of charter school competition on student achievement of traditional public schools after 25 years: Evidence from National District-level Panel Data. *Journal of School Choice, 14*(3), 429–467. https://doi.org/ 10.1080/15582159.2020.1746621

Hargreaves, A. (1994). *Changing teachers, changing times: Teachers' work and culture in the post-modern age*. Teachers College Press.

Harris, D. N. (2015). Good news for New Orleans. *Education Next, 15*(4), 8–15.

Harris, D. N. (2020). *Charter school city: What the end of traditional public schools in New Orleans Means for American education*. University of Chicago Press.

Hicks, B., & Lens, M. (2021). *Incoming! Spatial enrollment competition between charter schools and traditional public schools*. Lewis Center for Regional Policy Studies: University of California at Los Angeles. https://escholarship.org/uc/item/2bk6f7mc

Hopkins, D. (2007). Sustaining leaders for system change. In B. Davies (Ed.), *Developing sustainable leadership* (pp. 154–174). Paul Chapman.

Jabbar, H. (2015, April 28). "Every kid is money": Market-like competition and school leader strategies in New Orleans. *Educational Evaluation and Policy Analysis, 37*, 638–659. http://epa.sagepub.com/content/early/2015/04/27/0162373715577447.abstract

Khalifa, M. (2012). A re-new-ed paradigm in successful urban school leadership: Principal as community leader. *Educational Administration Quarterly, 48*(3), 424–467. https://doi.org/10.1177/0013161X11432922

Latten-Clark, S. L. (2022). *Charter school leaders' perceptions of school autonomy*. University of New Orleans Theses and Dissertations. https://scholarworks.uno.edu/td/3056

Leithwood, K. A., Jantzi, D., & Steinbach, R. (1999). *Changing leadership for changing times*. Open University Press.

Levin, B., & Fullan, M. (2008). Learning about system renewal. *Educational Management Administration Leadership, 36*(2), 289–303.

Meier, D. (2002). *The power of their ideas* (2nd ed.). Beacon Press.

Mitchell, C. (2015, August 19). *What happened to New Orleans' veteran Black Teachers?* Retrieved April 7, 2022, from http://www.edweek.org

Nir, A. E. (2009), "To seek or not to seek professional help? School leaders' dilemma." *Journal of Educational Administration*, *47*(2), 176–190. https://doi.org/10.1108/09578230910941039

Olsen, B., & Sexton, D. (2009, March 1, 2009). Threat rigidity, school reform, and how teachers view their work inside current education policy contexts. *American Educational Research Journal, 46*(1), 9–44.

Padamsee, X., & Crowe, B. (2017). *Unrealized impact: The case for diversity, equity, and inclusion*. https://www.promise54.org/wp-content/uploads/2020/10/Unrealized_Impact-ExecSummary-Final-072017.pdf

Stake, R. E. (1995). *The art of case study research*. SAGE.

Stelly, L. (2007). Excerpt from: 'National model' or 'flawed approach? A report by the United Teachers of New Orleans, Louisiana Federation of Teachers and the American Federation of Teachers, November, 2006. *The High School Journal, 90*(2), 23–26.

Warren, M. R., & Mapp, K. L. (2011). *A match on dry grass: Community organizing as a catalyst for school reform*. Oxford University Press.

CHAPTER 6

FAMILIES ACTIVELY MOBILIZING

School-Based Family Wellness Groups in Two Oakland Charter Schools

Cynthia Martinez
San Francisco State University

Rebecca Anguiano
Saint Mary's College of California

INTRODUCTION

Since the first charter schools were founded in Oakland, California in the early 1990s, thousands of charter schools have opened their doors with the promise of innovation, effectiveness, and ultimately improved student outcomes (Fuller, 2002). Some scholars and practitioners have asserted that because charter schools operate more autonomously than traditional public schools, charter school educators might be better able to engage families from these historically disenfranchised communities (Smith et al., 2011). However, individual charter schools, operating as completely standalone entities, may struggle to operate with a single campus revenue stream and limited operational support (Farrell et al., 2002). Furthermore, successful individual charter schools seem difficult to replicate. Therefore, these successful schools have not had the large-scale impact originally intended (Center for Research on Education Outcomes, 2009).

Such limited impact among charter schools has led to the establishment of Charter Management Organizations (CMOs). CMOs are nonprofit

Family and Community Engagement in Charter Schools, pp. 121–143
Copyright © 2025 by Information Age Publishing
www.infoagepub.com
All rights of reproduction in any form reserved.

organizations that oversee networks of charter schools in order to provide operational resources and ideas. However, CMOs led to a level of uniformity across networked schools (Lake et al., 2010). Interestingly, the standardization required by CMOs may hinder the very flexibility that community members and educators had hoped. One hope was that the flexibility of charter schools would meaningfully engage families of color living in urban poverty.

In this chapter, we share the stories of two Oakland, California charter schools that are attempting to engage this group. One serves 94% Latinx families, and the other serves an almost 50/50 split of Black and Latinx families. We examine their efforts to engage in a model of liberatory family engagement we developed, known as *Families Actively Mobilizing* (FAM). FAM is a model of school-based family wellness groups the authors created grounded in Freire's (1970) conceptions of popular education and grass-roots community organizing strategies (Warren & Mapp, 2011). We analyze the successes and failures of this model, as well as the experiences of families and school leaders at both schools, within the context of the larger political, cultural, and organizational backdrops. More specifically, we highlight how the constraints and benefits of belonging to one of the largest CMOs in the country, within the context of a quickly gentrifying Oakland with a rich history of progressive movements and abundance of charter schools, created the conditions that made space for Oakland families to come together, build community, and lift their voices in meaningful ways for a period of time.

Charter School Landscape in Oakland, California

Oakland, CA is a diverse city with a rich history and culture. Home to the Black Panther Party and staunch Occupy Movement, Oakland has birthed many activists and progressive movements (Stulberg, 2008). This city, like many other urban hubs, has struggled with homelessness and crime. In 2018, Oakland's crime rate was 2.5 times greater than the U.S. average, making crime a major issue that families and elected officials talk about (City-Data.com, 2018). Additionally, Oakland is seeing its highest rates of homelessness in years, increasing by 26% between 2015 and 2017 (Oakland Homeless Response, n.d.). *The World Population Review* (2020) reports that Oakland is one of the most ethnically diverse major cities in the United States, ranking fourth in this regard. Notably, Oakland's large African American/Black population made it the center of California's Black community (BondGraham, 2018). Yet, because of its proximity to high-wealth San Francisco and the Silicon Valley, Oakland residents are feeling the devastating effects of gentrification. Currently, the city of Oakland finds itself in a housing crisis in which, for the past decade, a majority of Oakland residents cannot afford to live there (PolicyLink, 2015). It is a familiar story: working-class families are priced out and displaced while Silicon Valley and San Francisco house tech industry workers and boast booming economies. The city's Black community has borne the brunt of gentrification as the African American population has plunged by 25% since 2000, many opting for other East Bay suburbs or southern states (BondGraham, 2018). Conversely, the Latinx population has grown exponentially at a rate of 132% in east Oakland (Community Assesment, Planning & Education Unit [CAPE], 2005). Interestingly, however, unlike most white and some Asian immigrants, Oakland's rapidly growing Latinx population is not economically advantaged. The per capita incomes remain well below all other ethnic groups in the area (BondGraham, 2018), painting a complicated picture in a rapidly changing city.

The Birth of Charter Schools in Oakland

With this history and context as our backdrop, we turn to the birth of the charter school movement in Oakland in the early 1990s. The California Charter Schools Act was enacted by the California legislature in 1992, with the goals of improving teaching and learning opportunities, expanding school choice, encouraging innovation, and ultimately improving student outcomes (National Charter School Resource Center [NCSR], 2015). The political landscape in California generally and in Oakland particularly made the area ripe for the change that charter schools promised. Within a two-year span the state saw the passage of conservative policies that reversed affirmative action (Proposition 209 in 1996) and eliminated bilingual education (Proposition 227 in 1998). At this time, the Oakland Unified School District (OUSD) faced state takeover as a result of declining school enrollments due to rising home prices and a devastating fiscal crisis just a few years later as a result of internal financial mismanagement (Stulberg, 2008). Amidst what many families of color considered political strife at the state level and poorly managed public schools at the city level, charter schools in Oakland, like in many urban areas, were a response to what were deemed inadequate and unequal schooling conditions for Black and Latinx communities (Fuller, 2002; Stulberg, 2008).

The first charter school in California opened in 1993, with the number of charter schools increasing exponentially in the years to come (NCRS, 2015). By 1998 a charter school expansion bill signed by then Governor Pete Wilson paved the way for an abundance of start-up charter schools, and eventually the state's first Charter Management Organization (CMO). Additionally, charter school growth in California is not as regulated as other states, permitting an additional 100 schools to open per year coupled with a strong appeals process if a charter application is denied (Lake et al., 2018). As a result, from 1992 to 2007 the number of charter schools in California rapidly grew to approximately 710 charter schools serving an estimated 238,593 students (Center for Education Reform, 2007). In this context, Achieve Schools[1] was established, a CMO, in California and the managing organization for the two Oakland schools we detail in this chapter, Marigold Academy and Washington Douglass Academy (WDA).

CMOs and the history of Achieve Schools. CMOs are nonprofit organizations that oversee a network of charter schools, typically with shared administrative support and a unifying mission or instructional orientation (Farrell et al., 2012). The first CMO was founded in 1999, growing significantly to an estimated 137 nonprofit organizations, managing almost 800 charter schools only one decade later (Miron & Urschel, 2010). CMOs tend to grow in urban centers—areas where charter schools have grown rapidly—because of the administrative and capacity advantages they offer (Lake et al., 2010). More specifically, CMOs have grown rapidly because individual charter schools often struggle with start-up costs, facilities access and maintenance, insurance costs, and other logistical and business costs associated with the running of a school usually overseen by a district. CMOs also provide a way to "scale-up" successful charter school models, supposedly for larger and lasting impact, often due to the infusion of foundation and philanthropic funding (Farrell et al. 2012).

Achieve Schools was established in 1998 by a former superintendent with start-up funding from an entrepreneur. The original intention of the founders was the expansion and replication of small, high-quality college preparatory charter schools located in low-income communities whose children and families were historically underserved. The first two elementary schools opened in 1999, the very first of which was Marigold Academy, and the third was Washington Douglass Academy (WDA). We will detail their unique histories later. The first charter schools under Achieve were highly successful, boasting higher test scores than their district counterparts, an over 90% re-enrollment rate, and a demand for spots that well exceeded capacity. Achieve Schools' early success speaks to a combination of high-quality instruction compared to the troubling conditions in the district schools and, thus, families' desire for alternative better schooling options for their children (Fuller, 2002).

Only four years later, Achieve Schools was overseeing 10 high-performing elementary and middle schools, with lofty goals for significant and continued growth throughout the state. This intention for scale-up is significant in that it motivated organizational goals, changes in leadership, instructional design and many other systemic practices that impacted the school leaders, teachers, families, and students at both schools. At the time of data collection in 2013 through 2015, Achieve Schools had indeed expanded significantly, with schools in southern California, the Central Valley, and throughout the greater Bay Area. This included 10 schools in the Bay Area (TK–12, serving approximately 4,530 students), 16 schools in the Central Valley (TK–12, serving approximately 6,650 students) and 11 schools in the Los Angeles area (TK–12, serving approximately 4,510 students).

Framing the Two Schools

The creation of Marigold Academy and Washington Douglass Academy (WDA) in Oakland is emblematic of the racial and schooling politics of the time—a highly segregated and quickly gentrifying Oakland, a financially bankrupt public school district, and the boom of charter schools and CMOs (Stulberg, 2008). Bay area charter schools, in particular, boomed in the late 90s and early 2000s, seeing steady growth and representing one of the nation's fastest growing charter regions (Lake et al., 2018). Marigold and WDA, founded in 1999 and 2005, respectively, are two of the earliest schools established under Achieve School's CMO. When family wellness groups utilizing the FAM model were created in 2013, both schools had survived changes in leadership and created some enduring systems of support for students and families.

Like many charter schools in urban centers (e.g., Fuller, 2002), active parents in the local community were integral to the founding of the original charters of both schools. The two front office managers, Latina women—matriarchs in the community—were also present at each school's founding and held important community and school history. Interestingly, both Marigold and WDA gained original support from the surrounding community with the endorsement of a local, trusted priest. This is consistent with research demonstrating the role of religious institutions generally, and Catholic institutions in particular. Religious leaders generate social capital in historically disenfranchised communities because of their concern for economic justice and the trust required to create ties that bridge low-income communities to other resources (Bryk et al., 1993; Foley et al., 2001). Once the priest in the community endorsed Achieve Schools, the community, parish, and surrounding neighborhood used grassroots efforts like word of mouth and door-to-door outreach to gain larger community (BondGraham, 2018).

Marigold Academy: History, community, and context. Marigold Academy, a kindergarten through fifth grade elementary school, was the first to receive its charter under Achieve's CMO, celebrating 20 years of being open in 2019. The school serves families from the surrounding community who endure the stresses associated with community violence and poverty. The school boasts a colorful facade covered with monarch butterflies and resides on a heavily trafficked street in deep east Oakland. This facade welcomes the neighborhood's local Mexican immigrant community. The school building is attached to a Catholic church and originally housed a Catholic school, which later became an individual start-up charter in the mid-1990s. That charter was not renewed by the district due to low performance. Afterwards, Marigold Academy was opened in that location. One of the few remaining African American grandparents at Marigold recounted how all her children had attended the previous Catholic school, and now her grandchild attended Marigold Academy. This speaks to the permanence of a school at this site in the neighborhood, but also the merry-go-round of operators as a result of the challenges facing public schools in this community in particular.

This area of east Oakland, like Oakland generally, has experienced rapid growth in its Latinx population (BondGraham, 2018). The school's demographics are representative of the surrounding community. To date, Marigold's enrollment is 394 students, with Latinx students making up 94% of the school community, followed by 4% Black students, 1% Other, and no White students; and Oakland neighborhoods and schools continue to be largely segregated (Gill, 2020). Ninety-seven percent of the student body qualifies for free and reduced lunch.

Since its opening in 1999, Marigold has had a total of seven principals, each with the goal of setting students on the college path. Marigold's achievement and success metrics are mixed in that the school has boasted tremendous academic growth over the years but still struggles to move the majority of its students towards proficiency on state assessments. For example, during the years of data collection, the school went from only 14% meeting state achievement performance expectations in English language arts (ELA) and 15% meeting achievement expectations in math to over 40% meeting expectations in ELA and 50% meeting expectations in math four years later. As a result, Marigold Academy has received awards specifically for their achievement growth. These include High Impact awards for high student academic growth awarded by California Core Districts and recognition as a Top Bay Area Public school for low-income Latino students in mathematics. However, despite this progress and recognition, the majority of students in attendance have not met state achievement standards to date.

Washington Douglass Academy: History, community, and context. Washington Douglas Academy (WDA) opened in 2005 under the Achieve CMO. Housed in an Oakland Unified School District (OUSD) building, the charter school pays rent to utilize the district space. The school also used to share the building with a private secondary school, which later relocated.

WDA absorbed the middle school grades of the private secondary school and became a K–8 school in its fourth year.

Middle school students, an overall larger school population, and demographics provide this school with a different culture than Marigold. For example, administrators report different disciplinary and school culture trends, such as more frequent out-of-school suspensions and expulsions and more serious disciplinary infractions. This is consistent with research that indicates secondary charter schools struggle more with these issues than their elementary school counterparts (Lake et al., 2010). Nonetheless, the school has been considered a safe haven in the community, even though this area of Oakland has experienced more drastic changes in the neighborhood than Marigold. Washington Douglas Academy is located in a more industrialized area where numerous local businesses have closed their doors and national discount chain stores have emerged in their place. In fact, in an effort to stave off surrounding crime in the neighborhood, the school's administration leveraged its relationship with a historically Black local religious organization. The administration contracted with this group to provide private security during the first few years of the school's founding, effectively keeping the school safe from surrounding activity. Homes in the area have recently sold and been renovated for astronomical prices, making it challenging for families with children at WDA to live in the area. Unlike Marigold, which serves families in the surrounding neighborhood, WDA has been a commuter school since the first few years it was established. Many children are driven in from neighboring cities, such as Richmond and El Cerrito. As a charter school, parents have the option to legally by-pass their district schools to enroll at WDA.

Currently, WDA has 534 students enrolled, with the student population being 47% Black, 43% Latinx, 2% Asian American, 1% Pacific Islander, and 1% White. Eighty-one percent of the school community receives free or reduced lunch. Historically, however, WDA's student body was predominantly Black, shifting to closer to 50% Latinx and 50% Black in the past five to seven years, reflecting similar shifts in Oakland generally (BondGraham, 2018). Families and school leaders report historical tensions between Black and Latinx families, specifically as it relates to Parent-Teacher-Association leadership and funding. These tensions had made many family engagement efforts unsuccessful, up until the time of the FAM groups, during which we, as facilitators, intentionally sought to bring both communities together.

Since its opening, WDA has had four principals representing somewhat less turnover and therefore more stability than Marigold academy. WDA's achievement metrics are similar to Marigold's in that they have experienced significant growth over the past five to seven years. However, teachers have continued to struggle to bring the majority of their students to state achievement standards. In the 2014–2015 academic year, only 20% of students met state achievement performance expectations in ELA and 17% met expectations in math. Four years later, approximately 44% of students met performance expectations in ELA and 37% of students met expectations in math, representing significant growth that has garnered recognition.

Researcher Context. The authors of this chapter were originally mental health practitioners whose meeting was both serendipitous and reflective of the charter context. Research on the operation of CMOs indicates that securing philanthropic support and private resources for funding as well leveraging partnerships with nonprofit and for-profit organizations are critical to the health and success of the charter schools CMOs manage (Scott & Holme, 2002; Toch, 2010). Achieve Schools had connections with private foundations, community agencies, hospitals, and universities, which resulted in both authors meeting on the Marigold Academy campus in 2013. The first author (Martinez) began working at Marigold as a postdoctoral fellow in clinical psychology at a teaching hospital, providing trauma-informed mental health services bilingually (Spanish-English) for children, adolescents, and their families at schools and in the hospital. Later, a private donor made it possible for the foundation to fund Martinez to work at Marigold Academy once her postdoctoral fellowship ended. When the foundation was no longer able to fund the position, the principals at Marigold and WDA banded together to fund Martinez to work at both schools. This financial autonomy at the individual school level provided these school leaders with the flexibility to hire Martinez based on their value of trauma-informed care and mental health services in schools. This is exactly the type of innovation and flexibility that charter schools were meant to enable (Gross, 2011; NCSR 2015; Wohlstetter & Smith, 2006), and would likely not have occurred in a traditional public-school context.

The second author of this chapter (Anguiano), a doctoral level school psychologist, was hired directly by Achieve Schools in 2012 to provide consultation, counseling, and psychoeducational assessment services at several Achieve Schools. As a school psychologist Anguiano was a part of the interdisciplinary team that oversaw the school's Multi-Tiered Systems of Support (MTSS), a framework of prevention and intervention systems meant to triage both academic and social-emotional services for students (Averill & Rinaldi, 2013). The presence of a well-established intervention system at several Achieve Schools is again reflective of the ways that successful charter schools have been able to create innovative intervention programming unique to their students' needs (Izumi, 2007). In the case of Marigold Academy this meant providing intensive reading intervention and mental health services. Given that the students and their families at Marigold Academy were disproportionately affected by poverty, incarceration, deportation, and community violence, Anguiano invited Martinez to join the MTSS interdisciplinary team given her expertise in complex trauma. It was during these team meetings that the two began to collaborate to bolster family engagement programming at Marigold Academy, and later at WDA. Similar to Martinez's position, the principal at Marigold valued Anguiano's services as a bilingual/bicultural school psychologist and provided funding so that Anguiano could work exclusively at Marigold Academy, instead of spreading services across several Achieve Schools. Both our unique positions illustrate how school leaders utilized the funding and programming flexibility they had to creatively meet the community's needs, paving the way for the establishment of family wellness groups at both schools under the FAM model described below from 2013 to 2018.

Data Sources

Our chapter includes information gathered from 29 semi-structured interviews with individual school community members from Marigold Academy and WDA. The largest group of participants included parents who attended school-based family wellness groups, based on the model developed by the authors of this chapter, *Families Actively Mobilizing* (FAM), at both charter schools ($n = 17$). Parent participants from Marigold Academy ($n = 10$) were all immigrant Latinx and Spanish-speaking, with one parent immigrating from Guatemala and the rest from Mexico. This reflects the demographic makeup of that school, with over 94% of the student body identifying as Latinx, the majority of whom were children born in the United States with parents who immigrated from Mexico. In contrast, WDA parents were almost evenly split between the Latinx and African American communities, with four Latinx and three African American parents interviewed, again reflecting the demographic makeup of this school. Other participants included the principal and vice principal at each school, school counselors, veteran teachers, and office managers from each of the schools ($n = 1$ 2).

Our interview data are supported by oral histories provided by a founding parent and staff member, during which we specifically asked for the history of each school's founding, neighborhood context and changes over the years, and family engagement history. Data were also supported by artifacts we collected from the family wellness groups (e.g., fliers for advertising or disseminating information) and observational notes from each of the wellness groups (approximately 9–10, two-hour meetings at each

130 C. MARTINEZ and R. ANGUIANO

school yearly). In essence, we helped facilitate as mental health practitioners in both schools.

Families Actively Mobilizing (FAM): Popular Education and Community Organizing in Action

Meaningfully engaging families in their children's education is recognized by researchers, educators, and policymakers as critical to academic achievement, academic engagement, and even the mental health of students (Jeynes, 2005, 2012; Wang & Sheikh-Khalil, 2014). Bridging the gaps between families and schools is especially important for families living in urban poverty because schools offer an important source of stability and a frontline point of intervention for families with limited access to resources (Crosnoe, 2004; Noguera, 2001). Charter school enthusiasts have claimed that fewer bureaucratic barriers might allow for more innovative strategies to engage parents from historically disenfranchised communities, though research in this regard is somewhat mixed. For example, Smith et al. (2011) found that parents in urban charter schools engaged in similar types of activities as their traditional public-school counterparts. However, the strategies charter schools used to attract parent attendance were more creative, including things like incentives, wrap-around services, technology, and focus groups. Relatedly, Beabout and Boselovic (2016) detail how two charter schools in post-Katrina New Orleans were able to purposefully and meaningfully engage with the surrounding community from their inception. Other research, however, suggests that charter school leaders lack confidence in engaging with families, especially in urban areas (Gross & Popchop, 2007). While parents may be critical to the initial founding of a charter, Fuller's (2002) case studies of charter schools across the nation indicate that charter schools are not necessarily more successful at engaging families equitably in school processes.

A common theme in the family engagement literature is the difficulties that low-income, historically disenfranchised communities of color face when interacting with schools. These challenges include a lack of financial resources (Cooper & Crosnoe, 2007), lack of awareness and time (Williams & Sanchez, 2011), incongruent cultural models and language barriers (Gallimore & Goldenberg, 2001), and community violence (Zhou, 2003). At the same time, schools and practitioners serving these same families have a tendency to operate under a deficit model of thinking—or identifying what parents and families lack as opposed to their adaptive abilities (Valencia & Black, 2002). This labeling results in educators' tendency to see families as barriers to overcome, a dehumanizing practice that blames families instead of holding schools accountable for creating accessible family programming (Mapp & Hong, 2010). Additionally, many schools utilize "banking methods" (Freire, 1970) of interacting with families, whereby parents are invited to school meetings that are didactic and rarely leverage parents' strengths and contributions to their children's learning. Likewise, traditional therapeutic group interventions are often based on western frameworks that do not factor in the wellness needs of people from collectivist ethnic backgrounds (Barrio & Yamada, 2010). Scholars and practitioners alike have called for therapeutic work with parents to be more culturally responsive (Forehand & Kotchick, 1996). Before becoming a clinical psychologist, Martinez had training and experience as an activist and community organizer with immigrant communities in San Francisco. Leveraging this training, we worked together to re-engage families in a culturally accountable and empowering wellness group grounded in the Freirean idea of popular education (Freire, 1970) and grassroots community organizing (Warren & Mapp, 2011).

Popular education is a pedagogical framework that stresses egalitarian relationships between teachers and students, dialogue, and reflection as a means to liberation, and the importance of content that is relevant to the learner's sociopolitical reality (Freire, 1970). This framework is a tool for building counternarratives to deficit-based narratives of parent involvement research and practice (Beckett et al., 2012). To that end, the starting point of the FAM groups was the context of the parent/learner—we wanted to know the issues families faced in their communities and how the school could better support them. We did outreach before school, after school, and at various school events, approaching parents and helping them fill out a needs assessment. Monthly meetings were based on topics families had picked. Parents crafted community agreements, and each month we collectively dialogued in partners, small groups, and whole group about each topic. These dialogues were central activities that created sustained relationships over time as we learned together in community. Popular education also emphasizes accessibility of teaching materials, so that everyone is able to create new knowledge (Arnold & Burke, 1983; Gadotti & Torres, 2009). Importantly, as facilitators, the authors were both bilingual/bicultural Latinx women; Martinez is a first-generation child of immigrant parents and Anguiano has deep Chicanx roots. Both our backgrounds and histories with the schools helped us to foster groups that were culturally congruent with parent communities. At Marigold academy, the FAM group was majority Spanish-speaking Latinx families, with a few Black African/American families also attending monthly, reflecting the demographic makeup of this school. Similarly, the FAM group at WDA was approximately half Latinx and half Black/African American, though the Latinx families were a mix of immigrant Spanish-speaking families and second and third generation Latinx families who were bilingual and bicultural.

132   C. MARTINEZ and R. ANGUIANO

Finally, a crucial piece of FAM groups were regular check-ins with families. Were the groups helpful? Were they serving their purpose? Did the parents feel heard and were school leaders being held accountable? As facilitators we also engaged in constant reflection and dialogue with each other.

Similarly, *community organizing* focuses on building relational power among marginalized communities to influence positive change and generate social capital (Mediratta et al., 2009). Community organizing efforts led by trusted individuals can ultimately repair historically damaged relationships and generate relational power (Abdul-Adil & Farmer, 2006; Vaandering, 2013). Our desire was to generate trust among families and between families and educators creating an authentic home-to-school connection; all organizing begins with relationships (Warren & Mapp, 2011). Both principals were excited by the high attendance rates (an average of 45 parents monthly) and the energy of the family groups, building in food and childcare costs into their school budgets after the first year. The groups thrived for five years at Marigold and three years at WDA. During this time families increased communication with administrators and teachers, often inviting school leaders or teachers to FAM group meetings when questions regarding school policies or announcements arose. Parents of special needs children educated the group on special education law and parental rights when interacting with the school about providing special education services. At WDA, families were also able to leverage their power to gain an audience with all teaching and support staff to share their concerns regarding punitive disciplinary policies and offer support for ways to better communicate with children who were struggling to follow school rules, ultimately influencing disciplinary policy and practice. At both schools, families brought in legal advocates to educate immigrant families about their rights in relation to police and Immigration and Customs Enforcement (ICE) as raids in Oakland increased during the Trump administration. Families also organized to attend demonstrations or local protests together in light of police violence against Black bodies. Through these activities at both schools, Black families learned about the immigration struggles facing Latinx families, and Latinx families learned about the legacy of violence and enslavement in the United States. Importantly, as Black and Latinx families understood each other's struggles, they also began to understand the ways in which their struggles overlapped, and the importance of compassion and solidarity.

In 2017, policy changes at the CMO level resulted in the mandatory creation of parent education meetings on required topics and the creation of an organization-wide family liaison position. Unfortunately, this mandate came down without consultation with administrators and family leaders at the school level regarding existing family engagement programming. This was also in direct conflict with the FAM model; parents could no longer dictate the topics of the family meetings nor the actions they wished to organize around. Parents were confused at the creation of family meetings organized by the district liaison, not understanding if the intention was to replace FAM groups or to have district programming in addition to the FAM groups. Parent leaders and the co-authors invited the district liaison to attend FAM meetings at both schools to explain the new position and the intention behind the new programming. Attempts were made to advocate for the FAM groups to continue, integrating required topics and parent-led topics, but unfortunately parent leaders were not incorporated into the planning and the disconnect between families' desires for family engagement and the CMO's thoughts on what parents needed continued to widen. Concurrently, funding for the co-facilitators' positions shifted, and the co-authors were no longer able to continue working at both schools. The timing of this, along with the CMO's policy changes regarding family engagement programming, led to the eventual dissolution of groups under the FAM model, and the organization returned to didactic parent education meetings.

Lessons Learned and Findings Across Both Schools

Relationships are foundational. The Spanish word *convivir* translates to meaningful time spent together in community. This was the word many parents used to describe the relational aspect of the FAM groups, and how being in community with other parents helped them to create authentic relationships that contributed to their wellness and led to their collective power. A Black parent from WDA spoke about FAM establishing a space for both Black and Brown parents to coexist together. She said, "Outside of [the FAM? group], I don't think the connection with the Hispanic community would've been a thing." This parent went on to say, "But just actually knowing people's names and deeper connections, collaborating on other things, I don't think that would've happened. And I think other people felt the same, that it kind of brought communities together through [the group] because no other group was doing that." Staff leaders also noted the way the groups bridged the two communities. The school counselor commented, "the family meeting is the one space on campus where both our Black families and our Latinx families come together in a space that is as least contentious as possible." Tensions between Black and Brown communities are well documented in cities across California (Pomfret, 2006) and Oakland is no exception, but the groups' community agreements promoted openness and a willingness to listen respectfully to each other.

Relationships were key in the founding of the schools and in the day-to-day operations. For example, the office manager and a founding parent from Marigold shared, "I think it's important to the families that when they come in, they see you talking to the student by name ... that we know them as a family as a whole ... I ask them a lot of questions ... to know them a little bit more ... I think that's what makes families be more en *confianza* [trust] with us because ... we ask and we're part of their family." The notion of trust and "seeing" each other is a critical piece of the FAM groups. The office manager's reasoning echoed values that the families' reflected back to us about why the groups were important to them.

Intentional spaces for families generate action. The FAM groups illustrated how intentional spaces for parents in their children's schools fostered unique opportunities for parents to voice their needs, have difficult conversations, and learn together about topics that were relevant to their sociopolitical contexts. Through storytelling (dialoguing) parents saw themselves reflected in each other and experienced moments of coming into self-awareness in community. This self-awareness inspired parents to get involved and take action in their children's schools. One parent said, "*Porque a veces lo despiertan a uno. Lo despiertan a uno a pensar más, a ayudar más* [Because sometimes it [the conversation] awakens you. It awakens you up to think more, to help more]." This awakening shaped parents' experiences in the group and humanized them to each other. As one school counselor said, "I think [it's been] a very humanizing experience for everybody in that room. I know it's highly valued by the parents who do attend and I think it's something that the attendees speak very highly of to other parents." Parents claimed the meetings as their own and this ownership continued to grow.

The group at WDA unified Brown and Black parents who, to date, could not recall any other collaborative spaces at their school. A parent said, "So that space really opened up the conversation and communication lines. So I feel that we need that space. I think that's the only space we have." The groups provided a space that was uniquely geared towards commonalities rather than differences. The overall culture of the groups planted seeds so that parents began to see themselves as leaders in their respective schools. Parents at WDA leveraged their newfound solidarity and prepared a presentation for administration regarding behavior management and school culture, and at Marigold, parents used their newfound power to obtain free immigrant rights training for the entire school community. One school counselor said of the meetings, "And it's been ever-evolving, right? Like it's sometimes kind of a psycho-ed group, where we're doing a lot of education work, and I think it's really been evolving into more of a parent-led space." Echoing Freire (1970), who argued that true liberation of the base could only occur if led by the base, our groups were primed to generate social capital and create opportunities for parents' empowerment.

Accessible methods matter. In order to create access, we always considered the community's language and literacy levels. To that end, we ensured all power points and outreach materials contained images that reflected the schools' families and contained words written in both English and Spanish. For example, fliers and presentation slides contained more images than actual words in order to promote access to all who attended the groups. One parent said, "*Porque sin las imágenes como que uno no se alcanza a expresar bien uno mismo, en cambio uno ya ve las imágenes y dice "iah!, empieza así." O demuestran, por ejemplo, cómo es lo que está pasando.* [Because without the images you aren't able to express yourself well, instead you see the images and you say, 'ah! It starts like this!' Or it shows, for example, what is going on.]" These images were intended to help pre-literate parents access the information written on the slides. For that parent in particular, the images assisted in her learning. The translation provided at meetings was sequential (one language then the next), as opposed to simultaneous, so that content was presented with the same fervor and for the same amount of time in both languages to ensure equitable delivery. Rather than see the need for bilingual groups as barriers to working with families (Smith et al., 2011) we saw it as an opportunity to lift parents' culture and languages as strengths.

Dialogue also served as a teaching method that helped parents talk about personal experiences that illustrated challenges and successes tied to the monthly topic. A parent explained, "*Yo creo que también me han servido mucho las conversaciones que tuvimos con los padres. Y también de que ellos han pasado por situaciones difíciles, y uno a veces se identifica con ellos.* [Also, I think the conversations we've had with other parents have helped me a lot. Sometimes they are going through a difficult situation, and you identify with them.]" She speaks of no longer feeling isolated by having the opportunity to identify with other parents who had similar challenges. We contend that taking the time to allow for dialogue and reflection in community primed the parents to come to a critical consciousness, the type of *conscientization* [awakening] that Freire (1970) wrote about.

FAM groups were held monthly at both schools, each for an hour and a half. Both schools offered back to school nights at the beginning of the school year where parents filled out a needs assessment conducted by the school mental health team to understand what topics parents wanted to focus on. Topics ranged from "*how to best support my child's learning*" to "*how do I understand anger in my child.*" Early in the school year, families generated community agreements that all participants agreed to follow. Unlike other school meetings that focused on district-led initiatives for curriculum and test scores, FAM groups were an intentional space for parents to build community and discuss topics that were most salient to their lived experiences. Most importantly, the meetings provide privileged parents' needs

136 C. MARTINEZ and R. ANGUIANO

and voices. In the end, these meetings provided a space for the parents to access self-care, psychoeducation, and learn advocacy skills.

One particularly important session involved a parent meeting at WDA. Parents at WDA began the session by discussing a concern regarding a lack of home-school connection. Feelings of mistrust and frustration surfaced as parents described a lack of meaningful collaboration between the school and families and a need for increased communication among teachers, administrators, and parents. Parents also expressed concerns about students being sent to the office for mild infractions (e.g., not raising their hand), a confusing new mathematics curriculum, and feeling unheard by school administrators. Above all, parents wanted to collaborate with teachers and school administrators, to co-create a community where they had some decision-making input and clearer understanding regarding how their children learned and were treated. Parents also had ideas about how to support self-care among teachers, recognizing the difficulty of their jobs and sincerely wanting to support them. Parents expressed a desire for more *humanized* interactions with school administrators and teachers. Parents in the FAM groups became excited as they generated ideas about how to better get to know their school staff. Moreover, all parents agreed that meeting with the school administration was necessary to begin to increase authentic collaboration. In keeping with community organizing strategies, facilitators offered that a parent-led meeting with school staff could have a lot of impact. Facilitators asked for volunteers from the group to present the group's needs and ideas to school leaders. Seven parents, three Black and four Latinx Spanish-speaking mothers, volunteered, meeting with coauthor Martinez outside the FAM group meeting to create the presentation. The mothers practiced their presentation with the FAM group and received glowing feedback from families, boosting their confidence to present to administrators and represent all of the families. On the day of the presentation, school administrators were extremely impressed by the mothers' presentation. School leaders were excited about the potential collaboration between the FAM group and the mothers representing the FAM group felt motivated and empowered. Later that month, the group was invited to present to all the teachers at a professional development training. Their presentation sparked great discussions about creative ways to spend time with families and build stronger relationships. Further, teachers were truly touched by parents' desire to support teacher self-care and retention in their presentation, which created stronger relationships between teachers and parents. When asked about her experience in organizing, creating, and presenting to school leaders and teachers this WDA mother recalled the following:

Well, I think that I learned many things, and I'm so happy to share this, but I think the biggest thing that I learned was that we need to voice our thoughts and our opinions and voice what we need and what we want for our children. That's the biggest thing, and I know that Dr. Cynthia has worked with us in the past in making our voices heard. So I think that we need to kind of—now we need to make sure that we never stay quiet.... And just what I was sharing with you about that, it actually happened. It took a while for our meetings with our principal, but that was one thing that we worked with you in the past. So we know that even though things take time, we still need to voice it, no matter what, even if you're just one person, even though I know there's more than one person that feels exactly like I do, but they don't want to, or because of whatever reason they don't want to say it, but I will.

The FAM groups naturally grew into a space that fostered values and tenets underscored by popular education and community organizing frameworks, creating space for parents to lift their voices and develop community power. Both Marigold and WDA FAM groups were framed around each of the school communities' distinct needs and became a collective effort. Parents from both groups felt a responsibility towards the school community to create a better experience for their children's learning and mental health. At first, many parents reported fear or intimidation around voicing their opinions to school leaders. However, with the encouragement and community they built with each other, this fear dissipated, and parents felt it critical to voice their needs at their school for the sake of their children. In the end, parents learned the power that can be generated in community. More importantly, parents created strong relationships with each other, which resulted in empowering and transformative experiences.

Family, charter, and CMO tensions are unavoidable. As families in the groups began to trust each other, parents also began to understand their own power and their right to make themselves heard on matters regarding the education of their children. One mother at WDA described, "the biggest thing I learned was that we need to voice our thoughts and our opinions and voice what we need and what we want for our children...we need to make sure that we never stay quiet." Freire believed that popular education should nurture critical thinking in students and not uphold oppressive structures, which is what we saw happening among families when, for example, they asked for more communication with administrators and became active in local protests and demonstrations. This type of critical community engagement is the goals of popular education and community organizing (Freire, 1970; Warren & Mapp, 2011) and of the FAM model. This means, however, that when parents feel empowered to voice their concerns, there will inevitably be tension between families' wishes and those of the school leaders. For example, FAM parents vehemently opposed classroom behavior management that involved teachers sending their child out of class and, as a result, the child missed valuable learning time, at times creating tensions between parents and the school principal, who often supported teachers' disciplinary decisions. Interestingly, however, the principal at WDA was a supportive administrator who understood how charter schools had the potential to disempower parents, even voicing this tension within the larger context of charter school education. He explained to us:

> Charter schools, in general, are kind of founded on this colonial style of education, right? We come in, we tell the community what's best for them. We tell them how their kids should learn, how their kids are or are not achieving.... And I think that's a huge problem, a real problem that I think FAM helps to disrupt because it's creating authentic space and partnership for families where it's grassroots. It's coming from the community. It's what they're feeling. It's what they're wanting. It's what they're wanting to discuss. And it's not a colonial method.

Despite this principal's support of the FAM group approach, eventually the FAM groups ended because the CMO wanted family programming to look a specific way at each school, resulting in a disconnect between the base (families) and the overseeing organization. This type of standardization speaks to the inherent conflict between the flexibility charter schools boast and the compulsion for consistency across schools under one CMO (Lake et al., 2010). It also perhaps speaks to a fundamental conflict between the FAM model, which is intended to be grassroots and liberatory model of family engagement, and any type of prescriptive family programming. Additionally, because at its conception, Achieve Schools was intended for replication and scaling up, it may be that this type of conflict was unavoidable (Farrell et al., 2014). Some researchers have argued that the regulated environment of public schools under CMOs may actually be harmful to some students, especially during instances when behavioral conformity is valued over the students' ability to express themselves contributing overtime to a student's lowered self-esteem (Goodman, 2013). While still others question whether the private funding often secured in charter schools constitutes a new type of colonialism, or acquiring control of urban areas (Lipman, 2015). Surveys of charter school leaders also indicate that CMO leaders tend to rank parent and community engagement as one of their lowest priorities, not seeing it as critical to student success, especially when compared to specific teaching methodologies (Lake et al., 2010). Indeed, it is ironic that it was the CMO's community partnerships and the principals' autonomy at each site that led to the creation of the FAM groups, but the same CMO's standardization practices that resulted in their eventual ending.

Implications and Recommendations for Practice

Achieve Schools was founded under conditions that paralleled national narratives on the birth of charter schools and CMOs in urban areas (Farrell et al., 2012; Fuller, 2002; Stulberg, 2008). The creation of Marigold Academy and Washington Douglass Academy were a response to Oakland families' desires for equitable schooling options for their children. Both schools opened with support from parents and trusted community members, and both principals had enough autonomy to be innovative in their budgeting and hiring. This eventually led to the creation of family wellness groups under the FAM model at both schools, which for several years made space for parents to come together, build trusting relationships, and take action toward shaping their school communities. Unfortunately, top-down policies regulating what family programming should look like across schools in the CMO eventually led to the dissolving of parent-driven family groups. It may be the case that there isn't room for models of grassroots, liberatory family engagement within the CMO context. Alternatively, if equitable family involvement is considered as high a priority as instruction, perhaps parent-driven family engagement would be more feasible. Both schools felt the negative effects of gentrification, which school leaders themselves acknowledged charter schools might be passive participants in. Critics of charter schools and CMOs question how the abundance of charter schools in urban areas may exacerbate segregation (Frankenberg et al., 2011) and even replicate oppressive colonial practices (Lipman, 2015).

Given the awakening, resilience, and resistance we witnessed among families participating in FAM groups, perhaps the way to combat these forces is to train school-based mental health practitioners, school leaders, and teachers in activism, community organizing, and popular education (Freire, 1970; Warren & Mapp, 2011). We saw how leveraging partnerships with hospitals and private foundations created access to mental health care at both schools, but prioritizing partnerships with local grassroots community organizations that represent the communities their charter schools serve might also ensure that families retain their voices within the CMO context.

REFERENCES

Abdul-Adil, J. K., & Farmer, A. D., Jr. (2006). Inner-city African American parental involvement in elementary schools: Getting beyond urban legends of apathy. *School Psychology Quarterly, 21*(1), 1–12. https://doi.org/10.1521/scpq.2006.21.1.1

140   C. MARTINEZ and R. ANGUIANO

Arnold, R., & Burke., B. (1983). *A popular education handbook: An educational experience taken from Central America and adapted to the Canadian context.* http://eric.ed.gov/?id=ED289024

Averill, O. H., & Rinaldi, C. (2013). *Research brief: Multi-tier Systems of Supports (MTSS)* Urban Special Education Leadership Collaborative: From RtI and PBIS to MTSS.

Barrio, C., & Yamada, A. (2010). Culturally based intervention development: The case of Latino families dealing with schizophrenia. *Research on Social Work Practice, 20*(5), 483–492. https://doi.org/10.1177/1049731510361613

Beabout, B. R., & Boselovic, J. L. (2016). Community engagement as a central activity. In M. P. Evans & B. B. Hiatt-Michael (Eds.), *The power of community engagement for educational change* (pp. 41-63). Information Age Publishing.

Beckett, L., Glass, R. D., & Moreno, A. P. (2012). A pedagogy of community building: Re-imagining parent involvement and community organizing in popular education efforts. *Journal of the Association of Mexican American Educators, 6*(1), 5–14.

BondGraham, D. (2018, February 14). The East Bay's changing demographics. *East Bay Express.* https://eastbayexpress.com/the-east-bays-changing-demographics-2-1/

Bryk, A. S., Lee, V. E., & Holland, P. B. (1993). *Catholic schools and the common good.* Harvard University Press.

Center for Education Reform. (2007). *National charter school data: 200—2008 new school estimates.*

Center for Research on Education Outcomes. (2009). *Multiple choice: Charter school performance in 16 states.*

City-data.com. (2018). *Crime in Oakland, California (CA): Murders, rapes, robberies, assaults, burglaries, thefts, auto thefts, arson, law enforcement employees, police officers, crime map.* Retrieved January 12, 2020, from https://www.city-data.com/crime/crime-Oakland-California.html

Community Assessment, Planning, and Education (CAPE) Unit. (2005, October). *East Oakland Community Information Book Update.* Alameda County Public Health Department. http://www.acphd.org/media/53459/eoakland05.pdf

Cooper, C. E., & Crosnoe, R. (2007). The engagement in schooling of economically disadvantaged parents and children. *Youth & Society, 38*(3), 372–391. https://doi.org/10.1177/0044118X06289999

Crosnoe, R. (2004). Social capital and the interplay of families and schools. *Journal of Marriage and Family, 66*(2), 267–280. https://doi.org/10.1111/j.1741-3737.2004.00019.x

Farrell, C., Nayfack, M. B., Smith, J., & Wohlstetter, P. (2014). One size does not fit all: Understanding the variation in charter management scale-up. *Journal of Educational Change, 15*(1), 77–97. https://doi.org/10.1007/s10833-013-9216-7

Farrell, C., Wohlstetter, P., & Smith, J., (2012). Charter management organizations: An emerging approach to scaling up what works. *Educational Policy, 26*(4), 499–532. https://doi.org/0.1177/0895904811417587

Frankenberg, E., Siegel-Hawley, G., & Wang, J. (2011). Choice without equity: Charter school segregation. *Educational Policy Analysis Archives, 19*(1), 1–96.

Foley, M. W., McCarthy, J. D., & Chaves, M. (2001). Social capital, religious institutions, and poor communities. In S. Saegert, J. P. Thompson J., & M. R. Warren (Eds.), *Social capital in poor communities* (pp. 215–245). The Russell Sage Foundation.

Forehand, R., & Kotchick, B. A. (1996). Cultural diversity: A wake-up call for parent training. *Behavior Therapy, 27*(2), 187–206. https://doi.org/10.1016/S0005-7894(96)80014-1

Freire, P. (1970). *Pedagogy of the oppressed.* Bloomsburg.

Fuller, B. (2002). *Inside charter schools: The paradox of radical decentralization.* Harvard University Press.

Gadotti, M., & Torres, C. L. (2009). Paulo Freire: Education for development. *Development and Change, 40*(6), 1255–1267. https://doi.org/10.1111/j.1467-7660.2009.01606.x

Gallimore, R., & Goldenberg, C. (2001). Analyzing cultural models and settings to connect minority achievement and school improvement research. *Educational Psychologist, 36*, 45–56.

Goodman, J. F. (2013). Charter management organizations and the regulated environment: Is it worth the price? *Educational Researcher, 42*(2), 89–96. https://doi.org/10.3102/0013189X12470856

Gill, B. (2020). *Charter schools and segregation: What the research says.* Future Ed. https://www.future-ed.org/work/school-choice-social-justice-what-the-research-shows/

Gross, B. (2011). *Inside charter schools: Unlocking doors to student success.* Center on Reinventing Public Education. https://eric.ed.gov/?id=ED519943

Gross, B., & Popchop, K. M. (2007). *Leadership to date, leadership tomorrow: A review of data on charter school directors* (NCSRP working paper #2007-2). Center on Reinventing Public Education.

Izumi, L. T. (2007). *What works: Inside charter schools.* Center on Innovation and Improvement.

Jeynes, W. (2005). A meta-analysis of the relation of parental involvement to urban elementary school student academic achievement. *Urban Education, 40*(3), 237–269. https://doi.org/10.1177/0042085905274540

Jeynes, W. (2012). A meta-analysis of the efficacy of different types of parental involvement programs for urban students. *Urban Education, 47*(4), 706–742. https://doi.org/10.1177/0042085912445643

Lake, R., Dusseault, B., Bowen, M., Demeritt, A., & Hill, P. (2010). *The national study of charter management organization effectiveness: Report on interim findings.* Mathematica Policy Research, Inc. & Center on Reinventing Public Education.

Lipman, P. (2015). Capitalizing on crisis: Venture philanthropy's colonial project to remake urban education. *Critical Studies in Education, 56*(2), 241–258. https://doi.org/10.1080/17508487.2015.959031

Mapp, K. L., & Hong, S. (2010). Debunking the myth of the hard-to-reach parent. In S. L. Christenson & A. L. Reschly (Eds.), *Handbook of family school partnerships* (pp. 345–361). Taylor & Francis.

Mediratta, K., Shah, S., & McAlister, S., (2009). *Community organizing for stronger schools: Strategies and successes.* Harvard Education Press.

Miron, G., & Urschel. J. (2009). *Profiles of nonprofit education management organizations: 2008–2009*. Education Policy Research Unit. https://eric.ed.gov/?id=ED507356

National Charter School Resource Center. (2015). *An analysis of the charter school facility landscape in California*. Safal Partners.

Noguera, P. (2001). Transforming urban schools through investments in the social capital of Parents. In S. Saegert, J. P. Thompson J., & M. R. Warren (Eds.), *Social capital in poor communities* (pp. 189–212). The Russell Sage Foundation.

Oakland Homeless Response. (n.d.). *The crisis*. Retrieved January 12, 2020, from https://www.oaklandhomelessresponse.com/the-problem

PolicyLink. (2015). Oakland's Displacement Crisis by the Numbers. Retrieved January 9, 2020, from https://www.policylink.org/sites/default/files/PolicyLink%20Oakland's%20Displacement%20Crisis%20by%20the%20numbers.pdf

Pomfret, J. (2006). *Black and Latino tensions on the rise*. Retrieved December 7, 2021, from https://www.nbcnews.com/id/wbna11467974

Scott, J., & Holme, J. J. (2002). Public schools, private resources: The role of social networks in California charter school reform. In A. S. Wells (Ed.), *Where charter school policy fails: The problems of accountability and equity*. Teachers College Press.

Smith, J., Priscilla W., Kuzin, C. A., & De Pedro. K., (2011). Parent involvement in urban charter schools: New strategies for increasing participation. *School Community Journal 21*(1), 71–94.

Stulberg, L. M. (2008). *Race, schools, & hope*. Teachers College Press.

Toch, T. (2010). Reflections on the charter school movement. *Phi Delta Kappan, 91*(8), 70.

Valencia, R. R., & Black, M. S. (2002). Mexican Americans don't value education! The basis of the myth, mythmaking, and debunking. *Journal of Latinos and Education, 1*(2), 81–103.

Vaandering, D. (2013). Implementing restorative practices in schools: What pedagogy reveals. *Journal of Peace Education, 11*(1), 64–80. https://doi.org/10.1080/17400201.2013.794335

Wang, M.-T., & Sheikh-Khalil, S. (2014). Does parental involvement matter for student achievement and mental health in high school? *Child Development, 85*(2), 610–625.

Warren, M. R., & Mapp, K. L. (2011). *A match on dry grass: Community organizing as a catalyst for school reform*. Oxford University Press.

Williams, T. R., & Sanchez, B. (2011). Identifying and decreasing barriers to parent involvement for inner-city parents. *Youth and Society, 45*(1), 54–74.

Wohlstetter, P., & Smith, J. (2006). Improving schools through partnerships: Learning from charter schools. *Phi Delta Kappan, 87*, 464–467. doi.org/10.1177/003172170608700615

World Population Review. (2020). Oakland, California Population 2020 (Demographics, Maps, Graphs). Retrieved January 9, 2020, from http://worldpopulationreview.com/us-cities/oakland-population/

Zhou, M. (2003). Urban education: Challenges in educating culturally diverse children. *Teachers College Record, 105*(2), 208–225.

ENDNOTE

1. Achieve Schools, Marigold Academy, and Washington Douglass Academy are all pseudonyms.

CHAPTER 7

FAMILY ENGAGEMENT IN CHARTER SCHOOL CLOSURE DECISIONS

Diana Ward
University of Holy Cross

INTRODUCTION

The word *choice* is often associated with charter schools. Proponents of charters tend to frame these schools as opening up the educational marketplace by offering more quality options to families of color and low-income families (Hoxby, 2003; Schneider et al., 2000; Wilson et al., 2019). Unlike private schools, which typically require tuition payments, and thus are frequently inaccessible to many families, charter schools provide a tuition-free alternative to traditional public schools. As such, charter schools have often been offered by proponents as a step towards greater equity, as they can provide low-income parents with a viable choice beyond just the traditional public school (Eden, 2020).

Charter schools might foster competition in the educational marketplace, but a premise of such a market orientation is that good performers will prosper, and poor performers will go out of business (Giroux & Saltman, 2009). In a system of choice with predominantly strong schools, school closure and the reassignment of students or re-selection by families might be likely to shift students from lower performing schools to higher performing ones. But in districts with many poor performing schools, school closure may lead to a scenario in which students arrive at schools

---

Family and Community Engagement in Charter Schools, pp. 145–170
Copyright © 2025 by Information Age Publishing
www.infoagepub.com
All rights of reproduction in any form reserved.

145

with similar level of instructional quality, but these students lose their social connections to staff, teachers, and peers that made their old school familiar. It is this double-edged nature of school competition and school closure which serves as the focus for this chapter examining the research base on parental engagement in charter school closure. While promising to place students in higher performing schools, charter schools also increase the likelihood of school closure impacting students and families.

Former Secretary of Education Betsy Devos (2017) once said of school choice that, "The point is to provide quality options that serve students so each of them can grow. Every option should be held accountable, but they should be directly accountable to parents." Given former Secretary Devos's assertion that schools should be accountable to parents, one would expect to see family engagement in the charter school closure process. However, this frequently is not the case.

School closures disproportionately impact students from lower socio-economic statuses and students of color (Brummet, 2014; De la Torre & Gwynne, 2009; Engberg et al., 2012; Lee & Lubienski, 2017). For students of color and poorer students, the following negative impacts of school closure tend to be especially pronounced: longer bus rides or travel time to school, less school accessibility, and decreased safety (Conner & Cosner, 2014; De la Torre et al., 2015; Graham et al., 2014; Lee & Lubienski, 2017; Tieken & Auldridge-Reveles, 2019). Charter school closure decisions and processes, however they are justified, depicted in policy, or implemented, can often be discriminatory and exclusionary.

Ultimately, school closures can carry significant disruption for students and families, from psychological maladjustment to transportation difficulties (Deeds & Pattillo, 2015; Witten et al., 2003; Witten et al., 2001). For example, Witten et al. (2001) interviewed parents after their child's school was closed. Many of these parents left environments they felt were welcoming and understanding at their old school, only to be met with social marginalization in their new school (Witten et al., 2001). Families also reported experiencing hardship related to new transportation costs (Witten et al., 2001). Despite these challenges, family engagement during school closures can help mitigate some of the difficulties parents may face in the transition. For instance, family input caused Chicago officials to address transportation issues that arose after schools were closed (Graham et al., 2014). Understanding the impact of school closure on families and the engagement of families in charter school closures can provide guidance in minimizing their negative effects on students. But first, this review begins with some brief general context on school closures, charter schools, and family engagement in charter schools.

Context of School Closures

Researchers cite three primary reasons for school closures: academic performance, equality, and cost efficiency (Ewing, 2018; Siegel-Hawley et al., 2017; Tieken & Auldridge-Reveles, 2019). A school might close for cost efficiency reasons when there is a declining population of school-age children in a town. Without demand, enrollment drops and schools (charter or not) may close when per pupil revenues can't cover a school's operating costs. An academically failing charter school might also close as an accountability measure. School choice advocates assert that students are better served by closing a failing or struggling school, but this is only true if a child's new school is of superior quality than the closed school (De la Torre & Gwynne, 2009; Han et al., 2017; Tieken & Auldridge-Reveles, 2019). If school closure results in more academic opportunities for children, then an argument could be made that school closure can further equity. School closures will likely have the opposite effect though if students are shuffled from one low-performing school to another. Further, school closures ultimately supersede parental choice, which has been critical among families and, thus, politically challenging to take away.

Parents and parental choice have been a founding piece of the charter school idea since their very inception (Nathan, 1996). In addition to charter schools' common pursuit of civil rights and social justice, their utilization of free-market mechanisms and limiting the role of government have made them a rare bipartisan policy darling in the last decade and a half. But it is clear that charter schools' deference to parents has its bounds.

While parents must actively choose a charter school their child will attend, popular charters are often oversubscribed, and lotteries ultimately make these choices (McEwan & Olsen, 2010). Parents on rare occasions have organized to create new charter schools when existing schools were found lacking (Beabout, 2014). But when charter school families are unhappy with aspects of school operations, there is no elected school board for parents to apply electoral pressure (Nelson, 2015). And charter schools may be as likely to tell disgruntled families to find a new school as they would be to authentically engage with a parent's concerns.

More broadly, family engagement in schools includes a wider set of behaviors than simply school entry and exit. The research base on parent engagement in schools covers homework support, communicating with teachers, volunteering in the classroom, and acting as conduits for community partnerships (Epstein, 2001; Sanders & Harvey, 2002). All of these arenas are applicable to charter schools, and are typically under-researched in the charter context, but a thorough examination of all of these exceeds the scope of a single research synthesis. Thus, the focus here is on the engagement of families in charter school closures.

Literature Review

There is, to date, insufficient research evidence about whether charter schools engage parents any better, or any worse, than other types of schools during normal operations. In an effort to bring the field closer to some answers on this topic, the following review seeks to answer the question: *what voice do parents have in the charter school closure decision and/or closure process?* While the detailed findings are outlined below, generally the answer is that parents have little voice in the closure decision and process. Charter school closure candidates are typically decided administratively and largely without input from students' parents (Briscoe & Khalifa, 2015; Deeds & Pattillo, 2015; Finnigan & Lavner, 2012; Han et al., 2017; Kretchmar, 2014; Weber et al., 2020).

Even when a parent makes a deliberate choice about where to send their child to school, this choice can always be overruled by a school closure decision. This is a highly constrained version of parental choice. With their school choice overturned, it is no surprise that most parents strongly disagree with charter school closure decisions (De la Torre et al., 2015; Ewing, 2018; Finnigan & Lavner, 2012; Green, 2017; Lipman et al., 2014).

Through a review of media reporting and scholarly publications on school closures, this literature review will explore the broad impact of school closures on families, the specific impact of charter school closure on parental choice, the ways families are, or in many cases *are not*, engaged in school closure decisions and processes. This review will also examine the ways families sometimes resist charter school closures. At the end of this chapter, lessons from prior school closures and consolidations will be drawn upon to provide recommendations for school leaders and families experiencing a charter school closure.

Impact of School Closures on Families

Although school closure is frequently depicted as a process that improves outcomes for students and their families, in practice, this is often not the case (Deeds & Pattillo, 2015). Even when a school closes because of academic concerns, most students will not subsequently attend a better performing school (De la Torre & Gwynne, 2009; Ewing, 2018; Han et al., 2017; Lipman et al., 2014). Further, when a school closes, families have reduced access to an important educational and community institution. Conner and Cosner (2014) posited that "school closure is a form of structural violence that further dehumanizes already marginalized students, families, communities, and schools" (p. 34). Like many ills in society, it seems the burden of school closure is typically most heavily felt by historically underrepresented

Family Engagement in Charter School Closure Decisions   149

communities. School closures are generally "unevenly distributed, disproportionately affecting places where poor communities and communities of color live" (Tieken & Auldridge-Reveles, 2019, p. 1). As a result, many communities of color and poorer communities view school closure as a targeted threat and as an example of structural inequity.

It is important to note that research shows white parents from middle and upper socioeconomic tiers often enroll their students in private schools or gain their child reassignment to a better public or charter school in the event of a school closure. Through these actions, the negative consequences of school closure are largely (or completely) mitigated, as displaced students typically see academic gains when they are sent to academically stronger receiving schools (De la Torre & Gwynne, 2009; Engberg et al., 2012; Han et al., 2017). Black parents and parents from lower socioeconomic statuses often cannot enroll their child in private school and often do not have the political or social capital to gain their child reassignment into a quality public or charter school (England & Hamann, 2013; Williams, 2013). These students then frequently move from one failing school to another (De La Torre & Gwynne, 2009). Such a phenomenon is not the exception but the typical story that accompanies charter school closure. Thus, in the event of a school closure, the impacts are typically inequitable, and much of the inequity appears to vary with the economic and social capital of students' families.

In communities where family resources are already scarce, school closures can usher in a host of other unintended negative consequences. An investigation by WBEZ, Chicago's public radio station, found that school closures contributed to general real estate decline in the community, which included the decrease in home property values (Ramos, 2013). Further, Elaine Simon (2013), co-director of the Urban Studies Program at the University of Philadelphia, found that school closings create educational deserts that deteriorate neighborhoods and force students to travel long distances to obtain an education. In urban areas where poverty rates might be high, "school closings press students and communities already vying for basic resources to struggle for educational access and opportunity" (Wilson et al., 2019, p. 21).

Additionally, students and their families may experience feelings of loss, uncertainty, anger, and trauma when their school closes (Brummet, 2014; Deeds & Pattillo, 2015; Lipman et al., 2014). Ashana Bigard, a charter school parent and community activist in Louisiana, was interviewed for another public radio story on school closures in the all-charter public school system of New Orleans:

> The constant churn and burn of schools is destabilizing for students and their families. "The way our system behaves is insane.... Children do not

need to be constantly upheaved, their education disrupted, their friendships [damaged], their relationships that they're just forming with teachers and administration." (Clark, 2019, September)

Research supports Ms. Bigard's observations. In the aftermath of a school closure decision, students and their families might feel confused and uncertain about their future, and their connections to teachers or even peers might be severed as well (Conner & Cosner, 2014; Deeds & Pattillo, 2015). These experiences of loss can be particularly damaging for students, well beyond whatever benefits are accrued in the new school setting.

School closures can also impact a family's presence in the receiving school. Studies highlight how parent participation is negatively impacted by school closure (Deeds & Pattillo, 2015; Lipman et al., 2014). Parents from the closed school are less likely to be involved in the new school (Deeds & Pattillo, 2015; Lipman et al., 2014). This declining parent participation after a closure does not bode well for increased student success.

School closure can ultimately disrupt educational progress for students, negatively impact families, and contribute to blight in the community, as well as further systemic racism (Briscoe & Khalifa, 2015; Conner & Cosner, 2014; Wilson et al., 2019). Despite the research on the negative impacts of school closures on students and their families, charter school closures are still happening. The prevalence of charter school closures varies greatly by region. From 2008 to 2014, between 6 to 21% of charter schools closed in states across America (Paino et al., 2017). Thus, a lot of families are being impacted by charter school closures. Beyond the negative tangible impacts closure may have on families, charter school closures are also overturning the choices of parents.

Impact of Charter School Closures on Parental Choice

Often, schools that are closed have been labeled as "failing" and the closure decision is framed around the idea of accountability. Closure is then generally depicted as an expansion of student opportunity (Han et al., 2017; Tieken & Auldridge-Reveles, 2019). While groups of policymakers, district officials, or charter school authorizers might have agreement on the performance metrics to be used in closure decisions, this is no guarantee that this agreement extends to parents. Parents may, and often do, oppose the decision to close a school based on a belief that the school was serving their children and not failing students (Deeds & Pattillo, 2015; Ewing, 2018). Charter school closures can represent a direct overturning of parental choice by district officials or charter school authorizers.

Many families select a charter school for their child based in part on its performance scores, but families may choose a charter school for reasons not related to performance. For example, parents might explore how students do socially and emotionally at the school or they might look at the suspension rates in the school (Deeds & Pattillo, 2015; Ewing, 2018). When making a determination about the overall quality of a school, parents might also consider if students' safety is valued, if students are nurtured and cared for at the school, and how well the school is preparing students for adulthood (Wilson et al., 2019). Research in the New Orleans Public Schools indicated that proximity to the family home, extended school hours, and extra-curricular offerings were important considerations in addition to measures of academic performance (Harris & Larsen, 2015). District officials and charter school authorizers may look to entirely different factors, like test scores and fiscal efficiency, to determine the quality of a school (Wilson et al., 2019).

The Catherine Ferguson Academy in Detroit provides an example of the disparity in opinion that can exist between parents and district officials. The once public turned charter school was viewed as a good school by students, parents, and the local community. It was even recognized nationally through a feature in Oprah Winfrey's *O Magazine* (Owens, 2008). And yet, despite opposition from parents, students, and community members, this Detroit school was still closed by district officials as part of a system-wide deficit reduction plan (Wilson et al., 2019). All too often, conflicting notions of what defines a successful school can result in a clash between parent values and the market-oriented values that frequently drive district leaders and charter school authorizers.

Some research suggests that parents do indeed look at a much wider variety of factors of school quality compared to district officials and charter school authorizers. Weiher and Tedin (2001) analyzed the responses from 1,006 charter school households. These researchers asked parents to identify which of these factors was most important when selecting a school: test scores, discipline, common race/ethnicity of students, location, teaching of moral values, or safety. African American parents were most likely to cite the teaching of moral values. Hispanic parents were most likely to cite the practice of good discipline in the school as *the* factor that most influenced their school choice. Further analysis revealed that their choices were also influenced by the racial/ethnic makeup of the student body; in other words, they were more likely to choose the charter school where the students would look like their child (Weiher & Tedin, 2001).

Other researchers found a different factor can impact school choice, a factor that district officials and charter school authorizers may not even take into account when making closure decisions. Through the use of GIS mapping and other spatial methods, Lubienski and Lee (2016) found that

152   D. WARD

the distance between a family's home and the school played a deciding role in the choice process. The closer the charter school was to the family's home, the more likely the parents were to select that school (Lubienski & Lee, 2016).

Distance from school to home was an important factor for Alongkorn Lafargue's family. While Alongkorn's father acknowledged the Medard Nelson Charter school his son attended in New Orleans had some problems, like frequent turnover in school leadership, the school was just down the street and was a good fit for the family. When the charter school was closed, the Lafarque family's school choice was rendered meaningless by district officials, and the family was forced to travel to a different school that was not their first choice. Mr. Lafarque was understandably upset.

> "This was a great school" Lafargue said. "Orleans Parish School Board [NOLA Public Schools] surely has not allowed me the *choice* to let him stay [...] in the neighborhood [...]." This year, getting to school isn't as simple as the six-minute walk Lafargue and his son used to make to Nelson [School]. Alongkorn's new school, IDEA Oscar Dunn, is in another neighborhood nine miles away. Lafargue said it takes an hour on the school bus, so he drives Alongkorn himself every day in his compact Chevy sedan. (Clark, 2019, September)

Unfortunately, the Lafargue family's experience with charter school closure, and the overturning of their school choice, is not unique. The Lafarque family's struggle with transportation difficulties after the closure is not uncommon either. With a school closure, research suggests that many families will struggle with new burdens like increased travel times or new transportation costs (Deeds & Pattillo, 2015; Witten et al., 2003; Witten et al., 2001). Thus, one practical reason why parents sometimes oppose a school's closure is that the receiving school is farther from the family's home (De la Torre et al., 2015; Talen, 2001).

It is not surprising that parents consistently disagree with charter school closures (Tieken & Auldridge-Reveles, 2019). Parents might oppose school closures due to concerns about how it will impact student and teacher relationships (Kirshner et al., 2010). Some parents may believe closure decisions are based on racism (Briscoe & Khalifa, 2015; Ewing, 2018). Charter schools with large numbers of poor students of color are more likely to be closed than those serving wealthier, whiter populations. Parents may also oppose closure because they believe their school was set up to fail due to a lack of resources or because a subpopulation of students, like those in special education, were not properly served (Freelon, 2018; Kretchmar, 2014). At Cypress Academy, a closed charter school in New Orleans focused on serving students with special-education needs, parent Sydney Longwell, Jr. believes this is exactly what shut the school down (Hechinger Report,

Family Engagement in Charter School Closure Decisions   153

2018). Parents lamented that the district's decision to close the school would discourage charter operators from trying to serve special education students in the future (Jewson, 2018, November 12). They felt the district determined that the cost of serving this subpopulation of students was too high (Jewson, 2018, November 12). And, the school was closed, in spite of the fact that many families had selected it.

Ultimately, parents may oppose a closure decision for many reasons, not the least of which is that they see it as a direct contradiction of their personal choice and, by extension, an erosion of democracy (Fontaine, 1998; Tieken & Auldridge-Reveles, 2019). A claim could reasonably be made that charter school closure decisions supersede a parent's choice. Despite this, many district officials and charter school authorizers still advocate for closures as a sign that charter schools are improving the district overall. This is ironic given that charter schools are often advertised as giving families more choices. Rather than boosting equity through increased choice, charter school closures might inadvertently result in more educational disenfranchisement (Briscoe & Khalifa, 2015; Conner & Cosner, 2014; Wilson et al., 2019). Given the potential risk of harm to students and families from school closure, there is a reasonable case to be made that families should have some say in closure decisions and that they should be engaged in the closure process. It is in this area of engagement that we turn next.

Family Engagement in School Closures

As has been established, families going through a charter school closure typically oppose the decision (Tieken & Auldridge-Reveles, 2019). This makes sense, given that parents must choose to send their child to a charter school. And when a parent's choice is overturned, it could be argued that the process of charter school closure is undemocratic—especially when families are not engaged at all in the closure decision or process. All too often,

> Closures mostly happen to, not with, students, families, and communities, typically without meaningful participation or consent. Those most likely to be affected by closure—poor communities of color—are also those least likely to enjoy adequate political representation, and so their objections go unheard, their interests ignored. (Tieken & Auldridge-Reveles, 2019, p. 22)

However, research shows some district leaders and charter school authorizers have engaged families in school closure decisions and the closure process by holding open forums and creating councils or committees to provide oversight of the closure process (Finnigan & Lavner,

154   D. WARD

2012; Kretchmar, 2014; Warner et al., 2011). Sometimes these efforts were genuine and served as positive examples of family engagement in the school closure process. Sometimes these efforts were inauthentic, and they serve as negative examples of family engagement in the closure process. Both positive and negative examples will be presented next.

Positive Examples. The first positive example, while not comprised of charter schools, comes from rural school consolidations in North Dakota. Sell and Leistritz (1997) surveyed families from four different schools experiencing closure. They found in one of the four schools that was closed and consolidated with another that the process was particularly smooth for the families involved. The interviews with the families experiencing the smoothest transition through the closure and consolidation process revealed that school officials did several key things.

First, the school leaders made "an extreme effort to communicate facts" (Sell & Leistritz, 1997, p. 12). Through transparency, trust can be established, which can allow school leaders and families to better function as a team for the benefit of students. School officials also established a fact-finding committee made up of students and parents. Such a committee can recommend ways district officials or school leaders can support families in the transition and can also bring legitimacy to the school closure process through the exploration and sharing of factors leading to the school's closure. In addition, school officials conducted weekly public meetings to allow for further family engagement.

While the families in this aforementioned community could not influence the final decision on closure, this example highlights that engaging families in the closure process can help families through the transition. For instance, public meetings can not only foster more transparency in the closure process but also allow families to directly voice concerns with school leaders. School officials can then work to address the specific concerns presented by families. Sunderman and Payne (2009) analyzed existing research on school closures and found that the emotional impact of closure on families *can be minimized* through transparency. Such efforts at transparency should at the very least include "adequate notice about the [closure] decision and information on the criteria used to make decisions" (p. 19).

Another way to allow for family engagement in the closure process is for schools to create a task force (Finnigan & Lavner, 2012; Warner et al., 2011). Such a task force can be partially or fully made up of parents who are given the opportunity to weigh in on closure proposals (Finnigan & Lavner, 2012; Warner et al., 2011). The next positive example of family engagement, also from a district, rather than a charter school, is in the closure process involved in this very tactic.

When a rural middle school in the Appalachian Region was up for closure, a task force made up of school personnel, parents, and community members was created by district officials (Warner et al., 2011). The task force adopted a mission to determine how to enhance the opportunities for student success. After reviewing research and visiting many other schools, the task force provided a list of recommendations to district officials, which included the blending of their school with another. This consolidation ultimately happened as recommended by the task force (Warner et al., 2011). Warner et al. (2011) found that while there was some disagreement among parents and community members on the location of the consolidated school, many families, even though their school closed and joined with another, were ultimately happy with the final outcome.

The first example in this section illustrates how family engagement can support parents during the always difficult closure process. The second example highlights how family engagement can positively influence the closure decision. With these lessons in mind, district officials and charter school authorizers might be able to avoid adversarial relationships with parents and instead work to engage with them on the closure decision and process for the benefit of students, families, and the broader community.

Negative Examples. As discussed above, a task force can be a good way to allow for parent input with regards to closure decisions. And public meetings can be a good way to engage families throughout the closure process. However, such efforts are for naught if charter school authorizers or district administrators do not hold themselves accountable to parent feedback. This next example illustrates the need for district officials to engage families in genuine and not merely performative ways.

In New York City, 19 public forums were held prior to the shuttering of several district schools (Kretchmar, 2014). Hundreds of parents and community members spoke against the narrow approach district officials were taking in deciding which schools to close. Their efforts resulted in some community oversight of the process. There was an examination into what factors made a school subject to closure and if these terms were justified. Questions were also raised regarding the motives behind the school closures and if there was an overlap with the interests of district officials. Despite critical questions and feedback from families, the final decision on the school closures remained unchanged by district officials (Kretchmar, 2014). This is not an example of meaningful family engagement. Superficial efforts to engage families are not likely to mitigate the negative impacts of school closure.

Families going through school closures frequently state that efforts at parent and community input are surface level or "performance" and decisions to close a school are made without consideration for the needs or wants of those most affected by the decisions (Finnigan & Lavner, 2012; Freelon, 2018). Finnigan and Lavner (2012) interviewed family members "involved" in the closure process at Lincoln Elementary School, a pseudonym for a district- run school in a mid-size urban district serving mostly Black students. The superintendent and school board approved the creation of an ad hoc committee made up of parents and community members. This ad hoc committee was tasked with compiling data and seeking further community input in order to create a list of schools to potentially close. This included examining the condition of school buildings. The ad hoc committee of parents and community members submitted the names of five schools for closure. The superintended ultimately selected Lincoln Elementary for closure, a school that had *not* been on the committee's list. This led several community members to question if their committee had been purely symbolic, with one parent saying,

> It was just a matter of being able to say by the Superintendent, the Board and the staff that we had a process. We had key people. They did a little name dropping. They did a little signifying in various communities to say that we had African American involvement, we had Latino involvement. [...] So this report is authentic, but when you look around it wasn't. (Finnigan & Lavner, 2012, p. 138)

Parents, with good reason, may feel shut out of the closure process even when they are included on committees if their voices or recommendations are ignored in the end.

Charter school leaders who do not develop plans for meaningful family engagement in the school closure process do so at the detriment of the school community and the families they serve. Media reports demonstrate that families facing charter school closures have lamented about not being included in charter school closure discussions in sincere ways. Lona Hankins, a parent and former Recovery School District employee, implored the board

> to hold its committee meetings—where board members discuss most of their policy decisions—at times and in places that are accessible to the public. They are often held early on Tuesday afternoons at the district's Algiers headquarters. "Parents and the public can't participate in that," Hankins said. "You're leaving parents out." (Jewson, 2018, November 15)

When incorporating parent voice, every effort should be made by district officials to ensure their efforts are not just performative. District administrators must also ensure these efforts are welcoming and inclusive so that a diverse set of parents, not just those with the most resources, are able to participate. Failure to do this may lead not only to discouragement, but to significant resistance from families with regards to the closure process; examples of this will be explored next.

Family Engagement in Charter School Closure Decisions   157

Families Resisting Charter School Closures

Families who are not engaged in closure decisions and the closure process by district officials or charter school authorizers may decide to actively resist the efforts to close their school. In New Orleans, parents who felt shut out of the school closure process demanded to be heard. During a board meeting in 2018, board members attempted to discuss actions items on an agenda *not related to charter school closure decisions*, but parents in attendance insisted on time to discuss the upcoming closure of several charter schools. As local reporter Marta Jewson writes:

> At one point, as the board asked a woman to stop talking the crowd reacted in a chant: "Let her talk! Let her talk! Let her talk!" At another moment, organizer Ashana Bigard spoke from the audience. "You represent us, when did you ask us?" Bigard asked. "Did anybody sit in a meeting where we discussed these changes?" A collective "no" was the response. [...] After the meeting, Bigard said she planned to help parents organize. "We are organizing parents that want to come together to get real democracy and real choice," she said. "We're going to start our recall campaign tomorrow." (Jewson, 2018, November 15)

These parents and community members are now mobilizing to unseat the very board members who approved charter school closures in the city.

> Some parents and advocates from a group called Erase The Board [...] questioned why the closing schools couldn't be put on improvement plans, too. Erase The Board is a group aiming to unseat current members of the Orleans Parish School Board, the elected body that oversees the school district. The group wants the district to help failing schools, not close them. (Jewson, 2019)

Beyond mounting recall campaigns, some students, parents, and community members have staged other forms of protest in the face of school closure decisions (Green & McEvoy, 2019). These protests have taken many forms, including organizing students and parents to pack school board meetings or participate in school walkouts (Green & McEvoy, 2019). Packing a school board meeting was the exact tactic parents in Louisiana recently used in light of charter school closure announcements.

> Dozens of students, parents and community members attended the meeting to show support for Coghill [School] after [Superintendent] Lewis last month recommended pulling [the charter] due to [its] failing grade from the state. They offered impassioned pleas to keep [the school] open under the same management next school year. Swayed by the public support, four

158   D. WARD

of the School Board's seven members [...] voted to keep Coghill's management in place. (Hasselle, 2019, December)

This effort was ultimately unsuccessful, as the motion would have needed a
supermajority of the school board to succeed. It fell one vote short. However,
this example speaks to the power parents can have when they make their
voices heard. Yet, packing board meetings is not the only act of resistance
families can undertake in light of charter school closure announcements.

Other resistance efforts have been at least partially successful in altering closure decisions. For example, in 2011, Chicago Public Schools (CPS)
announced that the district-run Dyett High School was scheduled for closure, which prompted community members, known as the Coalition, to
engage in a lot of back and forth with CPS (Stovall, 2015). According to
Stovall (2015), when community members realized talking with CPS "was a
sham process, the Coalition decided to take matters into their own hands.
The result was a thirty-four day hunger strike to enforce the community's
demand for a school that met their expressed needs" (p. 85). To the dismay
of the Coalition, Dyett was not revitalized in their vision—as a green technology school. CPS did, however, announce that Dyett would be revitalized
as an open enrollment, arts-based, technology school called Dyett High
School for the Arts (Stovall, 2015). Dyett is still open to this day.

Still, other forms of protest parents have taken up in the face of school
closure announcements, include marches and filing lawsuits (Stovall, 2015;
Tieken & Auldridge-Reveles, 2019). Many such actions of resistance involve
or require broad mobilization to build the necessary coalitions of stakeholders (Aggarwal et al., 2012; Conner & Cosner, 2014; De la Torre et al.,
2015; Ewing, 2018). These actions of resistance have more likelihood of
success once organized, but when the closure decision is the beginning of
that process, they are hard-pressed for short-term wins.

With a broad coalition of stakeholders, parents may be able to influence
change over the medium and longer-terms. There are many obstacles to
effective mobilization though including sometimes confusing or exclusionary closure processes. There is sometimes a sense that nothing can be done
to change the decision of closure, and there can also be social and/or political divisions that may split communities going through closure (Aggarwal
et al., 2012; Finnigan & Lavner, 2012; Pappas, 2012). Despite this, parents
might still find hope in stories of resistance which prompted change, or at
least transparency, in the school closure process.

The above discussion details cases of family engagement in closure decisions. Also significant, despite scant research literature, are discussions of
the guidance district officials and charter school leaders provide to families
once a closure is authorized. Ideally, families should not have to mobilize
for this support to happen; it should be readily offered by charter school

Family Engagement in Charter School Closure Decisions   159

leaders in the event of a closure. Recommendations for how school leaders can support and engage with families during a charter school closure will be provided next. This will be followed by recommendations for families.

Recommendations for Charter School Leaders

It is important that when a charter school closes, the risk of negative consequences to students and their families be mitigated as much as possible. As has been discussed at length, district officials and charter school authorizers can mitigate negative consequences to families by engaging with them throughout the closure process. Charter school leaders can also play an important role in supporting families through a school closure. The recommendations below provide concrete suggestions for charter school leaders hoping to engage and collaborate with families during a school closure.

Recommendation One: Create Two-Way Communication Channels

When a decision to close a charter school has been made by district officials or charter school authorizers, the school leader should consider how the closure will impact families. To provide tailored supports, they should gather information on things like the anticipated financial impact on students' families. To gather this data, school leaders should consider ways to establish two-way communication with families. When establishing two-way communication channels, charter school leaders must consider how and when parents will get information to and from the school. The two-way communication channels should allow for communication with *all* families, not just the families with the most time or resources.

Charter school leaders could set up individual and/or focus group interviews with families. Multiple times could be offered to accommodate parents who work. Childcare and rides could also be offered to ensure the effort is inclusive. Such interviews could help families by allowing parents to identify specific struggles the closure might produce for them and giving them a chance to voice their concerns directly to school leaders.

Charter school leaders could also hold public meetings in which they share information about the closure decision and allow families to ask questions. Attending to families in such a way could help parents and students to cope emotionally with the closure decision. This is important considering that if students are negatively impacted emotionally, they are likely to be negatively impacted academically as well (Basu, 2007).

160 D. WARD

Further, charter school leaders should set up a regular timetable of communication. Through continuous communication, charter school leaders could highlight the resources available to families throughout the closure process. For instance, charter school leaders could communicate with parents on how to select a new quality school for their child. Communication could also go out from school leaders regarding a transportation fund that will be available for parents who need support for travel costs to the new school. This idea will be expanded upon in a later recommendation.

By engaging in two-way communication with parents, charter school leaders could avoid potentially contentious relationships with families. This would help school leaders to operate as a team with parents for the benefit of students. Two-way communication channels could ultimately serve to keep families in the loop about decisions, processes and timelines related to the school's closure, as well as keep families abreast of resources available to them.

Recommendation Two: Hire a School-Family Liaison

As a way to take two-way communication a step further, a school-family liaison could specifically be hired or appointed by the charter school leader to relay information to and receive information from families. This could be particularly helpful for the charter school leader in providing families adequate support as the capacity of the leader could be constrained as they prepare for closure. In particular, the school-family liaison could work with parents to ensure they find a new school to enroll their child in that both meets the family's needs and is not at risk of closure. Variations in course offerings, curricular materials, and student supports within the receiving schools can create dramatically different educational opportunities for displaced students (Tieken & Auldridge-Reveles, 2019).

The school in which a displaced student ends up going after a charter school closure is extremely important to the student's future academic success. Research shows that displaced students sent to lower or even similarly performing schools saw significant declines in their test scores (Engberg et al., 2012; Han et al., 2017).

A school-family liaison can assist families to navigate the process of finding an appropriate and quality new school for their child could be immensely important in mitigating the negative impact of closure. A school-family liaison could also hold public meetings to provide parents with as much information as possible. While it was previously suggested that school leaders hold such meetings, families may have lost trust in the school leader due to the closure announcement. Families may be more apt to trust a school-family liaison, especially if this person has ties to the community. As such, it is important that school leaders consider the multiple ways they could facilitate transparent communication with families. Depending on the dynamics of the situation, a school-family liaison could be better suited than the school leader to hold public forums with families.

Ultimately, in the event of closure, getting information and resources to parents as quickly as possible is extremely important. As one parent in New Orleans facing a charter school closure said, "As a parent, I want to know—now. I don't want to be scrambling, [...] I hope I can avoid that, to do right by my child" (Monteverde, 2018). The hiring of a dedicated, full-time school-family liaison could provide families with immediate and ongoing support.

Recommendation Three: Avoid Publically Supporting Closure

Because parents often disagree with charter school closure decisions (De la Torre et al., 2015), one thing charter school leaders should avoid is publicly advocating for closure (Deeds & Pattillo, 2015). Advocating for closure could potentially cause a divide between charter school leaders and families. This could make it much more difficult for charter school leaders to support families.

McMillin (2010) suggests school leaders discuss closure decisions as early as possible with parents. Holding the news could make it seem like the decision is being hidden from parents, which could erode trust between the school leader and families. School leaders can share the closure announcement without seeming like they were or are advocating for it. For example, the school leader could explain that they too are dismayed by the news from district officials. However, they are unable to change it and will work to support families through the transition.

By avoiding publicly supporting the closure decision, charter school leaders will be better positioned to collaborate with families and successfully enact transition plans for the benefit of students. If the leader were to be seen as on the side of those making the closure decision, they may find that families cannot trust them. Without trust, it would be hard for the charter school leader to support families through the closure in any kind of meaningful way.

Recommendation Four: Create a Task Force

Charter school leaders should devise plans to include parents in the closure process in authentic ways. These efforts could take many forms

162   D. WARD

including but not limited to creating councils, planning committees, or tasks forces made up of parents (Ewing, 2018; Kretchmar, 2014). The creation of action-oriented parent task forces could be particularly helpful for families, as well as for charter school leaders whose capacities may be limited as they prepare staff and their buildings for closure.

For instance, parents could be allowed to create a specific transition task force where plans could be developed and implemented to support families in selecting a new school for their child. The selection of a new school after a closure has been discussed before. The ample discussion of this topic is warranted because the quality of the receiving school is particularly important to the future success of displaced students (Tieken & Auldridge-Reveles, 2019). Thus, the charter school leader should consider multiple ways they can support families in selecting a new school. A potential benefit of the option to allow a transition task force to form is that a parent-led task force will engender more trust with families than a school leader or staff member.

The parent transition task force could gather information about other school options. The information gathered could include school performance scores, suspension rates, extracurricular activities offered, and more. This information could be presented to all families in a public meeting. The members of the transition task force could then lead efforts to support parents in registering their student(s) at new schools.

Different parent task forces could be created to address multiple areas where families may need support. As another example, there could also be a transportation task force. Interested parents could research bus routes, ride shares, and other modes of travel. Their goal could be to assist families who may struggle with transportation once their student is in a new school.

Charter school leaders should provide the space for these parent task forces to meet. They should lend these groups to use the school's computers to conduct research and communicate with the school community. They should help the task forces to put on public meetings to share information with other families. In this sense, parents involved in a task force would have some power in the closure process and also empower other families through their work.

Recommendation Five: Provide Funds for Families in Need

Charter school leaders whose buildings will be closed may have the opportunity to sell school materials or properties. Much of these funds will likely be earmarked for certain things, like paying off existing debts. If possible, a charter school leader could set aside some of the funds though to go to families with financial need related to the school closure.

Family Engagement in Charter School Closure Decisions   163

For instance, some money from the selling of school materials or properties could go into a transportation fund. This fund could be used for families in the transition year. It could provide parents with financial assistance for transportation needs related to getting their student to and from the new school as the receiving school might be farther from their home than the charter school they originally selected. This might require additional bus fares or more money for gas.

Additionally, the new school may not have a bus route that includes the students in the displaced area or the school may not have buses at all. If public transportation in the city is poor, students might have to take taxis, Ubers, or Lyfts to school. This could be especially true if it is too far or unsafe for students to walk or bike to their new school. A transportation fund for families in such a position could help offset costs.

Finally, funds could also be given to families who cannot afford to buy new school items that may be required at the receiving school. For example, the new school could require a uniform. While many schools provide at least one free uniform for students, not all do. Students would likely need more than one uniform too. Providing some kind of monetary assistance to families facing a potentially costly school transition could help alleviate some of the burden on families due to the school closure.

Recommendation Six: Prepare the Receiving School

The receiving charter school also needs to have a strategy in place to support the displaced families. The charter school leaders in the closing school could help with this. The school leaders at the closing school should regularly reach out to school leaders in the receiving school to ensure comprehensive transition plans are crafted. They could proactively share student records to help the teachers in the receiving school prepare for the academic needs of their new students.

Additionally, research shows that parent participation is negatively impacted by school closure (Deeds & Pattillo, 2015; Lipman et al., 2014). As such, the receiving school needs to have a plan in place for engaging the parents of displaced students. The charter school leaders at the closing school should also help with this. The leaders at the closing school should host events before the closure to invite parents and the new leaders at the receiving school to interact. Such events would help families establish bonds with the new school staff. By doing this, the charter school leaders at the closing school would also show parents that they have trust in the receiving school, which could help further build the bonds between families and the new school staff.

164   D. WARD

Charter school leaders have a responsibility to serve the families who selected their school, and this responsibility should not end at the announcement of a charter school closure. Every effort should be made by charter school leaders to support families during the transition process. This support should not only include helping families to successfully transition to the receiving school, but also include preparing the new school to receive the displaced families.

Recommendations for Families

Charter school leaders should devise plans for family engagement in the event of a school closure. They should also implement student transition plans. But charter school leaders may not take these steps. In the event of inaction on behalf of the closing charter school's leaders, families must mobilize to take these actions themselves.

Parents should seek out community centers and online resources that will help them determine where their child can attend school and of those options which is the best fit for their student. They should feel empowered to ask the leaders at the closing charter school what resources they can provide during the transition, whether those resources be monetary or material. Parents should also feel empowered to ask officials in the receiving school what resources they can provide their family during the transition.

The adage "the squeaky wheel gets the grease," is likely accurate in the event of a charter school closure. Charter school families should feel empowered to make their voices heard. Charter school leaders should understand this. If their schools were meant to be avenues for parent choice, then they should expect that families are going to raise their voices during a charter school closure until they are heard. Ultimately, when schools do not provide clear avenues for family engagement, parents should feel emboldened to blaze their own paths to input.

CONCLUSION

In many ways, school closure decisions mirror the market principles in America's capitalistic society, in which competition is frequently prioritized over democratic participation (Aggarwal et al., 2012; Allweiss et al., 2015; Waitoller & Super, 2017). Greater competition through a proliferation of charter schools has increasingly led to a market perspective being applied to K–12 schools (Fitz et al., 2013). For charter schools that "lose the competition" for recruiting students and producing strong test scores, school

Family Engagement in Charter School Closure Decisions 165

closure will always be a possibility. In business, when a company closes, the employees are often negatively impacted; when a charter school closes, not only are employees often negatively impacted but so are students and their families, the community, and the broader educational system.

There is a special irony in a charter school closure: the charter school, likely built and branded around the idea of choice, is selected by families only to later close probably without any sincere input from the very parents who picked it. When a charter school is closed, students don't simply lose their school. The community loses a site that could help families exercise political voice and local control as well as support the growth of racial liberation (Ewing, 2018; Sell & Leistritz, 1997). This very human aspect of charter school closure cannot and should not be overlooked by district officials or charter school authorizers.

For families facing charter school closure, hope might be found in the stories of resistance from others who have faced this same process. This hope is evident in the comments of many parents in the public record who have faced school closure. When a parent with a student at New Orleans' McDonough 35 High School spoke of closure efforts related to her alma mater, she said, "You could try to give it fire, you can try to freeze it, and you can try to dismantle it, we will always come back to being that iron eagle [(the school mascot)]" (Clark, 2019, April). This sense of hope can help parents and students press on in the face of school closure decisions and certainly should be anticipated and recognized by district officials charged with making charter school closure decisions.

As this chapter presented, it is not unusual for families to organize and make their opposition to closure decisions known to district and school officials. Families often work together to fight to change or even stop the school closure process through large demonstrations, marches, and hunger strikes as well as through lawsuits, civil rights complainants, or other legal action (De la Torre et al., 2015; Ewing, 2018; Lipman et al., 2014; Siegel-Hawley et al., 2017). For such actions to be successful in halting school closure decisions or altering school closure processes, researchers agree that organized resistance is one of the biggest keys to success (Finnigan & Lavner, 2012; Green, 2017; Tieken & Auldridge-Reveles, 2019).

Despite the hope these stories of resistance may provide to families, the impact of resistance on charter school closure decisions is varied. Resistance efforts can result in delayed closures, reopening of schools, parents gaining representation on decision-making bodies, or changes being made to the closure process, but sometimes organization and resistance do not result in any change at all (Briscoe & Khalifa, 2015; Finnigan & Lavner, 2012; Siegel-Hawley et al., 2017). As such, every effort needs to be made by district officials and charter school authorizers, as well as charter school leaders, to reduce the harm to students and their families when a charter

166   D. WARD

school closure occurs. To reduce harm, district officials, charter school authorizers, and school leaders must actively and meaningfully engage families in the charter school closure process.

In the event of a charter school closure, families must also take power into their own hands by gathering information and using that knowledge to best transition their student to a new school. While charter school closure is likely to be hard, as change often brings seen and unforeseen pain, families should not lose hope for their children. Tulane University Researcher Douglas Harris has spent years researching charter school closures, and he says,

> School closures and takeovers should be a last resort, but they also show some promise when schools are consistently low-performing. [...] Certainly there's gonna be an initial disruption [in a school closure], but if [students] end up moving to a better school, that may all be OK in the long term. (Hasselle, 2019, August)

In the end, it is possible for students to not just survive but to thrive after a charter school closure. This seems demonstrably more likely if charter school authorizers, district officials, and school leaders engage with families during the process.

REFERENCES

Aggarwal, U., Mayorga, E., & Nevel, D. (2012). Slow violence and neoliberal education reform: Reflections on a school closure. *Peace and Conflict: Journal of Peace Psychology*, *18*(2), 156–164.

Allweiss, A., Grant, C. A., & Manning, K. (2015). Behind the photos and the tears: Media images, neoliberal discourses, racialized constructions of space and school closings in Chicago. *Race Ethnicity and Education*, *18*(5), 611–631.

Basu, R. (2007). Negotiating acts of citizenship in an era of neoliberal reform: The game of school closures. *International Journal of Urban and Regional Research*, *31*(1), 109–127.

Beabout, B.R. (2014). Community leadership: Seeking social justice while re-creating public schools in post-Katrina New Orleans. In I. Bogotch & C. M. Shields (Eds.), *International handbook of educational leadership and social (in) justice* (pp. 543–570). Springer.

Briscoe, F. M., & Khalifa, M. A. (2015). 'That racism thing:' A critical race discourse analysis of a conflict over the proposed closure of a black high school. *Race Ethnicity and Education*, *18*(6), 739–763.

Brummet, Q. (2014). The effect of school closings on student achievement. *Journal of Public Economics*, *119*, 108–124.

Clark, J. (2019, April 29). *Charter schools nearly destroyed this New Orleans School. Now it will become one.* The Hechinger Report. https://hechingerreport.org/charter-schools-nearly-destroyed-this-new-orleans-school-now-it-will-become-one/

Clark, J. (2019, September 6). *Closing a failing school is normal, but not easy, in charters-only New Orleans.* NPR. https://www.npr.org/2019/09/06/756456951/closing-a-failing-school-is-normal-but-not-easy-in-charters-only-new-orleans

Conner, J., & Cosner, K. (2014). School closure as structural violence and stakeholder resistance as social justice. *Journal for Peace and Justice Studies, 24*(2), 27–49.

De la Torre, M., Gordon, M., Moore, P., Cowhy, J., Jagsic, S., & Huynh, M. (2015, January). *School closings in Chicago: Understanding families' choices and constraints for new school enrollment.* The University of Chicago Consortium on Chicago School Research. https://consortium.uchicago.edu/sites/default/files/2018-10/School%20Closings%20Report.pdf

De la Torre, M., & Gwynne, J. (2009). *When schools close: Effects on displaced students in Chicago public schools.* The University of Chicago Consortium on Chicago School Research. https://consortium.uchicago.edu/sites/default/files/2018-10/CCSRSchoolClosings-Final.pdf

Deeds, V., & Pattillo, M. (2015). Organizational "failure" and institutional pluralism: A case study of an urban school closure. *Urban Education, 50*(4), 474–504.

Devos, B. (2017). *Prepared remarks by U.S. Secretary of Education Betsy DeVos to the American Federation for Children's National Policy Summit.* U.S. Department of Education.

Eden, M. (2020, January 28). *Issues 2020: Charter schools boost results for disadvantaged students and everyone else.* Manhattan Institute. https://www.manhattan-institute.org/issues-2020-charter-schools-benefits-for-low-income-minority-students

Engberg, J., Gill, B., Zamarro, G., & Zimmer, R. (2012). Closing schools in a shrinking district: Do student outcomes depend on which schools are closed? *Journal of Urban Economics, 71*(2), 189–203.

England, W., & Hamann, E.T. (2013). Segregation, inequality, demographic change, and school consolidation. *Great Plains Research: A Journal of Natural and Social Sciences, 23*, 171–183.

Epstein, J. L. (2001). *School, family, and community partnerships: Preparing educators and improving schools.* Westview Press.

Ewing, E. L. (2018). *Ghosts in the schoolyard: Racism and school closings on Chicago's South Side.* University of Chicago Press.

Finnigan, K. S., & Lavner, M. (2012). A political analysis of community influence over school closure. *The Urban Review, 44*(1), 133–151.

Fitz, J., Gorard, S., & Taylor, C. (2013). *Schools, markets and choice policies.* Routledge.

Fontaine, C. (1998). *Democracy, schools, and communities.* Clearinghouse.

Freelon, R. (2018). Transformational resistance and parent leadership: Black parents in a school district decision-making process. *Urban Education.* https://doi.org/10.1177/0042085918801886

Giroux, H. A., & Saltman, K. (2009). Obama's betrayal of public education? Arne Duncan and the corporate model of schooling. *Cultural Studies, Critical Methodologies, 9*(6), 772–779.

168   D. WARD

Graham, B. C., Keys, C. B., McMahon, S. D., & Brubacher, M. R. (2014). Transportation challenges for urban students with disabilities: Parent perspectives. *Journal of Prevention & Intervention in the Community, 42*(1), 45–57.

Green, M., & McEvoy, J. (2019, January 29). *Why is the closure of a small school in Oakland causing such a stir?* KQED. https://www.kqed.org/news/11721015/the-big-fight-over-a-small-school-in-oakland-what-you-need-to-know

Green, T. L. (2017). "We felt they took the heart out of the community:" Examining a community-based response to urban school closure. *Education Policy Analysis Archives, 25*(21), 1–30.

Han, C., Raymond, M. E., Woodworth, J. L., Negassi, Y., Richardson, W. P., & Snow, W. (2017). *Lights off: Practice and impact of closing low-performing schools*, (Vol. 1). Center for Research on Educational Outcomes (CREDO). https://credo.stanford.edu/sites/g/files/sbiybj6481/f/closure_final_volume_i.pdf

Harris, D. N., & Larsen, M. F. (2015). *What schools do families want (and why)*. Education Research Alliance for New Orleans.

Hasselle, D. (2019, August 20). *What's driving better school performance in New Orleans? Tulane researchers say it's school closures.* The Times Picayune-The New Orleans Advocate. https://www.nola.com/news/education/article_f2fbbc40-c35b-11e9-a03d9ba3203b0bb1.html

Hasselle, D. (2019, December 19). *Charters for two New Orleans schools will not be renewed this year after contentious board meeting.* The Times Picayune-The New Orleans Advocate. https://www.nola.com/news/education/article_1eef3aa4-22cd-11ea-a580-ef775e951d01.html

Hechinger Report. (2018, August 30). *These schools are opening their arms to special education students. Can they afford it?* The Lens. https://thelensnola.org/2018/08/30/these-schools-are-opening-their-arms-to-special-education-students-can-they-afford-it/

Hoxby, C. M. (2003). School choice and school productivity. Could school choice be a tide that lifts all boats?. In C. M. Hoxby (Ed.), *The economics of school choice* (pp. 287–342). University of Chicago Press.

Jewson, M. (2018, November 12). *Cypress Academy will close, students to transfer to Foundation Prep next year.* The Lens. https://thelensnola.org/2018/11/12/cypress-academy-will-close-students-to-transfer-to-foundation-prep-next-year/

Jewson, M. (2018, November 15). *Public frustration boils over at meeting on school closures, but board policy stifles comments.* The Lens. https://thelensnola.org/2018/11/15/public-frustration-boils-over-at-meeting-on-school-closures-but-board-policy-stifles-comment/

Jewson, M. (2019, March 13). *Class dismissed: The final year in a closing school.* The Lens. https://thelensnola.org/2019/03/13/class-dismissed-the-final-year-in-a-closing-school/

Kirshner, B., Gaertner, M., & Pozzoboni, K. (2010). Tracing transitions: The effect of high school closure on displaced students. *Educational Evaluation and Policy Analysis, 32*(3), 407–429.

Kretchmar, K. (2014). Democracy (in) action: A critical policy analysis of New York City public school closings by teachers, students, administrators, and community members. *Education and Urban Society, 46*(1), 3–29.

Family Engagement in Charter School Closure Decisions   169

Lee, J., & Lubienski, C. (2017). The impact of school closures on equity of access in Chicago. *Education and Urban Society*, *49*(1), 53–80.

Lipman, P., Vaughan, K., & Gutierrez, R. R. (2014, June). *Root shock: Parents' perspectives on school closings in Chicago.* Collaborative for Equity and Justice in Education. https://ceje.uic.edu/wp-content/uploads/2014/06/Root-Shock-Report-Compressed.pdf

Lubienski, C., & Lee, J. (2016). Geo-spatial analyses in education research: the critical challenge and methodological possibilities. *Geographical Research*, *55*(1), 89–99.

McEwan, P. J., & Olsen, R.B. (2010). Admissions lotteries in charter schools. In J.R. Betts & P.T. Hill (Eds.), *Taking measure of charter schools: Better assessments, better policymaking, better schools* (pp. 83–112). Rowman & Littlefield Education.

McMillin, E. (2010). *Closing a school building: A systematic approach.* National Clearinghouse for Educational Facilities.

Monteverde, D. (2018, October 17). *Parents stunned to learn Gentilly school might close.* 4WWL. https://www.wwltv.com/article/news/local/parents-stunned-to-learn-gentilly-school-might-close/289-605391711

Nathan, J. (1996). Early lessons of the Charter School Movement. *Educational Leadership*, *54*(2), 16–20.

Nelson, S.L. (2015). Gaining "choice" and losing voice: Is the New Orleans charter school takeover a case of the emperor's new clothes? In *Only in New Orleans* (pp. 237–265). Brill Sense.

Owens, M. (2008, April). Gardening to save Detroit. *O, the Oprah Magazine.* https://www.oprah.com/world/gardening-in-the-city-changing-detroits-landscape/all

Paino, M., Boylan, R.L., & Renzulli, L. A. (2017). The closing door: The effect of race on charter school closures. *Sociological Perspectives*, *60*(4), 747–767.

Pappas, L. N. (2012). School closings and parent engagement. *Peace and Conflict: Journal of Peace Psychology*, *18*(2), 165.

Ramos, E. (2013, February 18). *Which comes first? Closed schools or blighted neighborhoods?* WBEZ Chicago. https://www.wbez.org/stories/which-comes-first-closed-schools-or-blighted-neighborhoods/50662c2f-4b12-4b6a-a58c-da3a043822f1

Sanders, M., & Harvey, A. (2002). Beyond the school walls: A case study of principal leadership for school-community collaboration. *Teachers College Record*, *104*(7), 1345–1368.

Schneider, M., Teske, P., & Marschall, M. (2000). *Choosing schools: Consumer choice and the quality of American schools.* Princeton University Press.

Sell, R. S., & Leistritz, F. L. (1997). Socioeconomic impacts of school consolidation on host and vacated communities. *Community Development*, *28*(2), 186–205.

Siegel-Hawley, G., Bridges, K., & Shields, T. J. (2017). Solidifying segregation or promoting diversity? School closure and rezoning in an urban district. *Educational Administration Quarterly*, *53*(1), 107–141.

Simon, E. (2013, March 6). How closing schools hurts neighborhoods. *Washington Post.* https://www.washingtonpost.com/news/answer-sheet/wp/2013/03/06/how-closing-schools-hurts-neighborhoods/

Stovall, D. (2015). The fight that must be fought: Reflections on race, school, struggle and sacrifice on the south side of chicago. *Public Interest Law Reporter*, *21*(1), 78–86.

Sunderman, G. L., & Payne, A. (2009, December). *Does closing schools cause educational harm? A Review of the Research. Information Brief.* Mid-Atlantic Equity Center. https://files.eric.ed.gov/fulltext/ED543514.pdf

Talen, E. (2001). School, community, and spatial equity: An empirical investigation of access to elementary schools in West Virginia. *Annals of the Association of American Geographers*, *91*(3), 465–486.

Tieken, M. C., & Auldridge-Reveles, T. R. (2019). Rethinking the school closure research: School closure as spatial injustice. *Review of Educational Research*, *89*(6), 917–953.

Waitoller, F. R., & Super, G. (2017). School choice or the politics of desperation? Black and Latinx parents of students with dis/abilities selecting charter schools in Chicago. *Education Policy Analysis Archives*, *25*(55), 1–46.

Warner, W. M., Brown, M. W., & Clark Lindle, J. (2011). Micropolitics, community identity, and school consolidation. *Journal of School Public Relations, 31*(4), 303–318.

Weber, R., Farmer, S., & Donoghue, M. (2020). Predicting school closures in an era of austerity: The case of Chicago. *Urban Affairs Review, 56*(2), 415–450.

Weiher, G. R., & Tedin, K. L. (2002). Does choice lead to racially distinctive schools? Charter schools and household preferences. *Journal of Policy Analysis and Management: The Journal of the Association for Public Policy Analysis and Management, 21*(1), 79–92.

Williams, S. M. (2013). Micropolitics and rural school consolidation: The quest for equal educational opportunity in Webster Parish. *Peabody Journal of Education*, *88*(1), 127–138.

Wilson, C. M., Bentley, T., & Kneff-Chang, T. (2019). School closure, racial politics, and vulnerable youth: Challenging the shuttering of a Detroit school for teen parents. *Urban Education*, 1–31 .https://doi.org/10.1177/0042085919842611

Witten, K., Kearns, R., Lewis, N., Coster, H., & McCreanor, T. (2003). Educational restructuring from a community viewpoint: a case study of school closure from Invercargill, New Zealand. *Environment and Planning C: Government and Policy*, *21*(2), 203–224.

Witten, K., McCreanor, T., Kearns, R., & Ramasubramanian, L. (2001). The impacts of a school closure on neighborhood social cohesion: Narratives from Invercargill, New Zealand. *Health & Place, 7*(4), 307–317.

ABOUT THE AUTHORS

EDITOR

Brian Robert Beabout is the RosaMary Professor of Education at the University of New Orleans. He served as a teacher in urban schools in the USA and Mexico for six years before earning a PhD in Instructional Systems at Penn State University. He is the author of 16 peer-reviewed journal articles and 9 book chapters. He was a contributor to the 2015 IAP volume entitled *The Power of Community Engagement for Educational Change* (Edited by Michael Evans) He was the co-editor (with Mirón & Boselovic) of *Only in New Orleans: School Choice and Equity Post Hurricane Katrina* (Sense, 2015). He was a founding board member of the Morris Jeff Community School in New Orleans and has served on the boards of the Coalition of Diverse Charter Schools as well as the School Leadership Center of Greater New Orleans. His research focuses on community engagement in contexts of school choice, the unintended consequences of educational reform, and urban school leadership.

AUTHORS

Rebecca Anguiano is an Associate Professor in the Counseling Department at Saint Mary's College of California, and the Program Director of the School Psychology specialization. She earned her PhD in School Psychology from the University of California, Berkeley and is a credentialed,

172 ABOUT the AUTHORS

bilingual (Spanish-English) school psychologist and licensed educational psychologist. As a Brown Chicana woman, Dr. Anguiano's personal experiences have motivated her to focus her research and clinical work on lifting the voices of historically marginalized communities, especially Black and Brown children and their families, as they interface with prek-12 schools. At Saint Mary's she teaches Cognitive, Learning, and Development in the Social Context, Organizational System's Consultation, and School Psychology Seminar and Supervision. Dr. Anguiano's research has explored the translating practices of immigrant families, community organizing and popular education as methods for family engagement in schools, and culturally responsive data-based decision making to inform interventions for emergent bilingual students. She has been published in outlets such as the *School Community Journal*, the *Journal of Youth and Adolescence*, and *Cultural Diversity and Ethnic Minority Psychology*. Dr. Anguiano has provided trainings to community agencies and schools on trauma-informed practices, strength-based psychoeducational evaluations of bilingual children and youth, socially just family engagement, and anti-racist self-care for school leaders during the COVID-19 global pandemic.

Brian Beabout is the RosaMary Professor of Education at the University of New Orleans. He served as a teacher in urban schools in the United States and Mexico for six years before earning a PhD in Instructional Systems at Penn State University. He is the author of 16 peer-reviewed journal articles and 9 book chapters. He was a contributor to the 2015 IAP volume entitled *The Power of Community Engagement for Educational Change* (Edited by Michael Evans). He was the co-editor (with Mirón & Boselovic) of *Only in New Orleans: School Choice and Equity Post Hurricane Katrina* (Sense, 2015). He was a founding board member of the Morris Jeff Community School in New Orleans and has served on the boards of the Coalition of Diverse Charter Schools as well as the School Leadership Center of Greater New Orleans. His research focuses on community engagement in contexts of school choice, the unintended consequences of educational reform, and urban school leadership.

Delia Castillo is the Assistant Superintendent of Administrative Services for SIATech Charter Schools. Previously, she was project director II, Title I and Data for the Division of Student Programs, Los Angeles County Office of Education. During the COVID-19 pandemic, she supported the emergency efforts as a director II for the COVID-19 testing team, a federally funded grant program that supported school districts and charter schools in augmenting COVID-19 testing programs in schools. Her career has been marked by significant roles in the educational landscape. She has served as a coordinator at the Charter School Office of the Los An-

About the Authors 173

geles County Office of Education (LACOE), where she supported county-authorized charter schools and reviewed charter appeals. Prior to this, she spent five years in the Charter Schools Division of the Los Angeles Unified School District, overseeing up to 24 independent and affiliated charter schools and reviewing charter petition applications. Her extensive background in the field of education spans almost 25 years of site-, district-, and county-level experience, having served as an administrator, teacher, school plan writer, and a school founding team member. She earned her Doctorate in Education from Pepperdine University.

Elise Castillo is an Assistant Professor of Educational Studies at Trinity College in Hartford, Connecticut. She conducts qualitative research on school choice policies, focusing on their possibilities for, and limitations to, advancing equitable, democratic, and racially integrated public education. As an interdisciplinary scholar, Dr. Castillo employs concepts from sociology, political science, and critical policy analysis. Her work has been published in various academic journals, including *American Journal of Education*; *Education Policy Analysis Archives*; and *Race, Ethnicity, and Education*. In addition, her research has been supported by a National Academy of Education/Spencer Foundation Postdoctoral Fellowship and a Spencer Foundation COVID-19 Related Research Grant. Dr. Castillo holds a PhD in Education Policy from the University of California, Berkeley, an MST from Pace University, and a BA in English from Barnard College; and is a former New York City public school teacher.

Elif Sisli Ciamarra is a professor of business administration and serves as the finance department chair in the Leo J. Meehan School of Business at Stonehill College. She joined the College in 2017. She is also an adjunct associate professor of finance in the Heller School for Social Policy and Management at Brandeis University. She also serves in the academic team of Our Generation Speaks (OGS), a fellowship program and incubator to create high-impact ventures. Her scholarly interests include corporate finance, corporate governance, corporate social responsibility, entrepreneurship and financial technology and her research has been published in leading academic journals including *Review of Finance*, *Journal of Corporate Finance*, *Financial Management*, *Journal of Financial Stability* and *Journal of Financial Research*. Dr. Sisli Ciamarra received her BS from Bogazici University (Istanbul, Turkey), MBA from International University of Japan (Niigata, Japan), and PhD from the Stern School of Business at New York University.

Charisse Gulosino is a professor in the Leadership and Policy Studies Program at the University of Memphis. She earned her doctorate in education from Columbia University and completed postdoctoral training at Brown University's Taubman Center for American Politics and Policy. Her research focuses on assessing educational policies and programs, with a particular emphasis on school choice initiatives aimed at improving educational access, equity, efficiency, and accountability. She has also contributed as a visiting scholar/professor at the Graduate School of Education at the University of California, Berkeley. In addition, she is an affiliate faculty member at the Center for Research in Education Policy (CREP) within the College of Education at the University of Memphis and the Utah Education Policy Center at the University of Utah.

Laura E. Hernández is an interdisciplinary scholar who synthesizes political and sociological theories to investigate educational policies and the factors that affect the equitable and democratic character of their implementation. To date, her research has examined the systems, factors, and processes surrounding a range of reforms, including school choice, community schools, deeper learning school design, and relationship-centered schooling initiatives. Her work has appeared in scholarly journals such as the *American Educational Research Journal*, *Educational Policy*, *Urban Education*, and *Teachers College Record*. For her research, Hernández has received many honors, including being named a National Academy of Education/ Spencer Dissertation Fellow and Research Development Awardee. Hernández holds a PhD in Education Policy from the University of California, Berkeley, an MST from Pace University in New York City, and a BA in Political Science from the University of California, Los Angeles.

Elisabeth (Betsy) Kim is an Assistant Professor of Education and Leadership at California State University, Monterey Bay. Previously, she was a Robert Curvin Postdoctoral Associate at the Joseph C. Cornwall Center for Metropolitan Studies at Rutgers University–Newark. She holds a PhD in Education Policy from Teachers College, Columbia University. Dr. Kim's research uses a mixed-methods approach to explore the links between education policy and educational equity, with a particular focus on how contemporary policies moderate or exacerbate inequities in districts that serve low-income students of color. Her research interests include equitable leadership, student discipline policy, bilingual education, access to STEM coursework and FAFSA completion. Her work can be found in the *Review of Educational Research*, *Journal of School Choice*, *Leadership & Policy in Schools*, *Language & Education* and *Teachers College Press*. She is co-editor of a volume entitled *Equity Doesn't Just Happen: Stories of Education Leaders Working Toward Social Justice* published by Rowman & Littlefield in February 2023. In addition, she taught first grade in a public school in Harlem as part of the New York City Teaching Fellows program and served as a

Peace Corps volunteer in the Dominican Republic, where she focused her work in the areas of youth development and education. She is currently a California Education Policy Fellow.

Cynthia S. Martinez, PsyD is an assistant professor in the Department of Counseling at San Francisco State University (SFSU). She received her bachelor's degree from the University of California, Berkeley and her doctoral degree in psychology from the Wright Institute in Berkeley, CA. Her pedagogical frameworks include community organizing, popular education, trauma-informed clinical/school supports, decolonizing critical praxis and antiracist advocacy. At SFSU, she teaches Seminar on Child Treatment, Advanced Counseling Practicum, Counseling Skills and Process and Practicum. All courses are taught with a trauma-informed lens and an emphasis on intersectional and social justice analysis. Dr. Martinez's scholarship lies in participant action research focused on collaborating with Latinx Spanish-speaking immigrant families and Black/African American families to create non-traditional therapeutic wellness groups. Additional scholarship also includes trauma-informed, anti-racist advocacy, and radical self-care for practitioners and educators experiencing collective trauma. As a psychologist, her clinical training and expertise is in providing trauma informed care, with feminist-narrative and social justice frameworks. Prior to graduate school, she worked as an immigrant rights activist and obtained extensive experience in grassroots community organizing. As a first generation child of immigrants from Guatemala, Central America, Dr. Martinez is committed to working towards social justice and uplifting historically marginalized voices in higher education and in the mental health field.

Diana M. Ward is a therapist at the New Orleans Institute for Trauma and Compulsive Behaviors at River Oaks Hospital. Prior to entering the field of counseling, she worked in education for 13 years. She was a sixth-grade teacher in an urban K–8 community school before serving as an instructional coach for new teachers in the greater New Orleans area. After earning her PhD in educational administration from the University of New Orleans, she moved into higher education, serving as an administrator at Loyola University New Orleans for several years. She has also been an adjunct professor at the University of New Orleans and currently helps teach courses at the University of Holy Cross. She is a contributor to the second edition of *Counselor Self-Care* (Corey, Muratori, Austin II, and Austin), as well as to the upcoming 11th edition of *Groups: Process and Practice* (Corey, Corey, and Corey). Her research primarily focuses on issues facing students, teachers, and counselors from historically underrepresented and marginalized communities.

176   ABOUT the AUTHORS

Priscilla Wohlstetter is a Distinguished Research Professor at Teachers College, Columbia University, and also a senior researcher with the Consortium for Policy Research in Education (CPRE). Wohlstetter was the Tisch Distinguished Visiting Professor at Teachers College prior to her faculty appointment in the Department of Education Policy and Social Analysis. Before coming to TC, she held the Diane and MacDonald Becket Professorship in Education Policy at the University of Southern California, where she also founded and directed the Center on Educational Governance. Her research and writing has focused broadly on the policies and politics of K–12 education reform and specifically on charter schools, public-private partnerships, school decentralization, school networks, and, most recently, the implementation of the Common Core State Standards. She has served as principal investigator for numerous national and international studies focusing on federal, state and local reforms. She directed a national study of charter schools and public-private partnerships and served as co-director of the National Resource Center for Charter School Finance and Governance, both funded by the U.S. Department of Education. With support from several foundations, she developed a state accountability system (USC School Performance Dashboard), which rates California charter schools on both academic and financial performance. Her book *Choices and Challenges: Charter School Performance in Perspective* was published by Harvard Education Press in 2013.

Printed in the United States
by Baker & Taylor Publisher Services